Men in

Men in White Coats
Treatment Under Coercion

George Szmukler
Emeritus Professor of Psychiatry and Society
Institute of Psychiatry, Psychology and Neuroscience
King's College London, UK

OXFORD
UNIVERSITY PRESS

Great Clarendon Street, Oxford, OX2 6DP,
United Kingdom

Oxford University Press is a department of the University of Oxford.
It furthers the University's objective of excellence in research, scholarship,
and education by publishing worldwide. Oxford is a registered trade mark of
Oxford University Press in the UK and in certain other countries

First Edition published in 2018

Impression: 1

Published in the United States of America by Oxford University Press
198 Madison Avenue, New York, NY 10016, United States of America

British Library Cataloguing in Publication Data

Data available

Library of Congress Control Number: 2017941743

ISBN 978–0–19–880104–7

Printed in Great Britain by
Ashford Colour Press Ltd, Gosport, Hampshire

Acknowledgements

The ideas in this book have had a long gestation, during which they have been influenced by far too many people for to all be named here. Indeed, there have been many whose names I don't even know. In the course of my involvement in numerous lectures, seminars, workshops, and discussions during conference coffee-breaks, many people, from a range of disciplines, by sharing their thoughts with me and through their criticisms have helped me enormously to develop my ideas. I am furthermore extremely grateful to the large number of patients (or 'service users' as they are known in the United Kingdom) for their interest in my proposals and for their forthright views on coercion. Here I must mention especially Diana Rose at the Institute of Psychiatry, and the many service user collaborators in the Mental Health Research Network, who, not being my patients and through our relationship as colleagues, were able to speak openly about their experiences. This could be extremely discomforting for me (and even more so for them) but I appreciate their frankness. I must also mention Mark Lockyer for his powerful dramatization of the experiences of being coerced and bringing home to a wider audience their gravity, their pain, and sometimes (I hope often) their value.

Frank Holloway and Paul Appelbaum were most helpful in the earlier phases of my work and forced me to think through some basic questions. Paul continues to be helpfully probing in his questioning whenever we meet. I am enormously indebted to John Dawson for insisting that my ideas make sense from a practical legal point of view and for our joint work on the 'Fusion Law' proposal. We were then joined by Rowena Daw who also demanded the rigor necessary for drafting key sections of a Fusion Law. She also brought a huge experience in disability and discrimination policy and law.

Genevra Richardson has been a huge influence ever since she became a colleague at King's College London. We first made contact when she was the chair of the Expert Committee set up in 1998 to advise the government on reform of mental health law in England and Wales. 'Capacity' has been an endless subject of discussion for us ever since. She has been very important to me.

Numerous psychiatrist colleagues have engaged in stimulating discussion and debate with me concerning a 'Fusion Law'. I am grateful to them for this. My closest colleagues, particularly in work on the concept of 'decision-making capacity', have been Gareth Owen, Matthew Hotopf, and Tony David. They have pushed me hard to justify a capacity-based mental health law, and perhaps by now they are more or less convinced. Graham Thornicroft, Claire Henderson, Kim Sutherby, and Simone Farrelly have been valued colleagues, especially in relation to work on 'advance statements' in mental health care. Tony Holland has always been a valuable source of advice.

I have benefited enormously from many discussions with Jonathan Glover, Wayne Martin, Tania Gergel, Natalie Banner, Jill Craigie, and Derek Bolton. These philosophers have, I hope, sharpened my ability to deal with some of the complex concepts I have struggled with in formulating my ideas. Similarly, when it comes to the law, in addition to Genevra, Peter Bartlett, Jill Peay, Alex Ruck Keene, and Lucy Series have been important guides and critics. Peter Jackson has given me valuable insights into the perspective of a judge.

Michael Bach, Oliver Lewis, and Felicity Callard have helped me to understand the finer points of the United Nations Convention on the Rights of Persons with Disabilities as well as its significance in non-Western countries. Few people have had a deeper involvement in the study of abuses of psychiatry than Robert van Voren; his accounts have left an indelible impression on me.

Nikolas Rose and Diana Rose have been my ever-present guides to the sociology of psychiatry, particularly in illuminating for me the less obvious ways in which power can be exercised.

I am especially grateful for the support and comments from a number of friends, in the role of 'intelligent lay-persons', who have read various versions of the manuscript: Jo Wodak, Faye Crossman, Zellman Warhaft, Bob Weiss, Denise Asen, Eia Asen, and Jennie McDonnell. Tania Gergel, Jonathan Glover, and Gareth Owen have also been kind enough to look at the manuscript.

Peter Stevenson at Oxford University Press has been most supportive of the book.

I must express my gratitude to two people, who while not involved in work directly relevant to this book, have nevertheless had a lasting influence on my approach to psychiatry and to research. Sid Bloch was important in stimulating my interest, going back to my medical student days, in the potential of psychiatry as a tool of social control; Gerald Russell was an important mentor, always insisting on an unsparing meticulousness in psychiatric research as well as aiming for absolute clarity in writing. Even today, often when I write, I imagine him sitting at my elbow, critically scrutinizing every sentence.

Finally, I thank my wife, Linnet, for graciously putting up with my endless preoccupation with, and ramblings about, 'coercion'. At times I'm sure she must have feared I was afflicted with an '*idée fixe*'.

Contents

Part II **A solution**

Part IV **How practice would change**

PART V **The future**

Introduction

I cannot capture how truly terrifying, isolating and excruciating it is to be caught in the grip of these experiences. I cannot capture the relentless intensity of the suicidal obsession, which hangs over every minute of the day, with the force of some nefarious addiction, or the fear which comes from knowing that you are truly and existentially alone, detached from a world in which you have some physical presence. These experiences took place over many months and years and it would be impossible to give any true impression of their extent or duration. Yet, if there is one element, I have tried to evoke, it is the irrationality of this all—this strange and utterly overwhelming combination of control and its absence ...

Nothing, though, could be more sobering than the ringing of the ward alarm bell. Within a few seconds a group of large nurses, male and female, would gather around the offending patient. A screen would be pulled round and there was often screaming. Behind the screen, we all knew that the patient was being held, face-down, bottom stripped and injected. I am certainly no outright opponent of psychiatric coercion. Indeed, I am fully convinced that my own life depends on this being a lawful provision. All the same, when it happens to you and when you witness it first-hand, especially if you are yourself in a state of paranoia, it is an unspeakably shocking and terrifying experience.

(Excerpts from a patient's account of her mental illness)

Involuntary treatment

Overriding a person's refusal of a treatment represents a serious intrusion into that person's life. At its base lies a conundrum. On the one hand we aim to respect the 'autonomy' of persons, their right to determine what should or should not be done to them, and their right to define their own goals based on their particular personal values; on the other hand, the consequences to their well-being of a refusal of treatment may be grave, even fatal. How can this dilemma be resolved? I will show that we have resolved the dilemma for a particular category of people in a way that is not morally defensible.

When we think about treatment against a person's wishes, most of us will automatically think about psychiatry. Such measures have a very long history. Statutes allowing magistrates to detain 'pauper lunatics' (together with 'rogues, vagabonds, sturdy beggars, and vagrants') date from the early eighteenth century in England. An Act of 1774 added a new requirement—a medical certificate—for committing private patients to a 'madhouse'. By the early nineteenth century the laws governing the detention of persons with mental disorders were essentially similar in their general structure to those we have today.

The grounds for involuntary treatment have been long-lived—first, that the person has a 'mental disorder', usually no more specific than that, which warrants treatment; and second, the person needs to be treated in the interests of his or her safety or for the protection of others. James Parkinson, after whom Parkinson's disease was named, was for many years also a visiting physician to a private madhouse, Holly House in Hoxton, London. In 1811, he wrote a report entitled *Observations on the Act for regulating madhouses, and a correction of the statements of the case of Benjamin Elliott, convicted of illegally confining Mary Daintree; with remarks addressed to the friends of insane persons*. He stated that the leading principle of the 1774 Act was 'to place a medical man, as a competent judge, between society and the unfortunate patient; to prevent him, on the one hand, from the commission of any act injurious to himself, his family, or to any member of society; and on the other, to prevent him from undergoing unnecessary imprisonment'. Furthermore, it had to be 'proper [for the person] to be received into such house or place as a lunatic', that is, such placement should offer the appropriate type of care and control.

Some changes have been made in the mental health laws governing involuntary treatment over the past 200 years or so—but at the level of principle they have been relatively minor. A good example is French law. France's 1838 mental health law was not revised until 1990. Even then, the basic structure and procedures remained very similar. In many countries, the degree of discretion given to doctors versus the weight given to formal legal procedures has fluctuated to varying degrees across time—but again, not greatly. The largest change was probably that from the 1890 Lunacy Act to the 1959 Mental Health Act in England and Wales. This was characterized by a substantial reduction in 'legalism' (for example, no longer requiring authorization by a magistrate) and an increase in medical discretion (detention based largely on medical say-so). However, the basic criteria for involuntary treatment remained just as in Parkinson's day. I will reproduce a copy of a medical recommendation for the involuntary admission of a patient that I could have written yesterday, and that is in all significant respects the same as one written by a doctor concerning Camille Claudel, Rodin's one time co-sculptor, lover, and muse, in 1913. She spent the next 30 years in a mental hospital.

Justifying compulsion

Detention and treatment are nowadays usually based on medical recommendations following a request from a family member, an independent non-medical professional such as a social worker, a magistrate, or an administrative officer; in some countries a judicial hearing is also required, in others, appeals to a court or tribunal may be made after the admission. Medical certificates must support the criteria—the presence of a mental disorder and the need for treatment in the interests of the health or safety of the person, or for the protection of other persons. I will call these criteria the 'mental disorder criterion' and 'risk criterion', respectively.

We will see that both criteria have very serious short-comings when they come to serve as grounds for detention and involuntary treatment. The blurred boundary of what counts as a 'mental disorder' has provided a tempting gateway in a number of countries for a non-judicial or quasi-judicial short-cut to the incarceration of people who are seen as representing a threat to the social order. The political abuse of psychiatry in the Soviet Union was a gross example, but in various less dramatic forms it continues in some places to this day. We have a recent example in England. People with what can only be called a 'state-defined diagnosis'—'Dangerous Severe Personality Disorder'—were to be detained without a fixed limit of time, even if they had not committed a serious offence and even if there were no treatment available, other than custodial 'care'. Fortunately the programme was abandoned. The second criterion, 'risk', is similarly a slippery notion. It is a sad consequence of brute mathematics that we cannot usefully predict who will perpetrate the very events that we would most like to prevent—suicides, homicides, or acts of serious violence. Fortunately these are rare events; but as we shall see, it is this rarity that makes them unpredictable, even with state-of-the-art risk assessment techniques. For instance, the number of people detained because of their purported risk of suicide or serious violence who would in fact never have committed such an act, I shall show, vastly exceeds those who would.

What conclusions can we draw from the consistency over approximately two centuries of the legal criteria for involuntary treatment of persons with a mental illness? Should we feel reassured? Perhaps it indicates that the grounds for detention and the processes for its implementation work well enough and need no revision. No, I don't think so. There is a much less worthy reason for their persistence—that persons who are subject to such detention, persons with a severe mental illness, have been so marginalized in society, so lacking in a 'voice', so subjected to prejudicial stereotypes, that the principles justifying their detention and treatment have slipped under our civil rights radar systems. Scandals involving ill-treatment in mental hospitals and care homes occasionally make the news, but the reasons for people being detained there in the first place are rarely questioned. In recent years, the scandals that have made the biggest news in many places have focused on acts of serious violence by persons with mental disorders, rather than on abuses to those hospitalized. Recent reform of mental health law, in England at least, has largely sought to reassure the public that it is protected from 'dangerous' patients, especially those the media call 'community care patients', who have been 'released' (note, not 'discharged' like all other patients) from hospitals.

Like more or less all of my medical colleagues, as well as nurses, social workers, psychologists, occupational therapists, health service managers, lawyers, judges, policymakers, and the general public, I used to accept the compulsory admission arrangements as reasonable. There were certainly troubling cases when the decision whether or not to detain a person was hard to resolve. Implementing the process was usually sorely distressing for the patient, as well as very disquieting for the professionals involved. I disliked it intensely. Indeed it was this kind of 'social control' element of psychiatry that put me off joining that speciality for some time. Goffman, Foucault, and Szasz were prominent influences at the time and they posed some significant challenges. In the end I realized that psychiatry was, for me, by far the best specialty. I could not imagine spending the rest of my medical career listening to hearts, looking down tubes into the gastrointestinal tract, or wielding saws and drills against bones.

Professional rivalries could be played out around the respective roles of those involved in mental health assessments for involuntary treatment. Social workers accused doctors of being too 'paternalistic', of not taking sufficient account of the social context. Doctors sometimes accused lawyers who represented patients at hearings aimed at contesting their detention of ignoring the (to them, at least) obvious need for the proposed treatment. But the basic principles underlying the grounds for compulsion were rarely, if ever, questioned. Indeed, to my embarrassment now, though my doctoral thesis involved a study of 150 compulsory admissions of patients from the London Borough of Camden between 1976 and 1978, even by the end of it, I still thought the law was reasonable. My attention was drawn, above all, to the large proportion of the detained patients who were subsequently detained again—and then sometimes again—but who received little in the way of effective follow-up care between their admissions.

The main debate at that time and into the early 1980s centred on whether the protections of mental patients' civil liberties needed to be strengthened by introducing stricter, formal legal procedures, more like those characterizing the criminal justice system. Critics argued that medical discretion had gone too far. Again, the 'mental disorder' and 'risk' criteria justifying involuntary treatment were not in dispute. The major criticism of the law was that the 'risk' (or 'dangerousness') criterion should be narrower in scope. It was proposed, for example, that the risk of harm bar should be raised—requiring, for example, that the harm should be physical and the risk should be 'imminent'.

Questioning the orthodoxy

In the late 1980s and early 1990s, I began to have serious doubts about the orthodox view. An important trigger was an invitation to take part in a debate related to an aspect of 'informed consent' in medicine. This concerned the question of when, if ever, seeking fully informed consent could be skipped for fear that the patient might become so disturbed by the disclosure of facts about their illness that their judgement would be overwhelmed and their ability to make treatment decisions would consequently suffer. This is termed 'therapeutic privilege' and is certainly a tricky subject. But the importance of the debate for me lay in its directing my attention to the meaning of 'informed consent'. This notion has evolved steadily from the 1970s and is now adopted as a doctrine in most places, certainly in the Western world. Apart from the question of how much information should be disclosed to the patient about their illness and the options for treatment, a key requirement for giving informed consent is that the person must have the ability or 'capacity' to use that information. Is their 'decision-making capacity' so affected by some kind of disturbance of mental functioning that they cannot make a meaningful decision about treatment? It is only when the person lacks such decision-making capacity that one starts to think about whether treatment can be imposed against the patient's wishes. I began to wonder why decision-making capacity played no, or virtually no role, in determining when involuntary treatment was appropriate in mental health care. If a person is capable of making a treatment decision for himself or herself, what right do we have to interfere and to override the decision?

Somehow the philosophical 'climate-change' in medical practice underlying the advance of 'informed consent', that is, a growing respect for patient 'autonomy' (or self-determination) at the expense of medical paternalism, had passed psychiatry by. So, I wondered, what was special about mental illness in this regard? Why do we ignore decision-making capacity when it comes to psychiatric treatment?

A new development in mental health care generated further doubts in my mind about the conventional grounds for involuntary treatment. From the mid 1980s there has been a growing policy movement for introducing involuntary outpatient (or community) treatment orders. Since the locus of psychiatric care, even for the most serious disorders, is increasingly in the community as opposed to the hospital, so the rationale goes, why should involuntary treatment be restricted to the latter? But, can the same criteria—the 'mental disorder criterion' and 'risk criterion'—stand up in an acceptable manner in this very different community context? I saw as particularly problematic community orders of a 'prophylactic' or 'preventive' kind—imposed on someone not currently a risk, that aimed to reduce the risk of a relapse of their illness that might, in turn, subsequently carry an unacceptable risk of harm to them or to others. The aim is to reduce the risk of a risk; and a risk of what kinds of harms? Would they now include lesser harms than those meriting hospitalization? How well could they be predicted? This is not to mention, of course, the problem of what might come to be included under the category of 'mental disorder'. Would there be a temptation, for example, to expand its boundaries to include behaviours that are troublesome or annoying to others, that might now be construed as the manifestations of a 'mental disorder' (such as a 'personality disorder'—that is, roughly speaking, a combination of enduring character traits that cause suffering to the person or to others). In a risk-averse society, this is always a possibility. Together with a number of others, I saw significant scope for a large increase in numbers of patients being treated under compulsion—as has indeed occurred.

Concerns about numbers led me to look at studies examining the frequency of compulsory psychiatric admissions, within and between countries, as well as changes in rates over time. As we shall see, the variation in rates between countries (even similar ones as in Western Europe) or between regions in the same country is huge. Sometimes there have been large increases in compulsory admissions in one country (such as England over the past decade or so), but not in another. These statistics show how important social and cultural factors—quite separate from the clinical manifestations of mental disorders themselves—are in determining who is detained. They also point to a disturbing degree of what looks like arbitrariness in instigating involuntary treatment. In turn, this helps to explain what has been termed the 'coercive shadow' that looms over mental health care. Patients in the mental health system know that the psychiatrist ultimately has a power to set in train a compulsory order if a proposed treatment is rejected. Even if such an action is not at all in the psychiatrist's mind, the patient may nonetheless fear it is, and accept treatment that is unwanted in order to avoid the distress, humiliation, and stigma of a compulsory order.

Discrimination

An important though largely neglected book by Campbell and Heginbotham, *Mental Illness: Prejudice, Discrimination and the Law*, published in 1991 (Dartmouth Publishing Company), helped to clarify the bases of my unease. The conclusion that mental health law as conventionally conceived discriminates unfairly against persons with a mental illness appears to me unassailable. Autonomy (or the recognition of a right to self-determination, or the right to pursue personal goals and values) for persons with a mental illness is not accorded the same respect as it is for persons with all other types of illness. For the latter, but not the former, the person's ability (or 'capacity') to make a decision about treatment is key to whether we can begin to justify overriding a treatment refusal. Furthermore, even when capacity is lacking, an involuntary intervention is only justified if it is in the person's 'best interests'. Although there are various definitions of 'best interests', the personal values, goals, and wishes of the patient, when well, play a major role. These two considerations—'capacity' and 'best interests'—play virtually no role in initiating detention and, usually, involuntary treatment in mental health care.[i] Here the 'mental disorder' and 'risk' criteria operate. The rules are totally different. Furthermore, the 'protection of others' in the risk-based criterion singles out persons with mental disorders as uniquely liable to a form of preventive detention (albeit usually, or eventually, in hospital) on the basis of risk *alone*. In other words, they can be detained without first having, like the rest of us, to have actually committed an offence; this, despite the fact that only a tiny proportion—a few per cent—of all 'risky' people or violent offenders have a mental illness.

How is it that we have accepted such an obviously discriminatory approach to persons with mental illness for so long? The most likely explanation is that we share particular negative stereotypes of people with mental illness, stereotypes that are deeply rooted in our culture. These paint such people as having qualitatively different, 'diseased' minds that make them incapable of rationality and whose values, beliefs, and wishes are thus not to be taken seriously: and, furthermore that dangerousness is intrinsic to, part-and-parcel of mental illness. Mental health law gives frank expression to these assumptions—people with a mental illness lack decision-making capacity and are a risk to others. However, we shall see that the research evidence resoundingly fails to support these stereotypes.

A solution

Can we come up with a legal framework that is non-discriminatory? With colleagues, from law and philosophy as well as psychiatry, I have worked on an approach that meets that need. We have called this a 'Fusion Law'. A key point is that it is 'generic'; that is, it applies to *all* persons who have a serious problem with decision-making, whatever their diagnosis—physical or mental—and in any setting—medical, surgical, psychiatric, or in the community. We see no need for a specific 'mental health' law. My colleagues have shown that around 50 per cent of patients on both psychiatric wards and medical wards lack capacity. Patients on medical wards with dementia or confusional states due to a variety of physical illnesses are regularly

[i] In some countries, some provinces in Canada, and most states in the United States, while detention itself is based on the presence of a mental disorder and risk, non-emergency involuntary treatment—even though the person is detained—requires the patient's consent or an additional procedure for overriding a refusal. In some states, this involves a judicial determination of incapacity to consent. How voluntary the 'consent' can be under conditions of detention is highly questionable.

restrained and involuntarily treated. On an average day, I strongly suspect there is more physical restraint nowadays on a medical or surgical ward, where a large proportion of patients are elderly and prone to mental impairments, than a psychiatric ward.

The Fusion Law framework is based on 'decision-making capacity' and 'best interests', modified in various ways to make it applicable across all medical specialities, from psychiatry to orthopaedics. This leads to a need to develop sufficiently robust assessments of these notions. Standard assessments, based on the person's understanding of the information disclosed about the illness and the proposed treatment, the person's ability to 'use and weigh' that information (for example, to reason with it in the light of what is important to the person), and the ability to communicate a choice will suffice in the majority of cases. However, sometimes the assessment needs to go beyond the ability of the person to 'process' the relevant information. The standard test for decision-making capacity may be passed, yet our intuition is that there is still something seriously amiss—decision-making is in some manner undermined. The person's beliefs and values against which the processing of information is examined may themselves appear to have become distorted in some way; that is, the person's treatment decision seems to be out of joint with their deep or enduring or 'real' beliefs and values. There are challenges in such cases that I will describe, but there are good reasons to believe that valid assessments can be made. A major concern from 'capacity sceptics' is that when patients disagree with their doctors, they will be judged to lack decision-making capacity. I will examine ways in which a person's beliefs and values can be taken into account and be given due weight without their being usurped by those of the assessor.

Being a generic law and thus applicable to all patients, the criteria for non-consensual and involuntary treatment need to be workable in all settings. How practice would need to change to accommodate the new framework needs to be thought through. Some people will also be concerned that a law based on decision-making capability and best interests might mean that the public will no longer be adequately protected from persons with mental illness who might be violent. I will show those fears can be laid to rest.

At the same time as my colleagues and I were working on a formulation of a non-discriminatory health law, the United Nations General Assembly in 2006 adopted a new convention, the Convention on the Rights of Persons with Disabilities. Some have described the Convention as representing a 'paradigm shift' in relation to the standing of persons with disabilities in society. The overall purpose, stated in its Article 1, is to 'promote, protect and ensure the full and equal enjoyment of all human rights and fundamental freedoms by all persons with disabilities, and to promote respect for their inherent dignity'. The elimination of discrimination by ensuring that rights may be enjoyed 'on an equal basis with others' is a fundamental aim. Mental health problems of a severe and persistent nature that lead to involvement with the mental health services system are taken clearly to be disabilities under the Convention. I welcome the Convention, especially its clear articulation of the social, economic, and cultural rights of persons with disabilities. I am delighted that a key purpose of the Convention chimes so well with the Fusion Law's similar aim of eliminating discrimination.

While the aims are similar, the demands to be met for laws or policies to be compliant with the Convention are challenging. Some authorities, including the Committee established by the United Nations and charged with the oversight and monitoring of the 160 (at the time of writing) signatory states' compliance with the Convention, interpret it as virtually ruling out what is termed 'substitute decision-making'—a person making a decision on behalf of another who is regarded as incapable of making a decision for him- or herself. Involuntary treatment is clearly an example of 'substitute decision-making'. I will indicate why such an interpretation is not credible—within the terms of the Convention itself; and why the Fusion Law—with a reformulation of the notions of 'decision-making capacity' and 'best interests' consistent with the Convention's touchstone requirement of respect for a person's 'will and preferences—should be seen as compliant. I will go on to describe the Fusion proposal as based on a 'decision-making capability–will and preferences' approach.

If we could minimize the number of instances where the question of compulsion arises in the first place, everyone would be pleased. There is unfortunately only a small research literature on this subject, but there are enough leads to stimulate further thinking.

Treatment pressures and 'coercion'

While the main focus of this book is on involuntary and non-consensual treatment, these need to be seen in the broader context of what might be called 'treatment pressures'. They comprise a kind of hierarchy of increasing pressures that might be exerted on a person who is rejecting treatment, apparently unwisely: the hierarchy comprises 'persuasion', 'interpersonal leverage', 'inducements', 'threats', and 'compulsion'. While little thought is generally given to these interventions, they play an important role in the practice of medicine. Threats—actual or perceived—are particularly significant in psychiatry. We currently lack an accepted framework for thinking about their justifications, if any. The 'decision-making capability–will and preferences' approach can help fill the gap.

Many of us will have been patients who at some time, due to illness, have lacked the capability of making treatment decisions according to the beliefs and values that to a large extent make us who we are—or we will at some time in the future be in such a position. Most of us will have family members or friends who have been, or will be, in such situations. We need to ensure that the justifications for intervening against a person's wishes at such times stand up to the most thorough scrutiny.

A few explanations

Since I am aiming at a multidisciplinary readership—which will include, I hope, 'experts by experience', that is, patients and their families and friends—I have tried to minimize the use of technical terms. Where I have considered them helpful in progressing a line of thought, I have tried my best to clearly define their meaning.

For the same reason, I have tended to be fairly spare with the number of references. I hope, however, that they will be sufficient to support my major claims as well as to form the basis of a more detailed search if that is what the reader should wish.

Although the book has quite a lot about health law, this is mainly at the level of principles and basic concepts. Where more detail is required, it is presented, I hope, in everyday language

I have illustrated many of the issues dealt with in the text with case histories. Apart from those whose details are in the public domain, they do not describe 'real' individuals, but represent typical clinical examples. I am confident that my colleagues would find them authentic.

I make no attempt to deal with coercive interventions involving children. This is not an area in which I have the necessary expertise.

The title of this book

'Carry on like that and the 'men in white coats' will come and take you away!'

Such reference to 'men in white coats' might be less common today, but nearly everyone knows what it means. When I've told people that this was to be the title of this book, most have thought it apt. However, others have objected: it's old-fashioned, psychiatrists and their 'attendants' don't wear white coats anymore, and in any case they are as likely to be women as men. True, but the disquiet so poignantly evoked by the expression—and the 'coercive shadow' of psychiatry to which it alludes—arguably remain as potent today as before. Many patients are highly likely to accept its metaphoric truth. Another reason for my liking 'white coats' in the title is that my discussion extends beyond psychiatry to coercion in medicine in general. Some doctors still wear white coats.

How the book is structured

Part I: 'The problem'. Chapters 1–5 deal with the problems associated with involuntary treatment in general, and the discrimination against people with mental illness that characterizes conventional legal frameworks.

Part II: 'A solution'. In Chapters 6–8, I propose a solution to the problems of involuntary treatment that aims to respect, on an equal basis, the autonomy and rights of all persons with a serious decision-making difficulty.

Part III: '"Coercion" viewed more broadly'. Compulsory treatment is not the only form of 'coercion'. Chapters 9 and 10 consider 'treatment pressures' more broadly and examine interventions aimed at reducing recourse to coercive measures.

Part IV: 'How practice would change'. Chapters 11 and 12 look at the ways in which the proposed reforms would change medical and psychiatric practice in some key areas.

Part V: 'The future'. Chapter 13 looks at some recent trends in thinking about coercive interventions and attempts to predict what the future might hold.

Part I

The problem

Chapter 1

A practice with a very long history

What follows is a 'medical recommendation', made jointly by two doctors, one with special expertise in psychiatry, for the involuntary admission of a person to a psychiatric hospital under the Mental Health Act 1983 for England and Wales. It was written in 2013. I have made many such entries over 35 years or so as a consultant psychiatrist.

A Section 2 admission, while called an 'assessment' order, nevertheless permits involuntary treatment against the person's wishes when it is deemed appropriate and necessary. Detention of the patient can be for up to 28 days. However, the patient can be discharged earlier if the consultant psychiatrist thinks the person is now well enough, or if the patient appeals successfully to an independent mental health tribunal. The tribunal comprises a judge who is the chair, an independent psychiatrist, and a lay person with experience in mental health matters (for example, as a social worker).

This was the medical recommendation for Ms Fear, giving the reasons for her detention:

Medical recommendation: Ms Fear

Section 2 (Admission for Assessment)

'In our opinion,

(a) this patient is suffering from mental disorder of a nature or degree which warrants the detention of the patient in hospital for assessment (or for assessment followed by medical treatment) for at least a limited period.

AND

(b) ought to be so detained
  - (i) in the interests of the patient's own health
  - (ii) in the interests of the patient's own safety
  - (iii) with a view to the protection of other persons

(Delete the indents not applicable)

Our reasons for these opinions are:

(Your reasons should cover both (a) and (b). As part of them: describe the patient's symptoms and behaviour and explain how those symptoms and behaviour lead you to your opinion; explain why the patient ought to be admitted to hospital and why informal admission is not appropriate)

> Ms Fear shows symptoms of a psychotic illness, probably schizophrenia. She states that for the past 3 months her ex-husband has organised a gang of persons who are spying on her, gathering evidence to ruin her reputation so she will lose her job as a school teacher (she is currently on sick leave, though she denies being sick). She says she hears members of the gang talking about her, conspiring, commenting disapprovingly on her thoughts and actions, and abusing her. These are clearly hallucinations. She suspects that gasses are being pumped into her flat to make her talk in a compromising way – probably about induced paedophile fantasies – in her sleep. All ventilation points in her flat consequently have been stopped up with newspapers. She yesterday shouted out to one of the 'spies' from her second floor window and threw an empty Coca-Cola bottle at him (fortunately, missing). Her sister brings her food as Ms Fear is frightened to leave her flat. Ms Fear's hygiene is poor. She appears not to have washed for some time; her hair is matted and she is malodorous. Her flat is in disarray with clothing and papers scattered on the floor in the bedroom, bathroom and lounge. She also has a large neck lump that she says does not worry her. She denies that she is ill in any way and refuses to accept the offer of treatment, which she clearly needs, including hospitalisation. She needs to be admitted in the interests of her own health and safety and for the protection of others.

And here is a copy of the medical certificate written 100 years earlier, in 1913, for the admission to the Ville-Evrard mental hospital, just outside Paris, for Camille Claudel, the highly gifted sculptor, as well as muse and former mistress of Auguste Rodin:

> I the undersigned, Dr Michaux, certify that Mademoiselle Camille Claudel suffers from very serious mental problems; that she dresses in scraggy clothes; that she is absolutely filthy, certainly never washing; that she has sold all her furniture apart from a bed and armchair; that she receives from her family, over and above the rent for her apartment paid directly to the landlord, 200 francs per month which would be ample to allow her to live comfortably; that she lives her life completely shut up in her airless apartment, the window shutters being tightly closed; that for several months she has not been out during the day but she does goes out rarely in the middle of the night;

> that according to letters recently written to her brother and statements to her concierge, she is constantly in terror of the 'Rodin' gang; that I have observed over the past 7 or 8 years that she believes herself to be persecuted; that her state, as well as being dangerous to herself on account of her poor self-care and even nutrition, is also dangerous to her neighbours. And that it is necessary to detain her in a 'maison de santé [the private section of Ville-Evrard asylum]. Paris, 7th March 1913, doctor Michaux. [1,p246] [author's translation]

With the outbreak of the war in 1914 and the advance of the German army, Ms Claudel was transferred to a hospital at Montdevergues, near Avignon. There she spent the next 30 years until her death during the Second World War, probably largely due to the starvation of patients in mental hospitals in Vichy France.

A certificate, essentially like those detailed, could just as well have been written 100 years before Claudel's.

It is worth noting that there was some disagreement about whether Camille Claudel's mental illness was constantly present, at least to a substantial degree. Her doctors at various times recommended that her family take her home. However, they didn't do so. Her brother, Paul Claudel, a celebrated writer, visited rarely during her 30 years' hospitalization; her mother until her death in 1929, never. We shall see later that what might be meant by a 'mental disorder' may sometimes not be very clear; and that the social circumstances of those with such a diagnosis may hugely affect their treatment and their fate. The significance of such segregation from society of people with a mental illness will become clearer later.

Reasons for detention: 'plus ça change'

The kinds of reasons described in the certificates I have quoted for the detention and treatment of psychiatric patients have a very long and consistent history. In England, for example, the Act for Regulating Private Madhouses of 1774 required that for admission to a 'private madhouse' a person should be: 'proper to be received into such house or place as a lunatic'—that is, they needed first, to be categorized as a 'lunatic', and second, the madhouse had to be the right place for them to receive the care—such as it was—they required (or to allow their removal from the vicinity of others on whom they were an intolerable burden or to whom they posed an unacceptable threat). At that time, the poor were usually sent to workhouses by the local municipal authorities rather than to madhouses.

The first half of the nineteenth century saw a huge growth of public asylums in one of the largest public building programmes England, for example, has ever seen. Confinement became more tightly controlled legally in terms of the necessary documentation and supervisory systems for the institutions. However, the basic reasons for confinement hardly changed. The Lunacy Act of 1845 required a 'Request' from a family member or other person with a close relationship to the patient. The Request for a private patient took the form: 'I, . . ., hereby request that you receive . . ., a lunatic (or insane person or idiot or person of unsound mind) as a patient in your house (or hospital)', and was accompanied with a rudimentary medical and social history of the patient. An innovation was the requirement of two medical certificates, but their language was similar to that of 1774: 'the said . . . is a lunatic (or an insane person or an idiot or a person of unsound mind) and a proper person to be confined, and that I have formed this opinion from the following fact or facts, viz.: . . . .'. The confinement of pauper patients had to be signed by a justice of the peace (or officiating clergyman of the parish), while the 'relieving officer' of the workhouse had to approve the admission. For the pauper, the issue was usually more about funding than about protections.

The historian Kathleen Jones, in her book *A History of the Mental Health Services* (1972)[2] saw the nineteenth century as bringing in a new standard of public morality by which the care of the helpless classes of the community came to be seen as a social responsibility. She referred to this as a slow social revolution which transformed the 'Lunatic or mad Person' of the eighteenth century into the 'person of unsound mind' of 1845.

The Lunacy Act of 1890 toughened legal protections against unjustified confinement while building up a complex detention bureaucracy including licensing, inspections, judicial procedures, and documentation. Kathleen Jones characterized the Act thus:

> The Act itself is an extremely long and intricate document, which expresses few general principles and provides detail for almost every known contingency. Nothing was left to chance, and very little to future development.[2,p176]

However, the request and medical certificate structure remained the same, as did the reasons for detention—the person was a 'lunatic' and needed to be detained for their own welfare or for the welfare or safety of others.

The Mental Health Act 1959 perpetuated the 'request' and 'medical recommendation' format, but introduced a significant change in the underlying philosophy. It promoted medical discretion at the expense of legalism: a magistrate no longer needed to approve detention. Instead, the patient could appeal to a special tribunal following admission. The criteria for admission were again similar, but now slightly elaborated: the medical practitioners needed to be of the opinion that the person 'suffered from a mental disorder of a nature or degree which warrants his detention' (for either observation or for treatment) and his detention was 'necessary in the interests of his own health and safety or for the protection of other persons'. The current Mental Health Act 1983 (amended in 2007) continues this approach, as can be seen in the medical recommendations for Ms Fear cited at the beginning of this chapter.

This continuity of the grounds for detention is even clearer in another country, France. Before the Revolution of 1789, the commonest form of detention was by a royal order (known as a *lettre de cachet*) made by a minister of the royal household at the request of the person's family or the public authorities. The Revolution put an end to the *lettre de cachet*. There followed a period of flux, during which the new administrative authorities, represented by the *prefets*—the senior civil servants representing the authority of the state—increasingly intervened. This was especially so in cases where there was a threat to the public order. A law was then passed in 1838 that is recognizably like contemporary mental health law. This law laid down two methods of involuntary detention. The first was an 'administrative' route via a *prefet*. This was for persons who endangered public order or the safety of others. The second required a family request accompanied by a medical certificate. The medical certificate needed to confirm that the person was mentally ill but was refusing the required care. The two reasons for detention of a person with a mental disorder in the English legislation were here more clearly demarcated—for the welfare of the person, on the one hand, and for the protection of others, on the other.

The 1838 law was not replaced for 150 years—not until 1990. Even then, the two modes of detention were retained in the 1990 law: one initiated by the family, but now requiring two medical certificates (*Hospitalisation sur demande d'un tiers*), the other ordered by a *préfet* (or in the case of emergency by a mayor or the *commissaire de police* in Paris (*Hospitalisation d'Office*). For the former, the medical certificates had to state that the patient was unable to give consent to treatment because of his or her mental disorder, and that their condition called for immediate treatment and constant supervision in hospital. In the case of the latter mode of detention—initiated as previously because of a danger to public order or to the safety of others—a medical certificate was also required. However, only the *préfet* could discharge the patient. In theory, according to the Code of Practice for Medical Practitioners, psychiatric patients were to be treated like other patients: that is, treatment required consent. In practice, they were an exception.

A new law was introduced in 2011 because the *Conseil Constitutionnel*, France's highest authority on the Constitution, ruled that the Law of 1990 was not compliant with the Constitution. It had taken over 50 years for recognition of this fact; the current French Constitution dates from 1958! The law was reformed in 2013, again at the behest of the *Conseil*. The two modes of detention—as in 1990, and more or less as in 1838—survive unchanged. There were two new provisions. Involuntary treatment in the community was introduced—more about that later—as well as an automatic judicial review of detention—belatedly seen as required by the constitution.

The routine, accepted criteria: 'mental disorder' and 'risk of harm'

The medical certificates cited at the beginning of this chapter depict the two criteria that are practically universally accepted for the involuntary detention or treatment of persons in psychiatric services—first, the presence of a 'mental disorder'—usually undefined or, at best, broadly defined—and second, a risk of harm to the person or to others—also rarely specified further. I shall refer to these criteria as the *mental disorder criterion* and the *risk of harm criterion*, respectively.

Nearly all countries that have specific mental health legislation base involuntary admission and treatment on these criteria. It may be of interest to note that 20 per cent of the world's population live in countries that do not have specific mental health law.[3] It was 41 per cent until 2012, when China, accounting for about 20 per cent of the world's population, adopted such a law for the first time. For compulsory treatment, China's new law requires, as we now come to expect, a 'severe mental disorder' plus a risk of harm to self or others. 'Severe mental disorder' is described in greater detail than usual: a condition 'characterized by severe symptoms that result in severe impairments in social adjustment or other types of functioning, an impaired understanding of one's own health status or objective reality, or an inability to cope with one's own affairs'.[4]

Do two centuries of no change mean no change is required?

My guess is that many readers, probably most, will say at this stage, so what? Doesn't the longevity of the 'mental disorder' and 'risk of harm' criteria indicate that they hit the mark and work well in practice? This appears to be a telling observation. Revisions of mental health law over time have certainly occurred. However, they have been concerned with other matters, especially the legal protections—for example, the timing and degree of involvement of magistrates or judges; reviews, and how they are triggered; where the person can be detained and for how long; rights of appeal and by whom they can be made; or the nature of additional protections for serious or irreversible treatments (for example, electroconvulsive therapy and psychosurgery).

The vast majority of my colleagues do not question the routine grounds for compulsion. The criteria are seen as a useful guide for allowing a difficult job to be done in a lawful manner. Whether they are the right criteria that lead to the right questions being asked are rarely interrogated. The problems that do bother the professionals and the lawyers are whether the criteria apply in a particular case. Such problems are quite common. An extreme, but nonetheless instructive, example is the case of Ian Brady, the 'Moors Murderer'.[5]

> Together with Myra Hindley, Ian Brady killed five children and then buried them on Saddleworth Moor, near Manchester. Three bodies were found. Both Brady and Hindley were found guilty of these murders in 1966 and sentenced to life imprisonment. After 19 years in prison, Brady's behaviour led to his receiving a diagnosis of a 'mental disorder' within the meaning of the Mental Health Act 1983. He was transferred in 1985 to Ashworth Hospital, a high-security psychiatric hospital. He appealed to a Mental Health Tribunal in 2012 arguing he should be discharged from the compulsory order and returned to prison. He asked for the hearing to be held in public, which was granted.
>
> The details of the hearing are in the public domain.[5] Brady's appeal was turned down. The Tribunal concluded that Brady 'continues to suffer from a mental disorder which is of a nature and degree which makes it appropriate for him to continue to receive medical treatment and that it is necessary for his health and safety and for the protection of other persons that he should receive such treatment in hospital and that appropriate medical treatment is available for him'.

A detailed analysis of the case is not relevant for our purposes at this point—for example, whether he had a mental disorder or not, and if he had, whether the diagnosis should be a 'personality disorder' with or without 'paranoid schizophrenia'. The Tribunal concluded he had both. I wish to draw your attention to the extraordinarily drawn-out nature of the deliberations:

> Seven mental health professionals gave evidence in the Brady hearing. All agreed that he had an antisocial personality disorder. However, some argued, on the basis of other symptoms—though there was

> disagreement whether they were truly 'symptoms' —that he also had schizophrenia; others said he did not. There was further disagreement on whether treatment was necessary in the interests of his own health or for the protection of others. The Mental Health Act (since an amendment in 2007) requires for detention of a patient that 'appropriate treatment' should be available for their disorder. It was agreed that medication was not indicated, and that Brady continued to refuse to engage in any structured psychological treatment. Could nursing care in a custodial setting with attempts —so far thwarted—to develop therapeutic relationships be considered 'treatment'?

The written decision of the Tribunal published in 2014 runs to 115 pages, nearly all of which are given over to the competing views of the experts. Sixty-two pages dealt with whether Brady had a 'mental disorder' (despite having been under observation as an inpatient for 28 years). Thirty-five pages dealt with what counted as 'treatment', whether it was available, and whether it was in the interests of his health or safety or for the protection of others—the others in this case being fellow prisoners if he were to return, as he wished, to prison. This case illustrates the difficulties—admittedly in an unusually extreme form—that can arise in determining whether the two criteria justifying compulsory treatment apply. A lot hinges on whether the person has a 'mental disorder', largely undefined, and what is considered to be 'treatment' and in whose interests it would be.

Like my colleagues, for many years—sadly, too many—I assumed these were the right questions to put when weighing up the case for involuntary treatment. How deeply this approach was fixed in my thinking, now with hindsight, takes me aback. As mentioned in the Preface to this book, I was deeply immersed in a large study of compulsory admissions from the London Borough of Camden between 1976 and 1978.[6] It formed the basis for my MD dissertation. Despite looking in detail at the history and circumstances of the detention of 150 patients, I saw nothing wrong with the legal grounds for their involuntary admission. There was certainly quite a lot wrong with the psychiatric services at the time, particularly a failure of adequate follow-up care following discharge. I could make the excuse that my attention was drawn to this practical problem, about which I believed much could be done to improve matters. I did, however, say something about the grounds for involuntary admission in my dissertation that is revealing:

> Some types of mental illness, by their nature, occasion an impairment of the sufferer's judgement about aspects of the world around him and of his own state .... As a result he may not be able to take a number of decisions

> responsibly. Compulsory admission would be warranted, on this view, where a patient is suffering from a mental illness that impairs his judgement and where as a consequence his welfare is significantly threatened.

Sadly, I failed to realize at that time that the 'impairment of judgement' was simply a supposition that I made—one that does not, however, make an explicit demand under the Mental Health Act. Crucially, the presumed impairment of judgement does not need to be directly tested. It is this omission that later began to worry me.

My aim in highlighting the problematic role of diagnosis in compulsory treatment is not to denigrate the value of psychiatric diagnosis in other contexts. Diagnosis is essential to clinical practice. It is what doctors use to help them decide what treatment should be given and what the prognosis of the illness might be. The current state of play with psychiatric diagnoses certainly has its weaknesses, but despite these, diagnoses still have clinical utility. My disquiet about the use of the diagnosis of a 'mental disorder' as one of the two fundamental bases for involuntary treatment is that its function has been co-opted well outside its comfort zone. Diagnosis becomes in this context an instrument of social policy rather than a clinical tool. It is hard to think of another place in medicine where it plays a similar role in opening the door to coercive interventions. The only other case I know is the compulsory quarantining of persons with a highly contagious infectious disease. I will discuss this practice later (in Chapter 11) showing how it differs in important respects from detention in mental health care. The fact that in England and Wales there were around 50,000 compulsory detentions for mental disorder in 2013, compared with seven detentions of persons with infectious diseases who posed a danger to others (but without an authority to treat) offers a clue.

The misuse of diagnosis in involuntary treatment in psychiatry is not a problem with diagnosis per se. It is with the role into which it has been marshalled. What should be at issue, I will later argue, is what the patient (or potential patient) does with a diagnosis after being given one; that is, the person's ability to decide what the diagnosis means for him or her, and what action he or she thinks should be taken as a consequence.

A better explanation for the lack of change

There is another reason why the 'mental disorder' and the 'risk of harm' criteria have persisted essentially unchanged for two centuries. I believe it is has exerted a stronger influence than the rather complacent view that the established approach works well enough. The late social historian of psychiatry, Roy Porter, in his book *A Social History of Madness*, noted the work of Michel Foucault, the famous French philosopher-historian who in

1961 wrote a highly influential history of 'madness' and who argued that up to the seventeenth century:

> Madness really did utter its own truths and engage in a full dialogue with reason. We need not go all the way with this romantic primitivism. But we can accept his further contention that from the seventeenth century onwards movements were activated which led for the next three centuries to mad people increasingly being segregated from sane society, both categorically and physically. In particular the institutionalization of the insane inexorably gathered momentum. [7,p14]

The accelerating movement to segregate those with mental disturbances from society from the seventeenth, through the eighteenth and, with special impetus, in the nineteenth century was regarded, as Porter puts it, as 'best for everyone'—essential for the well-being of the 'lunatic' and for the safety of society. From the late eighteenth century, the case for the asylum was reinforced by a new optimism about the effectiveness of treatment, although by the late nineteenth century this turned to pessimism as the numbers incarcerated grew inexorably. By the turn of the twentieth century they far exceeded the populations the asylums had been built to accommodate. The movement to close the crumbling institutions—'deinstitutionalization'—and to replace many of them with mental health care in the community did not commence until the late twentieth century in Western Europe, the United States, and Australasia. It remains at an embryonic stage in most other countries, and in some still at pre-conception.

What this segregation has meant is that those with a mental illness, those persons who are subjected to involuntary detention, have had practically no standing or 'voice' in society. Certainly there have been well-publicized scandals over the centuries that have led to gradual reforms of the mental health system. These reforms mainly involved requirements like the licensing and inspection of 'madhouses' and, later, of asylums, the requirement for medical certificates, and tighter legal protections against wrongful detention. But the grounds for detention, as we have seen, have not changed. Since the eighteenth century, as Porter points out, there have been a small number of accounts of their illness by patients who have been detained, but there has never been, until the past 20 years or so, anything like an organized, patient-led, social movement. Such a socially marginalized group has been in no position to demand change. In this regard, the reader might recall that it took over 50 years for the *Conseil Constitutionnel* in France to be prompted to examine the Law of 1990 and to conclude in 2010 that it was not compliant with the French constitution (1958) and that it required urgent reform. This surely says something important about a society's regard, or lack of it, for the standing of persons with a mental illness. France is certainly not unique in this respect. As one English legal authority put it in 1983: 'As far as society is concerned, the insane are "in it" but not "of it"'.[8]

The 'shadow of coercion'

Mental health law attempts to achieve a balance. It seeks to offer protection of the right to liberty of the patient, yet it permits treatment to be given against the person's wishes when he or she has a mental disorder and poses a substantial risk of harm to the self, or puts others at risk. The way this liberty versus protection balance is constructed is generally seen as reasonable.

Nevertheless, the powers that can be exercised generate a great deal of unease. For many patients, as well as for many observers of psychiatry, the potential for compulsion looms as an unsettling shadow over its practice. For patients, forced treatment is a deeply humiliating experience, for many one of the worst they will suffer. The account by the patient at the beginning of the Introduction to this book gives us an inkling of what it can feel like. At the same time, instigating compulsion is disturbing for the clinician. Seeing distress in others, especially distress that the clinicians themselves have initiated, is in turn distressing, even when they see it as justified in the interests of the patient. It certainly does not sit comfortably with the idea of a 'caring' profession. It is not why people have chosen to work in medicine. It can easily seem to smack of 'social control', of an intolerance of the unusual, of 'difference'. But, on the other hand, without an intervention of this kind, one that can offer effective treatment, the person might suffer needlessly and see their principal life projects destroyed. They may suffer serious physical harms, even death.

The repercussions of coercion extend beyond the actors directly involved—the patients and the clinicians. There are few families that have been untouched by a member, or a close friend, with a serious mental illness. What should one do in the face of a drastic transformation in a person's thinking or behaviour, one that doesn't seem to make sense and that threatens their well-being, when, despite the promise of an effective treatment, the person denies there is a problem? It can pose a terrible dilemma: becoming in a sense 'complicit' in involuntary treatment is usually a horribly disorienting and painful experience.

The impact extends further still—in the form of what can be called the 'shadow of coercion'. This refers to the knowledge patients have that their psychiatrist has the power to initiate the procedures, in all likelihood successfully, for involuntary treatment. Some patients may overestimate this power, but it is nevertheless there. It exerts its influence in conversations where statements are liable to varying interpretations. For example, a psychiatrist's proposal that a treatment would be the 'right thing' or would be the 'wise' choice might be interpreted (rightly or wrongly) by the patient as a veiled threat—saying 'no' could lead to a compulsory order. The coercive shadow may loom especially in the minds of patients who have had first-hand experience of coercion in the past. Is the doctor's proposal communicating an uncomplicated piece of information or advice, or is it really a subtle threat? It may be impossible for the patient to tell—unless, of course, the proposal is rejected, which in turn, risks the involuntary treatment order that the patient wishes to avoid. In a later chapter I will look at the variety of forms that 'coercion' can take. A threat is certainly one of them. In many countries, the United Kingdom being an example, threats of involuntary treatment to induce an acceptance of 'voluntary' treatment are regarded as unethical. Yet many patients with a serious mental illness will say they are common in practice—or, at least, what are perceived as threats.

Another aspect of the clinician's power to coerce is its effect on the clinician. As I said before, clinicians do not like doing it. I have rarely, if ever, encountered one who does. But there is a trap that they can easily fall into, especially when working under pressure and where time becomes limited. The power to coerce may curtail the discussion between clinician and patient concerning treatment. The clinician takes the decision. This is bad in itself, but there is more at stake still. What goes on in the background during a discussion about treatment is at least as important as the decision itself—the building of a 'therapeutic alliance'. Such an alliance requires trust, and building trust requires time—it depends on the clinician showing that he or she is competent, that he or she knows what they are talking about, and crucially, that his or her 'agenda' is the same as the patient's.[9] That agenda is to serve the patient's interests. The power to treat a patient on a compulsory order offers the possibility of a short-cut to compliance, but it may come at a huge cost. Establishing a therapeutic alliance afterwards may prove much more difficult. And if the relationship is going to be a long one, as it often will be, this becomes a major handicap.

However, as I will go on to explain in Chapter 2, my unease does not end there.

References

1. **Rivière A, Gaudichon B, Ghanassia D.** *Camille Claudel: Catalogue raisonné* (3e édition, augmentée) Paris: Adam Biro, 2001.

2. **Jones K.** *A History of Mental Health Services.* London: Routledge & Kegan Paul, 1972.
3. **World Health Organization**. *Mental Health Atlas 2011.* Geneva: WHO, 2011.
4. **Zhao X, Dawson J.** The new Chinese Mental Health Law. *Psychiatry, Psychology and Law* 2014; **21**:669–686.
5. **First Tier Tribunal.** *In the Matter of an Application by Ian Stuart Brady.* 2014. https://www.judiciary.gov.uk/wp-content/uploads/JCO/Documents/Judgments/ian-brady-mh-tribunal-240114.pdf
6. **Szmukler GI, Bird AS, Button EJ.** Compulsory admissions in a London borough: I. Social and clinical features and a follow-up. *Psychological Medicine* 1981; **11**:617–636; II. Circumstances surrounding admission: service implications. *Psychological Medicine* 1981; **11**:825–838.
7. **Porter R.** *A Social History of Madness: The World Through the Eyes of the Insane.* New York: Dutton, 1989.
8. **Unsworth C.** *The Politics of Mental Health Legislation.* Oxford: Clarendon Press, 1987.
9. **Brown P, Calnan M.** *Trusting on the Edge: Managing Uncertainty and Vulnerability in the Midst of Serious Mental Health Problems.* Bristol: Polity Press, 2012.

Chapter 2

Some troubling observations about involuntary treatment

People with a diagnosis of a mental illness can be placed in a vulnerable position, especially when treatment, or measures that claim to be treatments, can be imposed against the person's will. The vulnerability can take a number of forms.

Disturbing statistics on variation by place and time

The use of involuntary treatment in recent years has increased greatly in England and in many other European countries.[1] I have not been able to find numbers for the United States, but I would be surprised if they had not also grown. The number of people detained per annum involuntarily in hospitals in England and Wales rose from 21,897 in 1988 to 58,399 in 2015.[2] The increase from the previous year was just under 10 per cent. The increase from 5 years previously was approximately 26 per cent. Just over a quarter of those detained were patients admitted 'informally' (i.e. voluntarily) but who were then placed on a compulsory order when wishing to leave the hospital or when rejecting treatment. A 'snapshot' of the number of people detained in hospital on 31 March comparing 2011 and 2015 showed an increase of 20 per cent. Nearly 50 per cent of inpatients are now on an order. I recall that it was less than 10 per cent when I was a trainee psychiatrist in the late 1970s.

Furthermore, the idea has taken root that since the predominant locus of mental health care has shifted from hospitals to the community, involuntary treatment should not be restricted to the former.[3] Surely, it is argued, it is sensible to extend the possibility of compulsion to community treatment as well. Hence, many countries have recently introduced what is variably termed 'involuntary outpatient treatment', 'involuntary outpatient commitment', or a 'community treatment order'. Community treatment orders were introduced in England and Wales in 2008, and in

2015 were commenced for 4564 people. There were 5461 people on a community treatment order on 31 March 2015.[2] Before their introduction, the government—intent on introducing this order despite the misgivings of many mental health professionals—predicted that only a few hundred people per annum would require a community treatment order. The prediction was inaccurate by a factor of more than ten!

What is behind this startling increase in numbers of people on a compulsory order? The reasons are not entirely clear but what is certain is that they involve social factors rather than anything directly to do with mental illness itself. The natures of schizophrenia, bipolar disorder, and psychotic depression have not mutated over the past 20 years. Neither has their prevalence grown. In England, the key factors are probably, first, a huge reduction in inpatient beds[4] and, second, the emergence of a strongly risk-averse society. The number of psychiatric beds has fallen from 150,000 in the mid 1950s to 67,000 in 1987, and to just over 19,000 in 2016. The number has fallen by a staggering 10,000 (approximately 30 per cent) in the last decade alone. Fewer beds mean longer delays in admission for those for whom it turns out to be unavoidable despite the best efforts of their community mental health teams. Delays mean more severe symptoms by the time admission occurs compared to, say, 20 years ago. When bed availability becomes highly constrained, patients may be placed on an involuntary order as a manoeuvre to secure their admission.

Changes in attitudes to what comprises an acceptable risk, accompanied by escalating efforts at greater control, have been evident in society in many areas, and especially so in mental health care. Official guidance for practitioners and hospital managers from the Department of Health since the mid 1990s shows increasing references to 'risk assessment' and 'risk management'. By 2001, the Department declared that 'risk assessment and risk management is [sic] at the heart of effective mental health practice and needs to be central to any training'. The risk to others has been the number one concern. For a clinician like myself, practising psychiatry since the 1970s, it came as a shock that my medical education, though occurring in the very best centres, had apparently missed out on a 'central' training need. The term 'risk assessment' was virtually never used, except perhaps by those clinicians looking after mentally abnormal offenders whose task was to assess how dangerous such a person might be following discharge. Nowadays every patient who comes into contact with mental health services—not just forensic services—must have a risk assessment, both of the risk to him- or herself, and—representing a huge change in emphasis—to others.[5]

Why have we seen this shift in mental health services? Risk aversion has been fuelled by the mistaken belief, repeatedly trumpeted in the media and accepted by many politicians and policymakers, that 'community care has failed'. The greatest fear seems to have been of homicides perpetrated by people with a mental illness who now live in the community but in the past would have been, in the popular imagination, safely locked up in hospitals. (The statistics, though, indicate that the numbers of homicides committed by people with a serious mental illness, such as a psychosis, have not increased, and if anything, have fallen.[6]) Concern seems to have particularly focused on preventing patients in the community from 'falling through the net' of services, or defaulting from them. Discontinuation of treatment or escaping from surveillance by the clinical team is believed to indicate a serious risk of violence to others.

In Chapter 3, I will deal in some detail with the idea of 'risk' and its 'assessment'. It turns out to be a sad and costly story of folly—of our limited capacity for understanding and making sense of numbers.

There is another striking fact about the use of compulsion in mental health care. It is the huge variation in the rates of involuntary admissions to psychiatric hospitals between countries—and even within countries. A 2004 study of involuntary detention covering fifteen European Union countries found a thirtyfold difference between the country with the lowest rate per 100,000 population (Portugal, 6 per 100,000) and that with the highest (Finland, 218 per 100,000).[7] Of course, the relevant legislation varies between countries, as do the psychiatric services. But even within a single country where these should be a constant, rates vary as much as fivefold between different regions or even between hospitals within a region.[1] This range of variation applies also to the frequency of involuntary outpatient treatment.[3] Clearly powerful socio-cultural influences are at work here. However, the variation within social entities, such as a region of a state, indicate that what might be termed local 'custom and convention' also play a large role in determining when involuntary treatment is seen as appropriate.

These large variations in rates are disconcerting. If we saw variations of such magnitude in the rates of surgery for a particular cancer, or in the prescription of an established medication for cardiac failure, I think there would be cries of outrage. The problem is one of a considerable degree of arbitrariness in decisions about detention. Perhaps it's unrealistic to draw an analogy with surgery; one would expect stronger social determinants in hospitalization for mental illness. But it is the scale of the differences that astonishes.

An unfortunate history of abuse, misuse, or mistreatment

I will distinguish here two kinds of 'abuse' of psychiatry. The first is abuse for political ends, or for control of those who threaten the social order; the second is 'abuse'—perhaps better termed 'mistreatment' or 'misplaced therapeutic confidence'—perpetrated by doctors in good faith, in the belief that they are doing well by their patients.

Psychiatry as an instrument to control threats to the social order

This is a huge subject with which I can only deal briefly.[8] Prime examples where psychiatry has been used as an instrument of social control include the former Soviet Union, China, and Nazi Germany. The interests of the patient were subjugated to those of the state. A diagnosis of a 'mental disorder' and a purported role of psychiatry to protect society from harms perpetrated by those with such disorders provided a well-established 'rationale' for the incarceration and so-called treatment of people who represented a threat to the social order. I am not suggesting that this was the whole story—far from it. The states in which such abuses occurred on a large scale were totalitarian, oppressive, intimidating, politically policed, and with scant respect for law. However, recognizable procedures for detention and involuntary treatment facilitated the process.

Probably the best-known example was the subversion of psychiatry in the former Soviet Union for political purposes, especially from the 1960s to the 1980s. Statements of opposition to the Soviet Union, portrayed by the authorities as embodying an 'ideal state', were interpreted as a sign of mental disorder. How could any sane person object to a manifestation of the ideal? Diagnosis became extraordinarily inclusive of the kinds of beliefs and behaviours that came to be considered signs of 'mental illness'. For example, a type of schizophrenia unknown to the rest of the world, 'sluggish schizophrenia', could be diagnosed before the onset of clear psychotic symptoms. Signs of illness could include 'delusions of reform' or 'struggle for the truth'. Once a person with dissenting views was found to be 'mentally ill', this could warrant hospitalization and forced 'treatment' if they were considered to pose a 'social danger'. In the 1960s, one-third of all political prisoners in the Soviet Union were diagnosed as being mentally ill. Following discharge, 'patients' could be placed on a psychiatric register and were then subject to compulsory recall for examination. According to the journal *Ogonek* published in 1988, there were ten million names on this register. A single doctor, above any objection by the family, could order admission, but this had to be later approved by a panel of three psychiatrists.

With *perestroika* came an admission of abuses. However, problems though on a lesser scale continue. A report to the European Parliament in 2013, *Psychiatry as a Tool for Coercion in Post-Soviet Countries*, from the Directorate-General for External Policies, concluded:

> Regrettably, the political climate in some of the former Soviet republics, and notably the Russian Federation, is again such that local officials feel they have the liberty to revert to using psychiatry as a tool of frightening their opponents. In most cases, there is no attempt to revert to long-term hospitalizations and compulsory treatment, as in the Soviet period, but rather using psychiatry as a matter of '*profilaktizirovanie*' (prevention), as KGB-Chairman Yuri Andropov preferred to call it.[9]

In China, there is good evidence that during the 'Cultural Revolution' there were many detentions in institutions for the criminally insane of people who were diagnosed with 'mental disorders' such as 'counterrevolutionary behaviour' or 'behaviour that endangers state security'. According to a 2002 report, *Dangerous Minds: Political Psychiatry in China Today and its Origins in the Mao Era*, by Human Rights Watch and the Geneva Initiative in Psychiatry, official psychiatric theory in China continued into the twenty-first century to condone the involuntary treatment in custodial mental asylums of dissidents and non-conformists. These included Falun Gong members ('evil cult-induced mental disorder'), independent labour organizers, whistle blowers, and individuals complaining about official misconduct (referred to as 'petitioners'). While politically inspired abuse was not systematic, the report claimed that a small number of psychiatrists in the forensic services readily diagnosed as mentally ill people who were brought before them by government officials. A report in 2012 to the UN Committee on the Rights of Persons with Disabilities by the organization Chinese Human Rights Defenders (CHRD) provided evidence that the abuses described in the 2002 report continued as late as 2012.

I hesitate to include in this context the Nazi regime's killing of people with certain mental disorder diagnoses, regarded as 'lives unworthy of life'. It was of a different kind and had nothing to do with any idea of 'treatment'. It was simply murder, termed euphemistically 'euthanasia', instigated by the state. Over 200,000 patients were killed. The procedures were supervised by doctors. The killing began with disabled babies and children and was then extended to adult mental patients. It represents the all-time low point in the history of psychiatry—indeed of medicine, since others were also intimately involved, for example, in implementing mass sterilization and in the promotion of eugenics and 'racial science'. Among them were doctors of the highest status and reputation. Resistance was rare. How did psychiatrists come to participate in this killing? Pressures from peers and superiors were certainly important, as were careerism and various psychological mechanisms of 'denial'. However, in keeping with the theme of this section, the role of ideology was key—serving 'a greater cause' or 'sacred mission': fulfilling a duty to the state to protect it from those who would rent its fabric.

In these cases, the interests of the patient and the duty of care owed to them by doctors were subjugated to the interests of the state. A diagnosis of a mental disorder, even of the most fanciful kind, was crucial in creating this possibility. The 'status' of being a person with a mental disorder was the key that opened a gateway. Actions then followed, made possible as a result of that status, that were justified by a form of the 'risk' criterion—the 'protection of others'.

A recent case: 'dangerous severe personality disorder'

There are lesser versions of such an ordering of psychiatry's obligations to the state as opposed to the individual. England has its own, admittedly contested, example. While in an entirely different league to the cases described earlier—I am not suggesting they are comparable in their perversion of psychiatric practice—there is nevertheless something in common. Psychiatry and its powers of detention were recruited to assist in the state's aim of controlling a group of people seen as presenting a threat to the community. I am referring to people designated in 1999 by the Department of Health and the Home Office as having a 'dangerous severe personality disorder' (often referred to as DSPD). This 'diagnosis' does not appear even among the 300 or so 'disorders' listed in the fifth edition of the *Diagnostic and Statistical Manual of Mental Disorders*. The Home Secretary at the time, Jack Straw, said in the House of Commons on 15 February 1999:

> [T]here is, however, a group of dangerous and severely personality disordered individuals from whom the public at present are not properly protected ... there should be new legislative powers for the indeterminate but renewable detention of dangerously personality disordered individuals. These powers will apply whether or not someone was before the courts for an offence.

This was a response to a highly publicized vicious attack in 1996 on a mother and her two daughters by a man regarded as having a 'personality disorder' but who was deemed 'untreatable' and thus not legally detainable under the Mental Health Act by his psychiatric service. At that time, a person with 'psychopathy'—'a persistent disorder or disability of mind which results in abnormally aggressive or seriously irresponsible conduct', and one of the subcategories of 'mental disorder' under the Mental Health Act 1983—could only be detained if treatment 'was likely to alleviate or prevent a deterioration' of the disorder. (The other subcategories of 'mental disorder' were 'mental illness' and 'mental impairment'—a state of 'arrested or incomplete development of mind'—as well as the catch-all of 'any other disorder or disability of mind'.) The government responded to a perceived demand for better public protection with a consultation document in 1999. Proposals included a change in the law to remove the 'treatability' requirement for the detention in hospital of people with a personality disorder, and if necessary for the duration of the detention to be indefinite. This would involve an intensive specialist psychiatric assessment of the personality disorder and dangerousness 'resulting from the disorder' and the establishment of a new programme for people with a 'dangerous severe personality disorder', including an evaluation of the programme's effectiveness. Prisoners reaching the end of their sentences but who met the diagnostic entry criteria would be transferred on a compulsory order to the programme, or eligible subjects could be referred by the courts or from psychiatric services.

A trenchant criticism was offered in an editorial in the *British Medical Journal* in 1999 by Paul Mullen, a forensic psychiatrist. While noting that supporters of the programme welcomed the promise of new resources for a neglected group of people with a mental disorder, and which at the same time offered the inviting prospect of securing a safer community, he nevertheless argued:

> If dangerousness was really a characteristic of some personality disordered individuals rather than a characteristic of some acts by some of them; if the proposed special centres, with their multidisciplinary teams armed with 'batteries of standardised procedures', could reliably recognise dangerous severe personality disorder; ... and if health professionals were really judges and jailers charged with maintaining public order, then perhaps these proposals would be worth taking seriously. But none of these assumptions holds true.[10]

He went on to say in relation to the meaning of 'antisocial personality' (or 'psychopathy' or 'dangerous personality disorder'—all are equally imprecise) that such diagnoses are essentially circular, recycling a history of prior offending behaviours in the form of a diagnosis that, in turn, is supposed to explain the offending behaviours. Mental health variables, he argued, contribute little to the prediction of future violence.

In 2001, a costly programme was instituted at two prisons and two secure hospitals for detained people with 'dangerous severe personality disorder', whether deemed treatable or not.[11] An associated research programme was established, aimed at developing and testing possible, but so far unproven, treatments. Changes were eventually made to the Mental Health Act 1983 that dropped the requirement of treatability for the detention of people with a personality disorder. The amendment required only that appropriate treatment be 'available'—not that it might be effective. To many, myself included, the programme looked very much like an attempt to impose preventive detention under the guise of psychiatric diagnosis and treatment. Detention under mental health law was much easier to achieve than through the courts of the criminal justice system. The involvement of lawyers for the defence, and of judges who probe the evidence in some depth, rendered the former a simpler means of achieving legal detention. In fact, since the passing of the Criminal Justice Act in 1991 (and later in 2003), the judges already had the power to impose extended sentences, including 'discretionary life sentences', after conviction for a range of serious offences where there is a significant risk of serious harm to the public. But they rarely did so. Perhaps the government thought psychiatrists might prove more pliable and more easily induced to produce a more or less equivalent outcome.

But things did not turn out as expected. In 2012, the government announced it was phasing out the 'DSPD' programme. A review of the research findings concluded there were:

> a number of concerns regarding stigma, restrictiveness of the environment and indeterminate detention. ... No high-quality trials were carried out of specific treatments or service environments. The key question - what treatments are effective for high-risk personality disordered offenders - remains unanswered.[12]

Clearly the fact that this programme was implemented in a state that respects legal process makes it quite unlike the former Soviet Union or China examples. However, what it does illustrate is the weight that can be given to a diagnosis of a 'mental disorder' in rendering a person subject to coercive interventions, in these examples exercised primarily in the interests of other people. My objection here is not to preventive detention per se—though I am not in favour of it—but to its discriminatory nature in this case. Why should only those with a 'mental disorder' be detained because they are deemed risky, when there are many more equally risky individuals out there who do not have a 'mental disorder' and who are therefore not eligible for detention? Furthermore, it is entirely reasonable to offer treatment to those with a 'personality disorder' if there is one that could be effective—but most people would say it should be on a voluntary basis. It is not clear how 'voluntary' the treatment for DSPD was. Again, it is fine to research possible interventions for people with a personality disorder if there are some leads that show promise. The treatments also need to be carefully designed, well implemented, and systematic if they are to be evaluated meaningfully. The review cited earlier[12] indicates these standards were not met.

In later chapters, I will look in detail at the discrimination implicated in the detention in hospital of people with a mental illness on the basis of a purported 'risk' to others.

Mistreatment due to misplaced therapeutic confidence

The 'good faith' of doctors involved directly in the abuse of psychiatry in the former Soviet Union, Nazi Germany, and China is dubious, though, no doubt, some convinced themselves they were acting in a way that was consistent with the duties of their profession. In the 'dangerous severe personality disorder' example, my impression was that most of those directly involved believed they were acting in the interests of a marginalized group of people who might be helped. However, many had at least some misgivings.

I now look at treatments that were given, often without the consent of the patient, where the vast majority of doctors involved believed they were doing their best for the patient.

There are a number of historical examples that are chilling—surgery for 'focal sepsis' (where teeth, tonsils, segments of bowel, the cervix, and other organ parts were surgically removed as they were apparently the site of infection-derived toxins affecting the brain and causing mental illness)[13]; prolonged narcosis; insulin coma therapy; lobotomy; and various crude forms of 'shock therapy'.[14] We look back on them now as grotesque. However, they were not seen that way at the time, that is, between the 1920s and 1950s. Some were even requested by patients, but more often requests were made by their families. Most of the time the patients feared the treatments, but their lack of consent was not a serious obstacle. Other people could consent on their behalf, believing the treatment would prove effective. In England, the Board of Control for Lunacy and Mental Deficiency, set up by the government in 1913 to ensure that those detained under the various mental illness and mental deficiency laws received proper care, encouraged the introduction of some of these 'modern' treatments.

Before allowing ourselves to feel too smug, it is important to take account of some context. The early decades of the twentieth century saw no hope for the mentally ill. The eugenic movement was influential—mental illness was commonly seen as representing a genetically based form of degeneration. The spread of the bad genes needed to be controlled. The idea attracted leading intellectuals and prominent members of the medical profession. Segregation from the rest of the community was one method of protecting the 'stock of the nation'; sterilization was another. The United States led the way in the first decade of the twentieth century, with forty states having passed laws allowing involuntary sterilization by 1940. Other Western countries followed, including Germany in one of Hitler's first acts on assuming power in 1933. After a long debate, England did not pass such a law.

The numbers of patients in the asylums grew enormously. Medical and other staff working in these overcrowded institutions were overwhelmed by the misery and disturbance they had to manage. It was during this time of despondency about mental illness that exciting, new, radical remedies emerged. They had a biological 'scientific' rationale, they were introduced and supported by eminent physicians and bioscientists, they brought psychiatry into the fold of 'real' medicine where physical interventions were the rule, and—most wonderfully—they seemed to work. Lobotomy is a good example. Edgar Moniz, a Portuguese neurologist, reported in 1936 that severing segments of the brain's connections to the frontal lobes—essential for many higher cognitive functions—resulted in improvement in 70 per cent of patients with schizophrenia. This was an immensely impressive outcome. The operation was then taken up and technically modified in various ways by Walter Freeman, a respected American neurologist and his neurosurgeon colleague, James Watts. Again, marvellous results were reported. The treatment received support from Professor Adolf Meyer of Johns Hopkins University, perhaps America's most famous psychiatrist. A review in 1943 of the outcomes of 618 lobotomies reported that 84 per cent of patients were 'improved' or 'recovered' and 40 per cent were living in the community and working full- or part-time. Mortality was reported as 2 per cent. Governments and hospital administrators struggling to fund hospitals well past their sell-by dates were excited by the prospect of reducing patient numbers. Newspaper and popular journal articles celebrated the treatment as a revolution in mental health care. A further seal of approval came when Moniz was awarded a Nobel Prize for his work in 1949.

Freeman made further modifications to the procedure aimed at making it simpler and widely accessible. 'Transorbital lobotomy', introduced in 1946, did not require a neurosurgeon; indeed, it could even be done by a psychiatrist. First the patient was made unconscious by two or three electroshocks. Then an ice pick-like device was driven with a few taps of a mallet through the top of the eye-socket into the frontal lobe and then swept across its connections to the rest of the brain. This was repeated on the other side. A dozen operations could be done in an afternoon. Freeman called it a 'minor operation'.

By 1954, over 20,000 lobotomies had been performed in the United States. It became clear by the mid 1950s that the results were far inferior to those reported by the early enthusiasts. The mortality rate was now over 10 per cent and many patients were left with severe disabilities. Freeman and Watts' book on psychosurgery, seen from the perspective of what we would require of a 'successful treatment' today, described grossly unacceptable outcomes. It is likely that the early apparently spectacular results reflected the low baseline of expectation for what were seen as hopelessly intractable disorders.

My reason for looking at this example is to recognize that treatments, later shown to be useless or worse still, damaging, were prescribed by many doctors in good faith, with the best of intentions, to many patients who were not able to refuse them. There is a big difference between patients making a considered decision for themselves, for or against a treatment, and the treatment being given without their consent or against their will. The latter must make special demands on the clinician—for instance, that recourse to involuntary treatment should be kept to an absolute minimum; and if it is to be used, careful reflection is required about its justification. People with mental illness, being a marginalized group without a 'voice', have been especially vulnerable to various forms of mistreatment.

Unfortunately, overestimates of the therapeutic value of 'established' treatments probably continue today. I quote an example from my own experience. When I started in psychiatry, the antipsychotic drug, haloperidol, was commonly used in schizophrenia and the manic phase of bipolar disorder. A common starting dose for a patient ill enough to be admitted to hospital was 15 mg per day. Doses of 45 mg, 60 mg, or even 100 mg or more per day for those not improving with lower doses were not uncommon. This was regarded as standard treatment, supported by psycho-pharmacologist experts in the field. The side effects of haloperidol at doses of 15 mg or higher are often very unpleasant. When I was later involved in a study in which each patient and the clinical team discussed in detail the patient's preferences for treatment if a relapse of their psychosis were to occur, a common request was for haloperidol to be avoided. Those patients were ready to accept other antipsychotic drugs—but 'please, not haloperidol'. In the meantime, a new group of antipsychotic drugs, 'second-generation' or 'atypical' antipsychotics, was introduced. Many randomized controlled treatment trials showed that these new drugs did not engender the distressing side effects characteristic of haloperidol (though they had new ones of their own). Despite their expense, and helped by adroit marketing by their manufacturers, they became the medication of first choice. However, some years later it emerged that the side effect comparisons were often made against haloperidol at up to 20 mg doses. Re-analysis of a large number of studies where various doses of haloperidol were used showed that with low doses of haloperidol, 6–12 mg, the response was just as good as with the 'atypicals' and the side effects just as tolerable, though different.[15] The important point to be made here is that during the 1970s to the 1990s, practitioners like me were using unnecessarily high doses of haloperidol, thereby causing disabling side effects. Of course, many patients subjected to high doses of haloperidol were on a compulsory order. They could not refuse the treatment.

The phenomenon of excessive therapeutic confidence of course occurs in all medical specialities. It is by no means unique to psychiatry. New treatments, especially when therapeutic options have been limited, can be greeted with enormous enthusiasm—which sadly wanes as their weaknesses emerge following their use in larger numbers of patients, in the real world. We must be especially wary in psychiatry, though, because of a particular combination: the power we have to force treatment, and a disempowered, socially marginalized patient group whose experiences of their treatments can so easily be ignored as the ranting of disturbed minds.

Race, ethnicity, minority status, and involuntary treatment

I shall focus here on the situation in the United Kingdom with which I am most familiar. But, even here, behind some bald facts are complexities that are hard to unravel.

The facts are that people of African or African-Caribbean origin are over-represented among patients in psychiatric hospitals, and among those on an involuntary treatment order.[16] A 1-day census of inpatients in England by the Care Quality Commission (*Count me in 2009*)[17] found that 'African', 'African-Caribbean', 'mixed', and 'other Black' groups were two to four times more likely to be admitted than white British patients.

They were also 19–32 per cent more likely than the average to be admitted on a compulsory order, up to 55 per cent more likely to be on a medium or high secure ward, and over-represented by up to 106 per cent on community treatment orders. An emergency admission via an accident and emergency department or via the police or criminal justice system is more likely for these groups compared to white British patients, and is correspondingly less likely to be via a referral from a general practitioner. Not all ethnic minority groups are over-represented in this way. The same census found that those of Indian origin were less likely to be admitted than white British and no more likely to be detained on a compulsory order. Generally, though, patients from minority ethnic groups, including the Irish, were over-represented, overall, among those detained on an order by around 10 per cent.

Other studies indicate that black patients after discharge from hospital are more likely to be readmitted and readmitted on a compulsory order.[18]

In relation to higher admission rates and involuntary status it is the black patients who stand out. How this happens is the subject of debate. Most authorities agree that there is a higher rate of serious mental illness, particularly psychoses, in these population groups[19] and that this is related to cumulative social disadvantage, such as unemployment, poverty, and low socio-economic status.[20] Discrimination, certainly as perceived by those people, compounds this disadvantage and its associated social exclusion. Where there is large disagreement concerns the direct contribution of mental health services. Some claim that mental health services are 'institutionally racist', an allegation that is fiercely denied by others, especially those who work in those services. As a psychiatrist who has spent his career in public mental health services, and has been involved over many years as a Board member in their management, the claim is enormously disturbing. Nevertheless, we must look at what 'institutional racism' means. It does not mean that those delivering the service are individually racist. Indeed, I have very infrequently encountered staff whose attitudes or behaviour I would label 'racist'. 'Institutional racism' refers to something else. It is defined as: 'the collective failure of an organization to provide an appropriate and professional service to people because of their colour, culture, or ethnic origin … through unwitting prejudice, ignorance, thoughtlessness, and racist stereotyping which disadvantages people in ethnic minority groups'.[21] Perhaps this is a fair assessment of at least some service components. But certainly not all—a recent study in three regions of England found that once people had reached the point of being brought for an assessment of whether an involuntary admission was warranted or not—how they got to there was not studied—the effect of ethnicity on whether they were detained or not was not clearly evident, especially when account was taken of a small number of socio-demographic factors.[22]

Overall, I find it difficult to disaggregate the role of mental health services from that of the wider society and its institutions. For instance, by the time black patients enter the service, there has already been more police involvement—not a congenial way to start what might turn out to be a long-term relationship with the service. The inter-relationships I am thinking about have been well described as follows:

> The net result for Black patients of more aversive pathways to care, greater compulsory admissions and poorer medication adherence, unsurprisingly, seems to lead both to increased mutual distrust from both patients and care-providers, as well as a more costly experience for Black patients through mental health services. The finding that Black people are often reluctant to engage with mainstream mental health services with delays in seeking help, seems to create new risks, such as police involvement or use of the Mental Health Act, which leads to disproportionately high rates of hospital inpatient admission, compulsory admission, admission to intensive care and secure services and use of seclusion and restraint in all types of hospital. Such patterns of service-use are negatively experienced and associated with poor outcomes, as measured by relapse and readmission. In turn, these adverse consequences reinforce mistrust of mainstream services that is the initial cause of delayed engagement.[i]

This book is not about solving this larger problem, but about a specific aspect. The reason for raising ethnicity in relation to involuntary treatment is to further reinforce our worries about its exercise and the need to think carefully about how it is to be justified.

I will suggest a different approach that I believe would reduce discrimination in the exercise of compulsion, and take greater account of patients' socially and culturally related values.

References

1. **Hoyer G.** Involuntary hospitalization in contemporary mental health care. Some (still) unanswered questions. *Journal of Mental Health* 2008; 17:281–292.
2. **Health and Social Care Information Centre.** *Inpatients Formally Detained in Hospitals under the Mental Health Act 1983, and Patients Subject to*

---

[i] Reproduced from Chakraborty A, Patrick L, Lambri M., 'Racism and Mental Illness in the UK'. In: *Mental Disorders - Theoretical and Empirical Perspectives*, eds. Woolfolk and Lesley Allen. INTECH Open Access Publisher; 2013 under the Creative Commons Attribution 3.0 Unported License (CC BY 3.0).

Supervised Community Treatment. Annual Report, England, 2014–2015. London: HSCIC, 2015.

3. **Dawson J.** *Community Treatment Orders: International Comparisons.* Dunedin, New Zealand: Otago University Press, 2005.
4. **Holloway F, Sederer LI.** Inpatient treatment. In: Thornicroft G, Szmukler G, Meuser K, Drake R (Eds) *Oxford Textbook of Community Mental Health.* Oxford: Oxford University Press, 2011; 167–177.
5. **Department of Health.** *Best Practice in Managing Risk: Principles and Guidance for Best Practice in the Assessment and Management of Risk to Self and Others in Mental Health Services.* London: Department of Health, 2007.
6. **Large M, Smith G, Swinson N, Shaw J, Nielssen O.** Homicide due to mental disorder in England and Wales over 50 years. *British Journal of Psychiatry* 2008; **193**:130–133.
7. **Dressing H, Salize HJ.** Compulsory admission of mentally ill patients in European Union Member States. *Social Psychiatry and Psychiatric Epidemiology* 2004; **39**:797–803.
8. For details see: **Reddaway P, Bloch S.** *Russia's Political Hospitals: The Abuse of Psychiatry in the Soviet Union.* London: Gollancz, 1977; **van Voren R.** Political abuse of psychiatry—an historical overview. *Schizophrenia Bulletin* 2010; **36**:33–35; **van Voren R.** Comparing Soviet and Chinese political psychiatry. *Journal of the American Academy of Psychiatry and the Law* 2002; **30**:131–135; **Munro R.** Judicial psychiatry in China and its political abuses *Columbia Journal of Asian Law* 2000; **14**:1–125.
9. **Van Voren R.** *Psychiatry as a Tool for Coercion in Post-Soviet Countries.* Belgium: European Union, 2013.
10. **Mullen P.** Dangerous people with severe personality disorder. *British Medical Journal* 1999; **319**:1146–1147.
11. **Duggan C.** Dangerous and severe personality disorder. *British Journal of Psychiatry* 2011; **198**:431–433.
12. **Vollm B, Konappa N.** The dangerous and severe personality disorder experiment – review of empirical research. *Criminal Behavior and Mental Health* 2012; **22**:165–180.
13. **Scull A.** Desperate remedies: a Gothic tale of madness and modern medicine. *Psychological Medicine* 1987; **17**:561–577.
14. For details see: **Shorter E.** *A Short History of Psychiatry: From the Era of the Asylum to the Age of Prozac.* New York: Wiley, 1997; **Whitaker R.** *Mad in America.* Cambridge, MA: Perseus, 2002.
15. **Geddes J, Freemantle N, Harrison P, Bebbington P.** Atypical antipsychotics in the treatment of schizophrenia: systematic overview and meta-regression analysis. *British Medical Journal* 2000; **321**:1371–1376.
16. **Singh SP, Greenwood NAN, White S, Churchill R.** Ethnicity and the mental health act 1983. *British Journal of Psychiatry* 2007; **191**:99–105.

17. **Care Quality Commission**. *Count Me In 2009. Results of the 2009 National Census of Inpatients and Patients on Supervised Community Treatment in Mental Health and Learning Disability Services in England and Wales.* London: Care Quality Commission, 2010.
18. **Morgan C, Fearon P, Lappin J**, et al. Ethnicity and long-term course and outcome of psychotic disorders: the AESOP-10 study. *British Journal of Psychiatry.* In press.
19. **Tortelli A, Errazuriz A, Croudace T**, et al. Schizophrenia and other psychotic disorders in Caribbean-born migrants and their descendants in England: systematic review and meta-analysis of incidence rates, 1950–2013. *Social Psychiatry & Psychiatric Epidemiology* 2015; **50**:1039–1055.
20. **Morgan C, Kirkbride J, Hutchinson G**, et al. Cumulative social disadvantage, ethnicity and first-episode psychosis: a case-control study. *Psychological Medicine* 2008; **38**:1701–1715.
21. **Home Office**. *The Stephen Lawrence Inquiry: Report of an Inquiry by Sir William Macpherson of Cluny* (Cm 4262-I). London: The Stationery Office, 1999.
22. **Singh SP, Burns T, Tyrer P, Islam Z, Parsons H, Crawford MJ.** Ethnicity as a predictor of detention under the Mental Health Act. *Psychological Medicine* 2014; **44**:997–1004.

Chapter 3

The conventional grounds for involuntary treatment are highly problematic

As we have seen, in nearly all countries, two criteria form the grounds for detention and involuntary treatment—the 'mental disorder' criterion and the 'risk of harm' criterion. These have not changed fundamentally for two centuries. Furthermore, today they are supported by a number of key international human rights instruments (though as we shall see later in Chapter 8, not by the latest, the UN Convention on the Rights of Persons with Disabilities).

Human rights conventions and mental disorder

The 1950 European Convention on Human Rights (ECHR)[1] produced in the aftermath of the horrors of the 1930s and 1940s has been signed and ratified by the 47 Council of Europe[i] nations. Any person who feels their rights have been violated under the Convention by a state institution can take a case to the European Court of Human Rights. Judgments of the Court are binding on the states concerned and they are obliged to execute them. Article 5[1] states which groups of people can be deprived of their liberty, provided there is a legal procedure:

---

[i] Not to be confused with the European Union. The Council of Europe, founded in 1949, is an organization focusing on promoting human rights in Europe. It is responsible for the ECHR. The Convention created the European Court of Human Rights in Strasbourg. The Court supervises compliance with the ECHR and thus functions as the highest European court.

Article 5
Right to liberty and security

1. Everyone has the right to liberty and security of person. No one shall be deprived of his liberty save in the following cases and in accordance with a procedure prescribed by law:
   (a) the lawful detention of a person after conviction by a competent court;
   (b) the lawful arrest or detention of a person for non-compliance with the lawful order of a court or in order to secure the fulfilment of any obligation prescribed by law;
   (c) the lawful arrest or detention of a person effected for the purpose of bringing him before the competent legal authority on reasonable suspicion of having committed an offence or when it is reasonably considered necessary to prevent his committing an offence or fleeing after having done so;
   (d) the detention of a minor by lawful order for the purpose of educational supervision or his lawful detention for the purpose of bringing him before the competent legal authority;
   (e) the lawful detention of persons for the prevention of the spreading of infectious diseases, of persons of unsound mind, alcoholics or drug addicts or vagrants;
   (f) the lawful arrest or detention of a person to prevent his effecting an unauthorised entry into the country or of a person against whom action is being taken with a view to deportation or extradition.[1][ii]

I draw your attention to Article 5.1(e), which refers to 'persons of unsound mind'—tellingly, from the point of view of their standing in society—placed in the company of 'drug addicts' and 'vagrants'. Who is included under 'persons of unsound mind'? The European Court has ruled in a landmark case in 1979 (*Winterwerp v Netherlands*) that the person must be 'reliably' shown to have a 'true' mental disorder on the basis of 'objective medical expertise'. The disorder must also be of a 'kind or degree that warrants compulsory confinement'. The court recognized that over time, with developments in mental health research, diagnostic criteria could change. Thus the definition was not specified further. Much faith is thus invested in the diagnostic practices of doctors.

Another important document, this time issued by the General Assembly of the United Nations in 1991, is entitled *The Protection of Persons with Mental Illness and the Improvement of Mental Health Care.*[2] This lays out a range of fundamental freedoms and basic rights for persons with mental illness. Under Principle 11, 'Consent to treatment', it states:

---

ii © ECHR-CEDH.

6. ... a proposed plan of treatment may be given to a patient without a patient's informed consent if the following conditions are satisfied:

   (a) The patient is, at the relevant time, held as an *involuntary patient*;

   (b) An independent authority, having in its possession all relevant information, ... is satisfied that, at the relevant time, the patient lacks the capacity to give or withhold informed consent to the proposed plan of treatment or, if domestic legislation so provides, that, *having regard to the patient's own safety or the safety of others, the patient unreasonably withholds such consent.* [My italics.]

Under Principle 16, 'Involuntary admission', it states what is required for an involuntary admission:

1. A person may be admitted involuntarily to a mental health facility as a patient or, having already been admitted voluntarily as a patient, be retained as an involuntary patient ... if, and only if, a qualified mental health practitioner authorized by law for that purpose determines ... that *that person has a mental illness* and considers:

   (a) That, because of that *mental illness*, there is a serious *likelihood of immediate or imminent harm to that person or to other persons*; or

   (b) That, in the case of a person whose mental illness is severe and whose judgement is impaired, failure to admit or retain that person is likely to lead to a serious deterioration in his or her condition or will prevent the giving of appropriate treatment that can only be given by admission to a mental health facility in accordance with the principle of the least restrictive alternative.[iii] [My italics.]

We see in these principles continuing endorsement for the 'mental disorder' and the 'risk of harm' criteria. There is mention in the 1991 UN Principle 16 of an impairment of judgement on the part of the person but its role is clearly subsidiary. In Principle 6, while 'capacity' to give consent is mentioned, the person's refusal can be overridden if consent is 'unreasonably withheld'.

I wish to now highlight some fundamental problems surrounding the two conventional criteria for involuntary detention and treatment—the presence of a 'mental disorder' and the 'risk of harm' to the person or other people.

What is a 'mental disorder'?

A key question for our purposes is what should count as a 'mental disorder' or a 'mental illness'. As we have seen, much hinges on a person receiving such a diagnosis. Without a mental disorder being diagnosed, a person cannot enter the frame for being detained in hospital or, usually, for being treated involuntarily. How 'objective' (as the European Court has put it) is the diagnosis of a 'true' mental disorder?

Psychiatric diagnoses today are asked to serve a variety of functions: in clinical practice, in research, in a range of medico-legal cases, in mental health service planning and funding, in defining eligibility for insurance and state benefits (for example, for unemployment or disability), as well as providing rallying calls for advocacy groups and charities.[3] The different contexts require different forms of diagnosis appropriate to the particular function such a diagnosis is meant to fulfil.

There are two contexts where the role of diagnosis is more or less clear and necessary—in the clinic and in research. Diagnosis is an indicator, guide, map, or hypothesis for the clinician as to the nature of the disorder that afflicts a patient, and especially as a guide to treatment and the likely outcome. It thus has an essential role in clinical practice and is expected to evolve in the light of new, relevant knowledge. The second context is in research. Ideally, research should provide a solid foundation for clinical diagnoses. The majority of psychiatrists would agree that existing clinical diagnoses such as those in the *Diagnostic and Statistical Manual of Mental Disorders* (DSM), now in its fifth edition, have not been validated using a range of research methods aimed at establishing a consistent relationship with causal—especially brain-related—abnormalities or mechanisms. It is thus appropriate that research diagnostic criteria depart from existing clinical schemas and adopt forms that hold the greatest promise for a scientific understanding of the causes of mental disorders. The hope is that the research findings will eventually lead to well-validated clinical diagnoses that will be informative about causes, treatments, and prognoses.

'Disorder' and 'values'

The role of a diagnosis in involuntary treatment is different again. Here it carries heavy legal and human rights implications. The ECHR demands that the diagnosis needs to be 'true' and based on 'objective medical expertise'. Particularly relevant to our discussion is the extent to which mental disorders are based on 'hard', 'objective' phenomena that occur in nature—sometimes called 'natural kinds'. Do the abnormalities represent, for example, failures of function of an organ or organs—primarily the brain? Or do they involve, to a significant degree, questions of 'value'?[4] By 'value' I mean that what determines whether a mental state is regarded as abnormal or pathological depends on what is socially valued, not on any objectively measureable 'natural kind'. Some forms of mental functioning—clearly abnormal in a statistical sense—are not regarded as 'disorder', but may be highly valued; high intelligence is an example. Other statistically abnormal forms are regarded as 'disorders'. Examples include the various types of 'personality disorder', such as 'antisocial personality disorder'. Diagnostic criteria for this condition vary but the following conveys the general flavour:

> People with antisocial personality disorder exhibit traits of impulsivity, high negative emotionality, low conscientiousness and associated behaviours including irresponsible and exploitative behaviour, recklessness and deceitfulness. This is manifest in unstable interpersonal relationships, disregard for the consequences of one's behaviour, a failure to learn from experience, egocentricity and a disregard for the feelings of others. The condition is associated with a wide range of interpersonal and social disturbance.[5]

Two aspects of 'value' can be traced here: first, the nature of the behaviour. It is considered socially undesirable or unacceptable because of its effect on others; second, the degree to which the behaviour is present. The degree of 'impulsivity' or 'negative emotionality' or 'deceitfulness', traits we all share to some degree, is judged as excessive.

Outside the 'personality disorders' where social values are clearly implicated to a major degree (many would say, entirely), problems of a similar kind are involved in determining when a person's sadness is severe enough to be a 'depressive illness', or when shyness becomes a 'social phobia'. Even 'harder' symptoms may sometimes present a similar problem—how irrational and impervious to clearly contradictory evidence does a belief need to be to be called a 'delusion'? Falling in love with a person whom everyone we know thinks is totally unsuitable is a common example. Holding extreme political beliefs is another. A diagnosis of a mental disorder is not usually made on the basis of symptoms alone, but also pays regard to disturbances in everyday functioning—the ability to sustain relationships, to work, and to engage in social or pleasurable activities. These also involve, to a greater or lesser degree, the kinds of value judgements to which I am referring.

The report of the Ian Brady Mental Health Tribunal hearing I discussed in Chapter 1 offers many examples of these kinds of judgement. All of the experts agreed Brady showed the features of an 'antisocial personality disorder'. A question here might be how one distinguishes between acts that are 'mad' versus 'bad, but let's leave that for later (see Chapter 11). When it came to the question of whether Brady also had schizophrenia, there was substantial disagreement. The experts were not helped by his unwillingness to engage with anyone, with a couple of exceptions, in psychiatric interviews. However, he had been observed in Ashford High Security Hospital for 28 years. It was noted that his lifestyle was highly restricted. However, was this a product of the withdrawal from the world of someone with schizophrenia, or was it an understandable reaction to his incarceration in an unusual institution run by authorities he did not trust? Was talking in his room when no one was present a response to hallucinations, or was it an example of a fairly commonplace talking to oneself when upset after an unpleasant interaction with others, or being excited by something seen on TV? Did he suffer from paranoid delusions or were his episodes of suspicion and irritation with staff and other patients understandable given the nature of his prickly personality and a severely limited life in an exacting, closed institution? Could the awareness that staff were constantly on the lookout for signs of psychosis make him act self-consciously and unnaturally, producing a kind of self-fulfilling prophecy?

The influence of 'values' in psychiatric diagnosis can make the 'mental disorder' criterion in involuntary treatment shaky. It has allowed fanciful diagnoses to be devised—such as the historical examples we looked at in Chapter 2—'sluggish schizophrenia' in the Soviet Union, or 'evil cult-induced psychosis' in China. It risks an expansion of 'disorders' to include more subtle threats to the social order—'dangerous severe personality disorder' is an example. It also risks the 'medicalization' of psychological states or behaviours what were previously considered to be part of normal experience—severe shyness or childhood hyperactivity are frequently quoted examples. Even biological abnormalities do not point invariably to a current 'disorder'—a substantial proportion of people with mild to moderate brain abnormalities typical of Alzheimer's disease do not have the clinical features of dementia.[6]

Values in diagnosis are not restricted to psychiatry. Many conditions in medicine are similarly influenced: how high should blood pressure be to warrant being called a disorder—'hypertension'? What level of bone density constitutes 'osteoporosis'? In both conditions, the risk of severe complications is elevated—for example, stroke in the former, fractures in the latter. What level of risk then justifies drug treatment for hypertension or osteoporosis? Such decisions reflect value judgements. However, values are usually less problematic in other areas of medicine than in psychiatry. There is general agreement that pain, even of mild to moderate degrees, is a bad thing and merits treatment; there is less agreement about mild to moderate anxiety.

In general, I don't find the role of values in diagnosis and treatment especially perturbing. Certainly we must be aware of them and give regard to them into our thinking about illness and 'disorder'. In normal clinical practice, we hope, differences in values between doctor and patient will emerge in the course of a discussion of the diagnosis, possible causes, and the options for treatment. There is thus the opportunity for the patient to assert his or her values. But here is the rub: when it comes to detention and involuntary treatment, the patient's values become less likely to attract attention. There is certainly no requirement in the 'mental disorder' criterion that they be taken into account.

I will aim to persuade the reader in the chapters that follow that the grounds for involuntary treatment should not be based on the 'status' of having a diagnosis of a mental disorder. For the reasons explored earlier, coupled with the examples in Chapter 2, I maintain that its boundaries are too blurred. The grounds for compulsion should instead be based (in part, not entirely) on what the person does with that diagnosis—how he or she understands it, how relevant it appears to be in the circumstances in which the person finds himself or herself, and how it is used in making a decision to accept or reject the proposed treatment. Are there reasons for believing that there is a problem with the person's ability to use, or weigh, or reason with what they have been told about the diagnosis and its implications: a problem with their ability to see the information in the light of their personal values and commitments?

Risk: the grave limitations of its assessment

A person meeting the 'risk of harm criterion' for involuntary treatment may already have suffered obvious harms or caused harms to others sufficient to make us think seriously about an urgent intervention. More often, it is the risk of harms occurring in the future that are the main concern. I shall engage in a fairly lengthy discussion of risk since it has assumed a huge role in mental health care in general—and for that matter in social care, a prominent example being child protection.

We like to believe that we can predict, in a useful way, many of the bad things that may happen. In health and social care, much effort has been devoted to developing the methods of 'risk assessment'. A suicide, a homicide committed by a person with a mental illness, the death of a child as a result of abuse, are appalling events. Every reasonable effort should be made to anticipate them and act to prevent them. The key here is every *reasonable* effort.

The sad truth is that we are very poor at predicting the very events that are the most tragic and that we most wish to prevent. The main reason for this is their rarity: the less frequent an event is, the more difficult it is to predict its occurrence with a worthwhile degree of accuracy. This is a brute statistical fact.

Unfortunately statistics are not very intuitive, at least not for non-statisticians. Very intelligent people, including psychiatrists, psychologists, lawyers, judges, journalists, senior civil servants, and politicians, find statistics very hard to grasp. *Probabilities* are what statistics in health care are largely about; that is, the precise probability (or chance) of a particular event occurring. It seems to me that our brains are not 'hard-wired' so as to make it easy for us. As will be described later, we are driven by a need to create narratives to explain events. Constructing narratives dwarfs our appreciation of probabilities, yet, in the instances we shall examine, the latter offers a truer account of the real world.

So how does it work? How are our conjectures undermined by statistical realities? I will take as an example the tragedy of a suicide. There was recently a case that was heard in the Supreme Court of the United Kingdom where a young woman was allowed home on leave from a psychiatric hospital where she had been admitted following a suicide attempt in the context of a depressive illness.[7]

A tragic case

Twenty-four-year-old Melanie committed suicide by hanging on 20 April 2005. The previous day she had been allowed home leave from a psychiatric unit where she had been admitted on 11 April. She had suffered from depression since 2000. On 4 March 2005 she had been admitted to hospital after a suicide attempt where she tied a pillow-case around her neck. She was discharged on 18 March after an earlier overnight leave on 14 March. She then went on a family holiday to Egypt, but on 31 March, after her return, she cut her wrists with broken glass. She was not readmitted, apparently as no bed was available. Follow-up with the trainee psychiatrist on 6 April revealed that she had occasional thoughts of suicide and frequent thoughts of deliberate self-harm.

On 11 April Melanie tied lamp flex around her neck. Her face became swollen and there were ligature marks around her neck. Her parents also found a hosepipe and tape hidden in her room. The medical notes stated she had a 'severe depressive episode ... possible psychosis. High risk self-harm and suicide'. She was admitted informally, prescribed medication, and placed under 15-minute observations. A risk assessment using Trust documents was commenced by one of the nurses on the ward, but further information was required for it to be completed. On 13 April, Melanie's father 'expressed grave concern about Melanie's current condition and her being sent out on leave or discharged too soon'. There were further conversations involving her parents along these lines during the week. Nursing reports in the notes from 16 April stated that her mood was lifting, but her father phoned the ward on 18 April saying that she was not improving and that she had expressed fleeting suicidal thoughts. On 19 April, her consultant, who had been on leave when Melanie was admitted, returned from leave. The following was the record in the nursing notes of a meeting with Melanie and her mother:

'Present: consultant, Trainee psychiatrist, staff nurse. Melanie seen with her mother. She states she self harmed at home due to feeling angry at herself because of the thoughts she has. Realises that does not achieve anything. Feels trapped at home 'slightly'. Would like to be more independent. Stated enjoyed recent trip to Egypt. Does not regret leaving employment. Wishes to look for something else. Does not want to stay in destructive cycle. Struggling to recognise how she can stop same. Feels she is lacking in confidence and has low self-esteem. Identified ways of addressing issues herself. Would like to leave for up to a week. Would start looking for job and see friends. Leave agreed as long as Melanie when seeing her friends does not talk about herself and become centre of attention. Reasons for this also discussed. Mother concerned about same as unable to keep eye on her. The Consultant advised Melanie has to take responsibility for own actions and when has previously harmed herself it has been when parents keeping an eye on her. Melanie in agreement that will not self-harm.

Plan - for 2 days/nights leave.'

Melanie left the ward with her mother that evening, and sometime after 5pm on the next day she hung herself from a tree in a park. The hospital conceded the decision to allow home leave was negligent.

The question before the court was whether there had been a breach of the state's 'duty to protect life' under Article 2 of the Human Rights Act 1998. (The Human Rights Act is, in fact, the ECHR incorporated into domestic law.) Both the High Court and the Court of Appeal judged that an 'operational duty' under Article 2 did not apply in this case. The requirement for a breach of the state's obligations under Article 2 is for the presence of a 'real and immediate risk' not to have been reasonably ascertained, or, if it has been, for reasonable action then not to have been taken to avoid that risk eventuating in a death. Further appeal was allowed to the Supreme Court, the highest court in the land.

The hospital had admitted negligence, but the decision of the Supreme Court in 2012 went further, concluding that the state (through its agent, the psychiatric hospital) did have an operational duty under Article 2 to protect the life of Melanie and that it had failed to take reasonable measures to do so. The patient should not have been allowed leave, it decided.

An important reason for the judgment was that the risk of suicide was not adequately assessed by the hospital. Had it been, it was judged, the patient would not have been given leave. If she had refused to stay voluntarily, she should have been detained on a compulsory order, judged a reasonable and not inappropriately burdensome action.

What goes into creating a sound risk assessment?

To see where we often go wrong, we need to examine the nature of 'risk assessment' in detail. There are three key ingredients from a statistical point of view. I will make them as simple as possible, but appreciating them requires some effort. The first two are characteristics of the risk assessment test itself; the third is the rate of occurrence of the dreaded event, a suicide in this case, in the group of people who are being assessed:

1. Of the eventual suicides, what proportion is accurately predicted by the test? We want this to be as high as possible.
2. Of those who do *not* suicide, what proportion of these non-suicides is accurately predicted by the test? This ingredient is often ignored when people think about risk prediction. It is absolutely critical though in pointing to how many 'false positives' there will be—that is, how many people will be rated as being a high suicide risk, but who will not commit suicide. This characteristic has to be considered in conjunction with the first. For example, I could accurately predict every one of the suicides in the first test. I could do this by predicting that everyone will commit suicide. I will get all the suicides—but it is not very sensible. It will be right for everyone who eventually does suicide, but wrong for all those who do not, and they will hugely outnumber those who do. So the test must address whom to exclude—that is, those who will not suicide. We want this proportion also to be as high as possible.
3. The rate at which the event we wish to predict and thus avoid occurs in the group of people who might be at risk. In this case, this is the rate of suicide among psychiatric inpatients.

Let's give each of these three characteristics a name: the first is technically the *sensitivity* of the test—how sensitive it is at picking up those who eventually suicide. I'll call it the '*inclusion rate*'. The second is the *specificity*—how specific the test is, that is, how well it excludes those who will not suicide. I'll call it the '*exclusion rate*'. The frequency of the event to be prevented is called the *base rate*.

An example: inpatient suicide

So let's look at some basic figures concerning suicide among patients admitted to a psychiatric hospital. I did this for 2009. That year there were 120,000 admissions to psychiatric hospitals in England involving 108,000 patients (some of whom were obviously admitted more than once). In that year, according to the *National Confidential Inquiry into Suicides and Homicides by People with Mental Illness,* there were 100 suicides during the period of the admission. There are no statistics concerning how many of these occurred during a leave period, but the 100 suicides include those occurring during such leave periods.

Let's now try to estimate how many of the 120,000 admissions involved patients like the one in the Supreme Court case—that is, those who were admitted because they were regarded as posing a suicide risk rather than for other reasons, such as disturbed behaviour based on delusions or hallucinations. The best estimate comes from a study in London, United Kingdom, that looked in detail at reasons for patients being admitted to a number of psychiatric hospitals.[8] This study found that the prevention of suicide was a reason in 36 per cent of the admissions. In 21 per cent it was the 'major' reason for the admission, in the remaining 15 per cent it was a 'contributory' reason. It is important to bear in mind that suicides among inpatients are not restricted to those who are admitted because of a risk of suicide. Suicides may occur in patients with a psychosis or with alcohol or substance abuse where there might have appeared to be a minor risk beforehand. However, let's assume that all 100 suicides in 2009 occurred in the 21 per cent of admissions, that is, 25,200, who were admitted primarily because of the risk of suicide. The rate of suicide then was approximately 1 in 250 inpatients—and, given the allowances we have made, this has to be a significant overestimate of the rate.

The lure of narrative versus statistical reality

It is at this point that a very typical human trait needs to be examined—the need to construct narratives. The Nobel Prize-winning psychologist of economics, Daniel Kahneman, presents many examples in his book *Thinking, Fast and Slow*[9] of how our need to build narratives to explain the behaviour of others may, on occasions, lead us badly astray. In most everyday situations, such an approach works well enough. We can predict pretty well, although not perfectly, whether our partner or a friend will like a particular film, or a new recipe, or how they will react to a particular setback at work. We construct a narrative based on our knowledge of the person's history and previous reactions in similar circumstances. But sometimes our automatic narrative building becomes a serious handicap.

Kahneman gives a wonderful example, one that deserves wide recognition. He calls it the *Linda Problem*. This is the description of Linda:

> Linda is thirty-one years old, single, outspoken, and very bright. She majored in philosophy. As a student, she was deeply concerned with issues of discrimination and social justice, and also participated in antinuclear demonstrations.[9]

(The experiments were done in the 1980s, hence the reference to the antinuclear demonstrations.) Now to the nub of the issue. He posed the following question:

> Which alternative is more probable?
>
> a. Linda is a bank teller.
>
> b. Linda is a bank teller and is active in the feminist movement.[9, p54]

I am fairly sure that most readers will choose the second alternative as more probable. I know this because Kahneman found that 85–90 per cent of undergraduates at several major universities in the United States endorsed this alternative. He reports that even Stephen Jay Gould struggled with the problem, and felt troubled by the right answer though he knew it to be the right answer. In some way it goes against the grain. It is logically, nevertheless, more likely that Linda is a bank teller than that she is *both* a bank teller *and* active in a feminist movement—there must be more female bank tellers than females who are bank tellers *as well as* feminists. Just as it is more likely that someone has brown hair, than that they have *both* brown hair *and* brown eyes. It's obvious in an example where we do not feel somehow driven to construct a narrative.

So, what are the implications of our insistent need to construct explanatory narratives? For any one of the 25,200 patients admitted to a psychiatric hospital in 2009 primarily because of the risk of suicide, if they had indeed committed suicide, a very plausible explanatory narrative could have been constructed, with hindsight, which would have indicated the event was very likely to happen. They were admitted because the psychiatric history seemed to offer precisely such a narrative. Common in such narratives would have been suicidal ideas, a history of self-harm, depressive symptoms (such as pervasive sadness, inability to find pleasure in anything, insomnia, poor concentration, feelings of hopelessness or guilt), a family history of suicide, recent troubling life events or losses, social problems, and so on. It would have appeared more or less obvious, and it is very likely staff would be seen as having failed the patient, or as being culpable. Yet, at most, only 1 of the 250 for whom the plausible narrative could have been constructed actually committed suicide!

Herein lies a major problem with post-incident inquiries, the attempt to 'learn lessons' from what went wrong (but which, in effect, are often mechanisms for allocating blame). Such inquiries track the narrative, as it were, in reverse, pointing with the benefit of hindsight, to every 'error' that was made by those responsible for the treatment. They nearly always fail to consider what is known as the 'base rate problem'—the fact that 249 of 250 persons, in most relevant respects the same as the person who died, did not commit suicide during the admission.

Nevertheless, can we pick the 1 in 250 who did?

Two further factors normally exaggerate, often grossly, our responses to certain types of bad events, even though their probability of occurring is extremely low—say 1 in 1000, or even much less.[10] The first factor is how horrendous the event would be—the carnage of a plane or train crash, or a suicide-terrorist bomb, for example. The second is the level of outrage that the event evokes.[11] This arises when it is believed that someone has failed to act responsibly or with due care in their professional role—for example, a railway track has not been properly maintained, or a mental health team allowed a 'risky' patient to leave hospital. A suicide can easily appear to fulfil these conditions; a homicide by a patient with a mental illness even more so.

How the statistics of risk assessment unfold

How well then, using the best available tools, could the 1 in 250 suicide be predicted? Unfortunately, we need to use some mathematics rather than the more comfortable habit of narrative building. Matthew Large and colleagues in Australia recently examined the accuracy of risk prediction methods for inpatient suicide (including all periods of leave).[12] The best *sensitivity (inclusion rate)* and *specificity (exclusion rate)* that could be achieved taking into account all potential predictors—known as *risk factors,* such as history of suicide attempts, suicidal ideas, depressive symptoms, alcohol or substance abuse, family history of suicide, recent social difficulties, and so on—were 0.64 and 0.85, respectively. The best way of showing the statistics is by using a 'probability tree'. You will see, I hope, it is not too complicated. It shows the way in which the three characteristics of risk assessment tests come together to determine how many persons predicted to commit suicide by the test, in fact, turn out on follow-up to do so.

Consider 1000 patients admitted to hospital for the prevention of suicide, 4 of whom will eventually commit suicide as an inpatient (i.e. 1 in 250): Fig. 3.1 shows how the tree looks for predicting inpatient suicide.

The result comes as a shock to most of us. Using the best predictive tool available—one that under normal clinical circumstances, due for example to time constraints, is unlikely to be feasible—only 2 per cent, 1 in 50, of those considered to be at *high risk* will commit suicide. To make matters worse, about a third of those who will commit suicide will not be classed as 'high risk' at all (the *inclusion rate* being only 0.64) and will be missed. The conclusion must be that predicting who will commit suicide during their inpatient stay is in practice simply not feasible. Placing restrictions, perhaps including involuntary detention, on the freedom of 50 patients who are rated as 'high risk' to prevent one suicide, in the mentioned example, would surely not be acceptable. Furthermore, concentrating on the 'high-risk' group may lead to less treatment attention to those who are considered at 'low risk' who will nevertheless contain one-third of the suicides. Indeed, less attention to that group may result in more suicides in that group.

I am not arguing whether Melanie Rabone should have been given leave or not, nor whether she should have been detained or not. The expert risk assessment accepted by the High Court (and thus necessarily by the

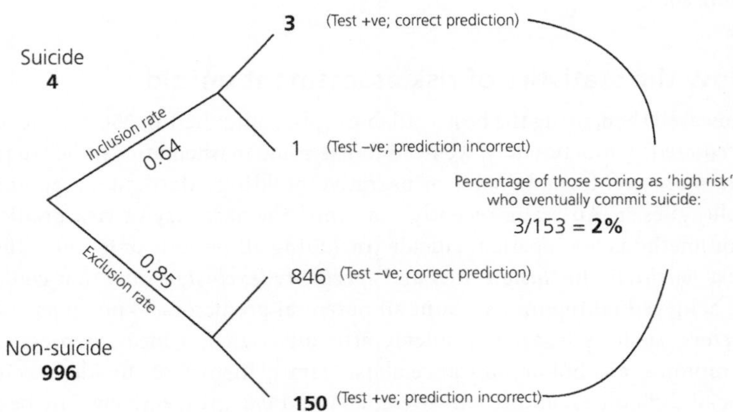

Fig. 3.1 A 'probability tree' for a test for risk of suicide. The 'probability tree' shows the relationships between the three key elements in a risk assessment—the 'inclusion rate' (sensitivity), the 'exclusion rate' (specificity), and the 'base rate' (here, 1 in 250) (the figures for suicides have been rounded up).

Supreme Court) was that the risk of suicide was 5 per cent on day one, 10 per cent by day two, and 20 per cent by day three. What I think should be clear from what I have said is that the 'risk assessment' evidence presented to the Court does not stand up. If the risk assessment had been accurate, the Court might not have concluded that the risk was 'real and immediate'.

At this point I must add a note of clarification. The reactions to these considerations from some of my collaborators who have been inpatients and who have made serious, indeed frightening, suicide attempts have reflected some disquiet. Suicides are clearly devastating events for near ones. These colleagues argue that serious suicide attempts greatly outnumber completed suicides, and some result in severe and lasting injury. They note that the lifetime risk of suicide is high, especially in those who have made previous attempts. They are correct on all points. Accurate figures on attempts in inpatients are hard to find. The mental health hospital in which I worked had recorded 37 in 2007/2008 while there were no actual inpatient suicides. The number of admissions that year was just under 5000. The lifetime risk of suicide in people with an affective (mood) disorder is around 2 per cent; for those who had had a past admission, 4 per cent; and for those with a past admission for suicidality, over 8 per cent.[13] I certainly do not wish to downplay in any way what is a tragic outcome. Nevertheless, we need to accept that our ability to predict suicide in the individual case, at a particular time, is very poor.

Predicting perpetrators of a homicide

When it comes to predicting homicides by people with a mental disorder, the figures are even more deflating. There are at any one time about 250,000 persons in England who have a psychotic illness such as schizophrenia. In any one year, about 25 homicides will be carried out by a patient with a psychotic illness—that is, 1 in 10,000. There are many violence risk assessment instruments, but rarely do they attain an 'inclusion rate' and 'exclusion rate' as good as 0.7 and 0.7, respectively. If the reader cares to construct a probability tree using these figures, he or she will find that 1 in 5000 patients classified as *high risk* will commit a homicide in a year. The tests are basically useless for predicting homicide.[14]

What about the prediction of serious violence? If serious violence, short of homicide, occurs in, say, 1 per cent of patients per annum, using this unusually good risk assessment tool—under research conditions and probably a far cry from the situation in the clinic—only 2 out of 100 patients who fall into the 'high-risk' category will commit such an act in a year.

(The reader can now easily show this by constructing a probability tree with the three key numbers—'inclusion rate', 'exclusion rate', and 'base rate'.) However, the narrative constructed for the two who do will be entirely plausible. It will feature the risk factors that are associated with violence—a past history of violence, substance abuse, paranoid delusions, poor compliance with treatment, a history of having experienced violence, living in a violent subculture, and so on. But so would the narratives of the other 98 persons rated as 'high risk'.

Some 'costs' of an unwarranted risk emphasis

My focus here is particularly on the risk of violence to others. For reasons that are somewhat puzzling, mental health care in England has placed an extremely strong emphasis on risk and its assessment. Other countries are less preoccupied with, for example, homicides perpetrated by persons with mental illness. In England, there have been fears that 'community care has failed', despite the absence of evidence this has been the case. Fears have nonetheless been generated that many dangerous mentally ill persons are now living in the community who in the past would have been safely locked up. Sensational stories in the media when a homicide has occurred have fuelled such fears. Politicians have reacted by insisting that public protection be a key aim, if not *the* key aim, of mental health services. What has been overlooked is that despite the shift to community care, and despite its considerable problems of implementation, the number of homicides by persons with mental illness has not increased; indeed, if anything it has fallen, most certainly as a much smaller proportion of all homicides perpetrated in England.[15] Suicide rates have remained about the same over the past 10 years.[16]

The emphasis on 'risk thinking' brings with it certain costs. It is an important principle that attempts at reducing uncertainty always carry a cost—even when the attempts are unsuccessful. There are four types of cost that I would like to mention that can be incurred in mental health care as a result of an emphasis on risk and its management: moral costs, changes in professional practice, threats to trust, and discrimination against persons with a mental illness.[17] These are in addition to the obvious costs in staff time spent doing risk assessments and preparing associated paperwork, or the deployment of additional resources to manage the designated 'risky' with less attention given to the 'non-risky'.

1 Our sadly limited ability to assess risk with a degree of practical utility and its bedevilment by a high rate of 'false positives'—that is, persons predicted to be seriously violent but who would never have done

so—mean that many people will be treated restrictively or coercively, but unnecessarily so. This obviously incurs a high *moral cost*.

2. There tends to be a negative impact on *professional practice*. Risk assessment offers a seductive illusion—of bringing the future into the present, of making it calculable and objective, and of bringing it under our control. We are lulled into imagining that actions taken today can prevent bad things from happening in the future. We may thus feel an obligation to act today. Risk becomes apparently 'objective', being based on scientifically constructed risk assessment tools derived from statistically established risk factors that are then combined into the most powerful cluster predicting the harm to be avoided. In the face of this 'objectivity', trust in traditional kinds of professional expertise declines. Practices change. Risk management becomes a new professional responsibility. Changing forms of accountability are favoured that are similarly 'objective'—checked, for example, through audit of forms completed, boxes ticked, or guidelines apparently followed. Ways of thinking about patients and ways of communicating about them with other professionals and agencies change. Risk language starts to infiltrate clinical talk. When referring a patient to a supported care home or hostel, I regularly had to provide details of a 'risk assessment'; in turn, some hostels had to complete a formal 'risk assessment' before a resident was allowed to go on a weekend group excursion, even when accompanied by a staff member.

   At the same time the risk focus based on discrete, unconnected, 'risk factors' that make up the items on a risk assessment form, moves us away from attempts to understand the person as an individual—the clinical account or formulation. This type of account focuses on the illness and the person who has it—what combination of past history, personality, and recent events led to it, what maintains it, what treatment is most likely to help, and what the prognosis might be and how it might be modified. Instead, risk thinking places the patient within a risk category—depending on the score on the risk assessment measure—which then starts to dominate thinking about the problem. This risk focus offers data that tend to narrow the range of interventions to modes of incapacitation—detention, community orders, surveillance, and the like—and away from treatment, as traditionally understood, based on understanding the patient as an individual.

3. There may also develop an erosion of *trust*. Trust helps the patient to deal with vulnerability and uncertainty. But the patient must believe that the clinician's agenda is the same as the patient's—that is, to further

the patient's interests and well-being. Recognizing that services are preoccupied with risk, patients may wonder whether the clinician's agenda favours a public protection interest over the patient's. Furthermore, the more time spent collecting risk-related data, completing forms, and protocols, the less time there is for communication—an essential ingredient in building trust.

There is another dimension related to trust: like an invasive organism, risk thinking tends to 'colonize' organizations. A pressure develops affecting all levels of staff, managerial through to clinical, to 'manage risk'. In reality, this easily slips into staff managing the risk to themselves, if something should go wrong. In England, for example, the consequences for the clinician and the organization if there should be a homicide by one of their patients are quite horrendous—protracted investigations and scrutiny of the case, blame, negative publicity, formal inquiries, and scores of recommendations requiring implementation. To manage risk, managers, from top down, seek assurance that others, accountable to them, are managing risk adequately. Paradoxically, attempts to strengthen such monitoring may lead to ignorance. Attempts to gain information concerning compliance with measures that clinicians see as obstacles to the 'real work' of patient care may motivate them to engage in subtle forms of *disinformation*. The organization may end up pervaded with unreliable information.

4. Finally, there is a problem of *discrimination*. This will be dealt with in more detail later in relation to involuntary hospitalization (see Chapter 5). But in brief, consider the example of the state's insistence, through the Department of Health in England, on a routine risk assessment for *all* persons referred to mental health services. There are many people in society, hugely exceeding in number those with a mental disorder, who present an equal, indeed often much greater risk of violence to others. But they are not selected for any form of routine, systematic risk assessment. Fairness demands that all people presenting an equal potential risk be treated equally. I suggest therefore that fairness requires risk assessment, if we are to have it, be only in response to some kind of reasonable 'trigger' event, applicable to *all*. Simply being referred to mental health services is not an acceptable trigger. So those who could be subjected to a risk assessment might include all who have been involved in violence of some kind, those with traumatic injuries, known substance misusers, those who have been threatening to neighbours or in the workplace, and so on. That would be fair—but obviously daft. However, societies seem well able to tolerate unfairness when it affects only those with mental illness. Their rights are easily discounted.

In later chapters I will discuss some of the implications of the limitations of risk assessment for clinical practice and for mental health law. The aim of this chapter has been to alert the reader to our very human fallibility in understanding the mathematics underlying 'risk'. Obviously clinicians must do everything they reasonably can to prevent serious mishaps involving their patients—but the emphasis must be on 'reasonably'. The management of risk, at least in the sense in which it has come so heavily to influence mental health care, I will claim, should not be a primary aim motivating involuntary treatment.

References

1. **Council of Europe**. *European Convention on Human Rights*. Council of Europe, 1950. http://www.echr.coe.int/Documents/Convention_ENG.pdf
2. **United Nations General Assembly**. *The Protection of Persons with Mental Illness and the Improvement of Mental Health Care*. A/RES/46/119. United Nations, 1991. http://www.un.org/documents/ga/res/46/a46r119.htm
3. **Szmukler G**. When psychiatric diagnosis becomes an overworked tool. *Journal of Medical Ethics* 2014; **40**:517–520.
4. **Bolton D**. *What is Mental Disorder? An Essay in Philosophy, Science and Values*. Oxford: Oxford University Press, 2007.
5. **National Institute for Clinical Excellence**. *Antisocial Personality Disorder: Prevention and Management* (Clinical Guideline CG77). London: NICE, 2009.
6. **Brayne C, Ince PG, Keage HAD**, et al. Education, the brain and dementia: neuroprotection or compensation? *Brain* 2010; **133**:2210–2216.
7. **UK Supreme Court**. *Judgment: Rabone and another (appellants) v Penine Care NHS Foundation Trust (Respondent)*. Hilary Term UKSC 2, 2012.
8. **Flannigan CB, Glover GR, Wing JK, Lewis SW, Bebbington PE, Feeney ST**. Inner London collaborative audit of admission in two health districts. III: reasons for acute admission to psychiatric wards. *British Journal of Psychiatry* 1994; **165**:750–759.
9. **Kahneman D**. *Thinking, Fast and Slow*. London: Allen Lane, 2011.
10. **Sunstein CR**. Terrorism and probability neglect. *Journal of Risk and Uncertainty* 2003; **26**:121–136.
11. **Wolff J**. Risk, fear, blame, shame and the regulation of public safety. *Economics and Philosophy* 2006; **22**:409–427.
12. **Large M, Smith G, Sharma S, Nielssen O, Singh SP**. Systematic review and meta-analysis of the clinical factors associated with the suicide of psychiatric in-patients. *Acta Psychiatrica Scandinavica* 2011; **124**:18–19.
13. **Bostwick JM, Pankratz VS**. Affective disorders and suicide risk: a reexamination. *American Journal of Psychiatry* 2000; **157**:1925–1932.

14. **Large MM, Ryan CJ, Singh SP, Paton MB, Nielssen OB.** The predictive value of risk categorization in schizophrenia. *Harvard Review of Psychiatry* 2011; **19**:25–33.
15. **Taylor PJ, Gunn J.** Homicides by people with mental illness: myth and reality. *British Journal of Psychiatry* 1999; **174**:9–14.
16. **National Confidential Inquiry into Suicide and Homicide by People with Mental Illness.** *Annual Report: England, Northern Ireland, Scotland and Wales, July 2015.* University of Manchester, 2015. http://research.bmh.manchester.ac.uk/cmhs/research/centreforsuicideprevention/nci/reports/NCISHReport2015bookmarked2.pdf
17. **Szmukler G, Rose N.** Risk assessment in mental health care: values and costs. *Behavioral Sciences and the Law* 2013; **31**:125–140.

Chapter 4

Challenges to the orthodoxy

During the late 1980s, there were two events that led me to question the way we justified involuntary treatment in psychiatry. The first, an invitation to participate in a debate on consent to treatment, was the most significant. As I shall recount, it opened my eyes to a huge gulf in how patients are treated when comparing psychiatry with the rest of medicine. The second, though less significant in undermining the basic assumptions underlying involuntary treatment in psychiatry, highlighted some problems that arise when compulsion is exported from the hospital to the community. 'Old wine in new bottles' doesn't work very well in this case; the 'new bottles' are liable to leakage.

I think it was in 1988 that I was invited to participate in a university debate about what is termed 'therapeutic privilege'. This relates to an important element of the practice of what is known as 'informed consent'. At issue was the disclosure of information to a patient about the nature of their illness, and the options for treatment, including the benefits as well as possible adverse effects of each one. Without such information a patient cannot make a sensible decision. 'Therapeutic privilege' refers to situations where it is claimed that the disclosure of information that might normally be given can reasonably be restricted. The justification would be that a full disclosure about the illness would so alarm the patient that their ability to reason about the treatment would be sufficiently badly affected to render them unable to make a valid decision, thus compromising their treatment. This is clearly a very thorny argument and reflects a historical tension between medical paternalism and patient self-determination that I will go into presently.

'Informed consent' and 'capacity'

The significance for me of the debate, however, was not the issue of 'therapeutic privilege'. The importance of the debate was that it drew me into the lively discussion that was going on in the late 1980s and 1990s in relation to another key element of informed consent—the person's 'capacity' to consent.[1] Disclosure of relevant information is all very well, but of little practical value if the patient lacks the ability, or capacity, to use the information in arriving at a treatment decision. A range of experts, especially from law, medicine, and psychology, were struggling to clarify the meaning of this 'capacity'—what abilities did a person require to exercise that capacity, and how that capacity could be validly assessed. Furthermore, it was asked, what should be done when a person lacks the capacity to consent, but if treatment were not to be given the person's well-being would be seriously harmed? Or further still—what should be done when the patient lacks the capacity to consent and rejects the treatment outright? I had only a vague appreciation of these issues; most of it was quite new to me. I am sure that I was not unusual in this regard as the vast majority of my colleagues were in the same boat. Notions of 'informed consent' and 'decision-making capacity' were very marginal to the practice of psychiatry; we had a Mental Health Act to deal with patients who were rejecting treatment. If the person had a 'mental disorder' and treatment was judged to be necessary in the interests of the person's health or safety or for the protection of others, involuntary treatment could be instigated.

I think it is helpful for our understanding of the deeper significance of 'informed consent'—especially for what it says about the relative standing of patients and doctors—to look at the history leading to the debate about disclosure and decision-making capacity. We will see a large shift in social policy, away from medical discretion or paternalism to patient 'autonomy' or self-determination.

A brief history of informed consent

Disclosure

In contrast to the unwavering grip of the long-established principles underlying involuntary treatment in psychiatry, consent to treatment in medicine evolved substantially over the twentieth century, and especially rapidly during the last 40 years or so. Until the mid twentieth century medical paternalism dominated. This ideology can be traced as far back as the Hippocratic corpus, around 400 BC:

> Perform [these] duties calmly and adroitly, concealing most things from the patient while you are attending to him. Give necessary orders with cheerfulness and serenity, turning his attention away from what is being done to him; sometimes reprove sharply and emphatically, and sometimes comfort with solicitude and attention, revealing nothing of the patient's future or present condition.[2,p299]

Hippocrates warned that 'many patients ... have taken a turn for the worse .... By the declaration ... of what is present, or by the forecast of what is to come'.[2]

This approach was echoed by the English physician, Thomas Percival, who wrote the immensely influential *Medical Ethics: Or a Code of Institutes and Precepts Adapted to the Professional Conduct of Physicians and Surgeons* published in 1803. He stated that the physician 'should be the minister of hope and comfort' who shapes conversations with patients to 'counteract the depressing influence of [the patient's] maladies'. This proposition held sway for a century and a half though, even then, it received some criticism from those who argued that veracity was a higher value. Percival recognized this value but maintained it was for the physician to decide when 'professional duty' was to outweigh truthfulness.

There were a few cases brought before the courts that seemed to limit the doctor's prerogative not to disclose information about a proposed treatment. There was a case in 1767 (*Slater v Baker and Stapleton*) where without the patient's consent, the surgeons re-fractured the patient's badly healing leg, then braced it in a new device. The doctors were found guilty of malpractice, but the court's rationale for informing the patient about the treatment is interesting: 'Indeed, it is reasonable that a patient should be told what is about to be done to him, that he may take courage and put himself in such a situation as to enable him to undergo the operation.'[1]

Nevertheless, Percival's ethics were to influence practice throughout the nineteenth century and well into the twentieth. For example, the American Medical Association code of ethics published in 1857 stated that physicians should 'so unite tenderness with firmness, and condescension with authority, as to inspire the minds of their patients with gratitude, respect, and confidence'. Revisions of the code into the twentieth century did not challenge the underlying paternalistic theme. Physicians saw the requirement for consent as minimal with little information needing disclosure before gaining the patient's permission to proceed with the treatment. Facts could even be spun to encourage the patient's cooperation with the course the doctor deemed best. Practice in the United Kingdom was similar to that in the United States.

It was not until the mid 1950s that the meaning of consent began to change significantly. The term 'informed consent' was coined in a famous case in the United States in 1957, *Salgo v University Board of Trustees*.[1] The patient suffered paralysis of the legs following the injection of dye to visualize the vascular system. He claimed he was not warned about this rare, but nevertheless well-recognized, complication. The court instructed the jury that the physician must disclose to the patient 'all the facts which mutually affect his rights and interests and of the surgical risk, hazard, and danger, if any'. However, subsequently the California Court of Appeals (October 1957) did not fully concur:

> The physician must place the welfare of his patient above all else and this very fact places him in a position in which he sometimes must choose between two alternative courses of action. One is to explain to the patient every risk attendant upon any surgical procedure or operation, no matter how remote; this may well result in alarming a patient who is already unduly apprehensive and who may as a result refuse to undertake surgery in which there is in fact minimal risk; it may also result in actually increasing the risks by reason of the physiological results of the apprehension itself. The other is to recognize that each patient presents a separate problem, that the patient's mental and emotional condition is important and in certain cases may be crucial, and that in discussing the element of risk a certain amount of discretion must be employed consistent with the full disclosure of facts necessary to an informed consent. (*Salgo v Leland Stanford etc. Bd. Trustees.* [Civ. No. 17045. First Dist. Div. One. Oct 22, 1957.] [5(b)])

Nevertheless, there was now no stopping a growing insistence in the United States, based on legal cases over the next 20 years or so, for a fuller disclosure of relevant information. But how full should the disclosure be? A famous case in 1972 (*Canterbury v Spence*)[1] stated that 'respect for the patient's right of self-determination on particular therapy demands a standard set by law for physicians rather than one which physicians may or may not impose upon themselves'. Despite this, a 'subjective or patient-oriented' standard along such lines has been very slow in being adopted.

In both the United States and the United Kingdom, until recently, what has been termed a 'professional' (or less flatteringly, a 'doctor-friendly') standard of disclosure has operated. In England this was known as the *Bolam* test: in deciding what information to give about risks a doctor was not negligent if he or she had acted in accordance with practice accepted at the time by a responsible body of medical opinion.[3] This standard was the one accepted by the court in a famous 1957 case, *Bolam v Friern Barnet Hospital Management Committee*, and was restated by the House of Lords in another famous case in 1985, *Sidaway v Bethlem Royal Hospital Governors*. (These cases have a personal resonance for me, since I have worked at both hospitals—perhaps this has subtly influenced my immersion in the issues this book addresses.)

We will see the nowadays discredited *Bolam* test reappearing soon in our discussion, but in a different guise.

Over the last 20 years or so, a number of legal cases and guidance issued by regulatory bodies such as the General Medical Council, British

Medical Association, and Department of Health in the United Kingdom, as well as the American Medical Association and the Australian Medical Council, have shifted the requirement for disclosure towards a 'subjective' standard—one tailored to the likely concerns of the individual patient—or, if not that far, at least to the 'reasonable person' standard—to provide that information that a hypothetical reasonable person in the position of the patient would want to know.

The important point I want to emphasize here is the now substantial shift over the past two decades from deference to doctors, medical paternalism or 'doctor knows best', towards patient autonomy or self-determination.

Decision-making 'capacity' or 'competence'

The initial focus in grappling with the meaning of 'informed consent' was on disclosure. However, no matter how excellent the disclosure, if the patient cannot understand or use the information provided, consent or failure to consent cannot be 'informed'. The ability to use the information in arriving at a decision is generally called 'capacity' or 'competence'. While, the former term originally referred to the clinical assessment and the latter to a legal adjudication, the terms are nowadays generally used interchangeably. I will use the term 'capacity'.

The major attempts to clarify the meaning of capacity are even more recent than those dealing with disclosure. Appelbaum, Lidz, and Meisel, in their book, *Informed Consent: Legal Theory and Clinical Practice*, published in 1987[1] stated: 'Making decisions in cases involving incompetent patients has been an area of great confusion, though the fog may be slowly beginning to lift'. Since the late 1990s there are signs of a growing consensus on the abilities underlying decision-making capacity.

In England,[3] prior to a famous and important legal case known as *Re F (1990)*, the principles for treatment of adult persons who lacked the capacity to consent to treatment were hazy and based on a small number of 'common law' damages cases brought by patients against their doctors. ('Common law' refers to 'judge-made' law, law based on precedent and reinterpreted as social mores change. Common law is unlike 'statutory law'—laws enacted by parliament.) At that time it was common practice to seek delegated consent from a relative though, in fact, this had no legal standing.

Re F concerned the sterilization of a 35-year-old woman with a very severe intellectual disability. She did not have the mental capacity to consent. F had formed a sexual relationship with another patient and all of her carers agreed that a pregnancy would be a disaster for her. Other forms of contraception were either impractical or ruled out on medical grounds. The case went through the lower courts until it reached the House of Lords, at that time the highest appeal court in the United Kingdom, for an authoritative judgement in 1989. The House of Lords declared that doctors had the power to treat patients who lack capacity when it was 'necessary' in the patient's 'best interests'. What was meant by 'best interests'? In deciding whether a treatment was necessary in the best interests of the patient, the doctor had to act in accordance with a responsible and competent body of medical opinion. This was the 'doctor-friendly' *Bolam* test we met earlier in relation to the standard of disclosure for informed consent.

One of the reasons why this was such an important case harks back to memories of the notorious sterilization laws enacted for eugenic reasons. The reader may recall the discussion on this subject in Chapter 2. Some sterilization laws from the 1920s and 1930s remained in place in some countries and some states in the United States until the 1960s, and even the 1970s. The important difference asserted in cases like *Re F* was that the sterilization was to be in the interests of the person and not in the interests of the state.

Re F thus provided a common-law basis for treating patients who lacked capacity. For routine cases, if treatment was necessary in the best interests of the patient, it could proceed. For non-routine or serious cases, such as sterilization or organ donation, or cases that posed unusual medical dilemmas it was accepted that good practice required a further step. Since there was no legal basis for allowing anyone to give consent to treatment in a patient's place, the appropriate course of action was to seek a 'declaration' from the High Court that the treatment was not unlawful. (There was an ancient mechanism dating from feudal times until 1959 called *parens patriae* or 'Royal Prerogative' which, after a finding in a jury trial that the person was of 'unsound mind and incapable of managing himself and his affairs', allowed the Crown and later the Court of Chancery to give power to a 'Committee of the Person' who could place the person in an asylum or hospital for treatment. By the end of the nineteenth century it was rarely used.)

Following *Re F*, the common law on treatment without consent started to take off. The same procedure was used to override frank refusals by patients who lacked capacity. *Re T (Adult consent to medical treatment) 1993* was a well-known example.[3] T was a pregnant young woman who sustained serious injuries in a car accident. She underwent an emergency caesarean operation after which her condition deteriorated. A blood transfusion was considered medically necessary. T had, however, refused a blood transfusion. The court decided that it was lawful for the transfusion to go ahead as T was found to lack capacity as a result of her physical and mental condition. She was drowsy and disorientated. Another important factor for the court was the judged 'undue influence' of T's mother, a committed Jehovah's Witness. In some cases, the High Court's 'declarative function' supported the patient's refusal. An important case was *Re C (mental patient: medical treatment)* where the key issue was whether the patient had capacity to refuse an amputation of a gangrenous leg, a potentially life-saving treatment strongly recommended by his doctors.[3]

Re C

C, aged 68 years, was a patient in Broadmoor Hospital, a high secure hospital for mentally ill persons who had committed a serious offence. He had a diagnosis of schizophrenia. C sought a declaration from the High Court that he had the capacity to refuse the amputation and a recognition that this treatment could not be given in the future without his express written consent—in effect, an advance directive. The court granted both orders. The judge held that C had the right to self-determination concerning the treatment for his gangrenous leg and that this had not been displaced despite the fact of his mental illness.

Importantly, a test for capacity was also proposed. This was based on the evidence given, apparently at short notice, by a respected forensic psychiatrist, Dr Nigel Eastman. Until *Re C* no test for capacity had been clearly specified. Three elements were identified:

1. Whether the person could comprehend and retain the treatment information;
2. Whether he believed it; and
3. Whether he could weigh it in the balance to arrive at a choice.

This test of capacity was then generally adopted in common law.

A significant section of this book will examine decision-making capacity in detail. At this point it is worth saying a little about the second element—what 'believing' the information was taken to mean. This element generated much controversy subsequently; could it be taken to mean that if a patient disagreed with the doctor, the patient lacked capacity? The same judge as in *Re C*, Justice Thorpe, in a later case distinguished 'outright disbelief', as might be seen in mental disorder—being 'impervious to reason, divorced from reality, or incapable of adjustment after reflection'—from 'the tendency which most people have when undergoing medical treatment to self-assess and then to puzzle over the divergence between medical and self-assessment'.

A codification of case law

At the time of *Re F*, it was becoming evident that decision-making involving persons who were unable to consent was a subject of growing concern. In 1989, the Law Society in England published a discussion document on the law relating to 'mental capacity' and decision-making in medicine, pointing out that English law did not possess a procedure whereby any person or court could take a medical decision on behalf of an adult person who lacked the capacity to take such a decision. The Law Commission then undertook an examination of this area as a programme of law reform.[4] It was generally accepted that the law at that time was 'unsystematic, uncertain, piecemeal and had failed to keep up with developments in thinking about the rights and needs of persons with mental impairments'. The High Court was in danger of being overwhelmed by applications for 'declarations' on proposed treatments for people lacking capacity for rulings on whether they were lawful or not. There was no provision for legitimating and regulating substitute decision-making for persons lacking capacity, though such decision-making was regularly taking place. The Law Commission received support for a root-and-branch rather than piecemeal approach to reform.

The Law Commission noted that many other countries also recognized the need for a framework for decision-making for incapacitated adults and that a number of law reform projects had been set up. The Law Commission in Scotland was in the process of examining the same issues. It also noted important social changes—care in the community meant that many more decisions needed to be taken by people with impaired capacity than was the case when they resided in institutions; and that, as a House of Lords Select Committee on Medical Ethics in 1994 had reported, the principle of patient autonomy had become important in relation to treatment and 'the relationship between doctor and patient had changed to one of partnership'.

After a set of detailed consultation papers in 1993, the Law Commission published a report in 1995 offering proposals for the ways in which decisions might lawfully be made on behalf of those who are unable to make decisions for themselves. Their work resulted in the drafting and passing in Parliament of the Mental Capacity Act 2005.[5] This piece of legislation has been well received, though there have been difficulties in its implementation. This is not surprising, given the major change in thinking that it embodies.

Capacity and best interests have also been the subject of reports and of law reform in other countries, and in many states of the United States and Australia, for example. They have followed similar lines of thought.

In Chapter 5, I will describe the main innovations of the Mental Capacity Act. For now, I wish to point to the two fundamental principles that are given effect in the Act—decision-making 'capacity' and 'best interests'. Much thought has gone into their characterization. The concepts are linked—when a person lacks 'capacity', an interference in their lives is only justified if it is in the person's 'best interests'. If a person retains capacity, their choices—no matter how unwise or imprudent they may appear to others—are to be respected.

Decision-making capacity and psychiatry

By now, the reader may be asking what all of this has to do with psychiatry and mental health law. The answer is: not much—and that, I suggest, is precisely the problem.

I began to ask myself why an approach embodied in the principles underlying, for example, the Mental Capacity Act should not apply equally to people with mental disorders who lack 'capacity' and who reject treatment? The Law Commission's final report (*Mental Incapacity*)[4] discussed the Mental Health Act 1983 and stated that the question of capacity was irrelevant to the detention and involuntary treatment of patients with a mental disorder. It went on to say:

> The distinction between the general law about decision-making capacity and the policy of the 1983 Act was made crystal clear in a recent case involving a patient detained under section 3 of the [Mental Health] Act. It was held by Thorpe J that the patient did have capacity to refuse the treatment being offered to her and was refusing it, but that she could nevertheless lawfully be given it by virtue of section 63 of the Act because it was 'for' her mental disorder within the meaning of that section. Our present report does not re-open the policy decisions embodied in the treatment provisions of the 1983 Act ... The law relating to mental incapacity and decision-making must address quite different legal issues and social purposes from the law relating to detention and treatment for mental disorder.[4,p7]

What exactly were these 'social purposes', I wondered. While it is true that the treatment of persons with a mental disorder falls under the provisions of the Mental Capacity Act as long as they accept or, at least, assent to the treatment, if the treatment is rejected and the person meets the Mental Health Act criteria for involuntary treatment, the principles of the Mental

Capacity Act cease to apply. Thus, even if the person's decision-making capacity is retained, the Mental Health Act permits his or her involuntary treatment.

In Chapter 5, we will look at the assumptions that lie behind this mental illness 'exceptionalism' and show how they entail unfair discrimination against persons with a mental illness.

Extending involuntary treatment into the community

At the beginning of this chapter I said there were two events that made me doubt the legitimacy of the orthodox approach to involuntary treatment in psychiatry. The first was the work that was being done on 'informed consent' as I have just recounted. The second was the introduction of involuntary psychiatric treatment into the community.[6,7] Especially troubling here is the use of compulsion—or more precisely the threat of compulsion—as a 'prophylactic' or preventive measure. The aim is to ensure the patient's compliance with treatment in order to reduce the risk of a relapse of the illness and so reduce the risk of harms to the person or to others that such a relapse might carry. Such orders are usually long term. Basing an intrusive treatment intervention on the risk of a risk when, as we have seen in Chapter 3, risk is so poorly understood, is one problem. But it became clear to me that what might be regarded as an unacceptable risk in the community was not necessarily what was previously regarded as a risk warranting detention in hospital.

I strongly support the philosophy behind the integration of people with mental illness in the community. However, at the same time I am aware of the fear, or at least the discomfort, that many members of the public feel about having such people in their midst. I noted from the late 1980s that my community mental health team was receiving an increasing number of calls from other agencies, or directly from members of the public, about people who appeared to be mentally disturbed and who, more importantly, were *disturbing*, as in the following example.

Non-acceptable risk?

I remember a call from a shopkeeper who said that a man who was 'obviously quite mad' was regularly loitering in the vicinity of his shop and, the shopkeeper believed, he was putting off potential customers. He asked if we could please do something about this as he 'obviously needed to be in a mental hospital'. On further inquiry, we found that the man was a patient known to the team, but though of unprepossessing appearance, there was no evidence that he had ever been violent, intimidating, or abusive in the past. Nor was he now. However, the shopkeeper saw him as a risk to his business.

Perhaps this was a fairly extreme example. But the general point is that what is perceived as an unacceptable risk in the community warranting some kind of preventive action, though not necessarily hospitalization, may be a lower level or different kind of risk to the one that would in the past have been seen as warranting detention in hospital. The level of risk required for inpatient detention is difficult enough to establish, but that level is certainly more straightforward than the level of risk attached to a patient based on past behaviour that warrants their long-term 'preventive commitment' in the community—and, indeed, the level of risk that warrants the 'recall' of this patient to hospital to forestall the original, unacceptable risk from arising. Adding a new power of involuntary community treatment to this broadening of the range of unacceptable risk looked troubling. It pointed to a likely increase in the use of compulsion.

An increase in the use of compulsion in the context of a social change that aimed to enhance the standing of people with a mental illness in the community was perturbing. It paints a troubling picture of people with mental illness; to live in the community it would appear they need special control and discipline. However, the main lesson I drew from the introduction of community treatment orders was the way they highlighted the shakiness of the 'risk criterion' for involuntary treatment. Furthermore, as discussed in Chapter 3, given the blurred boundary around notions of what constitutes a 'mental disorder' (especially when one includes the category of 'personality disorder') and an increasingly risk-averse society, the scope for involuntary treatment was greatly enlarged.

Were then the conventional criteria for involuntary treatment defensible? I concluded they were not. Exactly why is the subject of Chapter 5.

References

1. **Appelbaum PS, Lidz CW, Meisel A.** *Informed Consent: Legal Theory and Clinical Practice.* New York: Oxford University Press, 1987. [The reader will find detailed accounts in this book of the United States cases I discuss in this chapter.]
2. **Hippocrates.** *'Decorum'* **XVI** (WHS Jones, trans). Boston, MA: Harvard University Press, 1957.
3. **Fennell P.** *Treatment Without Consent. Law, Psychiatry and the Treatment of Mentally Disordered People Since 1945.* London: Routledge, 1996. [This

excellent book provides details of the cases and developments in the law in the United Kingdom that I discuss in this chapter.]

4. **Law Commission**. *Mental Incapacity* (Report No. 231). London: HMSO, 1995.
5. **Her Majesty's Government**. *Mental Capacity Act 2005*. London: The Stationery Office, 2005.
6. **Dawson J**. *Community Treatment Orders: International Comparisons*. Dunedin, New Zealand: Otago University Press, 2005.
7. **Szmukler G**. Fifty years of mental health legislation: paternalism, bound and unbound. In: Bloch S, Green SA, Holmes J (Eds) *Psychiatry: Past, Present, and Prospects*. Oxford: Oxford University Press, 2014; 133–153.

Chapter 5

How mental health law discriminates against persons with mental illness

Let's start by considering a case that was heard in the Court of Protection in England in 2014.

P was a woman with schizophrenia who, due to her unwillingness to accept treatment for this illness, was on a community treatment order. This meant that if she failed to take antipsychotic medication she would be liable to be recalled to hospital and to be then treated forcibly. However, at the same time P suffered from poorly controlled diabetes and hypertension, and was a heavy smoker. These, together with an infection, led to the development of gangrene in a leg. She had already lost the foot as a result of this disease, but was left with an unresolved wound. The expert medical opinions agreed that an amputation, below or above knee, was the right treatment. However, despite the potentially grave risk of the spread of the gangrene, P rejected surgery. The hospital referred the case to the court requesting its declaration that amputation against the resistance of the patient would be lawful, on the basis that she lacked 'capacity' and that it would be in her 'best interests'. After hearing the case, the judge concluded that she had retained decision-making capacity concerning the surgery and that her decision must stand. (Heart of England NHS Foundation Trust and JB. EWCOP 342; 2014.)

There are echoes in this case of *Re C*, the famous case also involving a patient with schizophrenia and a gangrenous leg, discussed in Chapter 4.

Two entirely different sets of rules governing involuntary treatment

There appears to be something odd in the case of P, an anomaly of some kind. The patient was on a compulsory order under the Mental Health Act 1983 for the treatment of her 'mental disorder' under one set of legal criteria, but was ruled ineligible for involuntary treatment for her 'physical disorder' under the Mental Capacity Act 2005 with its totally different set of criteria. Her 'mental disorder' presented a risk to her health or safety; the 'physical disorder' presented a grave risk to her health, indeed her life. Yet she could refuse treatment for the latter, but not the former.

England is not an exception in giving effect to this disparity. In the vast majority of jurisdictions, the circumstances in which treatment in medicine may be authorized without the consent of the patient are governed not by one set of legal principles, but by separate, distinct regimes. These different legal regimes tend to operate in parallel with different rules and legal standards governing their use.

The history and application of the 'mental disorder' and 'risk of harm' criteria for the involuntary treatment of persons under conventional mental health legislation have already been described in some detail. The criteria required under capacity-based legislation, such as the Mental Capacity Act, were introduced in Chapter 4 and I shall now expand on them. I wish to now draw your attention to the differences between the two regimes.

Capacity and best interests

Decision-making capacity

When does a person lack 'capacity' to make a specific decision? (It is important to note here that we are not talking about a capacity to make decisions generally, but to make a particular decision at a particular time.) To have decision-making capacity according to the Mental Capacity Act the person must be able:

(a) to understand the information relevant to the decision,

(b) to retain that information,

(c) to use or weigh that information as part of the process of making the decision, or

(d) to communicate his decision (whether by talking, using sign language or any other means).

These elements are very similar to those elucidated in an extremely influential account by Grisso and Appelbaum: *Assessing Competence to Consent to Treatment* (1998)[1] which reviewed the legal context in the United States. The abilities that are generally required are to:

a. Understand the relevant information

b. Appreciate the situation and its consequences

c. Reason about the treatment options

d. Communicate a choice.

Understanding requires that the person is able to grasp the basic meaning of the information provided by the doctor, in simple language where necessary. The information to be understood includes the nature of the patient's condition, the nature and purpose of the proposed treatment, the possible benefits and risks of that treatment, and alternative approaches (including no treatment). The patient must be able to *retain* that information long enough to be able to use it in arriving at a decision. The *use or weigh* criteria are essentially the same as the ability to 'appreciate' and 'reason' with the information provided. The person should be able to *use* the information by recognizing its pertinence to their predicament, for example, recognizing that they are ill or at least that there is a significant problem requiring attention and an important decision to be made. The ability to *weigh* the information focuses on the process by which a decision is reached. This is usually taken as the ability to reason with the relevant information. It covers the person's ability to generate and think through the consequences entailed in the various treatment options—in the light of what is important for that person.

A number of background conditions must also be observed when capacity is assessed. There must be a *presumption* that a person has capacity. The responsibility for proving that a person does not have capacity falls on the person who is challenging the presumption. Furthermore everything practicable must be done to *support* the person to make his or her own decision, before it is concluded that capacity is lacking. (This theme of support has become extremely important in the light of recent international law concerning the rights of persons with disabilities. It will be explored in detail in Chapter 8.) People also have the freedom to make apparently unwise decisions. Such a decision is not in itself proof that the person lacks capacity, though it may raise questions about whether this might be the case. The content of the decision itself—for example, whether most people (including the doctor) would agree with it or not—does not provide the basis for determining whether the person has capacity. The test depends on how the decision was reached, that is, the way in which the abilities described have been exercised.

The Mental Capacity Act requires that a decision that a person lacks capacity must be based on a 'reasonable belief' supported by objective reasons. Where there are disputes about whether a person lacks capacity that cannot be resolved using more informal methods, a special court responsible for issues arising from the Mental Capacity Act, the Court of Protection, can be asked for a judgment.

Best interests

If a person is found to lack capacity, this does not mean that a recommended treatment can automatically be given without the person's consent or against an express refusal. A second requirement must be satisfied. The intervention must be in the person's 'best interests'. The Mental Capacity Act does not offer a definition of best interests; the variety of interventions is so large that this would prove an impossible task. Instead it provides a statutory checklist of factors that must be considered when a best interests judgement is made.

The assessor must consider all the relevant circumstances and include the following:

- Whether it is likely that the person will at some time have capacity to make a required decision. If it appears likely that he will, when is that likely to be.
- The assessor must, so far as reasonably practicable, permit and encourage the person to participate, or to improve his ability to participate, as fully as possible in any act done for him and any decision affecting him.
- The assessor must consider, so far as is reasonably ascertainable: (a) the person's past and present wishes and feelings (and, in particular, any relevant written statement made by him when he had capacity); (b) the beliefs and values that would be likely to influence his decision if he had capacity; and, (c) any other factors that he would be likely to consider if he were able to do so.
- The assessor must take into account, if it is practicable and appropriate to consult them, the views of: (a) anyone named by the person as someone to be consulted; and (b) anyone engaged in caring for the person or interested in his welfare, as to what would be in the person's best interests and, in particular, concerning the person's past and present beliefs and values and any other factors that the person would be likely to consider if they were able to do so.

The Mental Capacity Act allows for a person, when they have capacity, to give a 'lasting power of attorney' to another person, empowering that person to make decisions on their behalf. The Court of Protection may also under certain circumstances appoint a 'deputy' to take on such a role. Such appointees must also follow the points listed when judging what is in the person's best interests.

It is only if the person lacks decision-making capacity and a treatment is in their best interests that such treatment may be given without the person's consent or against a refusal.

How does mental health legislation discriminate?

As we now see, countries with well-developed legal regimes, as in England, a mental capacity scheme, such as the Mental Capacity Act, is usually the legal regime for authorizing involuntary treatment of general medical conditions. On the other hand, mental health legislation (or 'civil commitment') such as the Mental Health Act is the preferred regime covering the involuntary treatment of psychiatric disorders. Such mental health law does not usually permit the treatment of physical disorders, unless the physical disorder is the cause of, or sometimes the consequence of, the mental disorder. An example of the latter would be the physical complications of a deliberate drug overdose by a person with depression.

As we have seen, entirely separate grounds support the use of the two schemes. The law governing involuntary treatment of general medical conditions relies on the concept of the impaired 'capacity' of the patient to make necessary treatment decisions, plus the notion of the 'best interests' of the patient if capacity is impaired. Note that capacity is what has been termed a *functional* criterion—meaning that the person is unable to carry out particular tasks that demonstrate their capacity. In this case, the person is unable to make a decision because of an impairment of one or more of the abilities listed previously. On the other hand, the criteria governing involuntary treatment under mental health legislation will usually incorporate some concept of 'mental disorder' or 'mental illness' (a *status* criterion) plus some notion of 'risk' (to the patient or others). A 'status' criterion means that the person is classed as being a member of a particular category, which is defined on the basis of a set of characteristics shared by people who fit that category.

To see how these differences play out, consider these two patients[2]:

Louise

Louise is a 47-year-old woman with stage II cancer of the cervix. Her doctor recommends treatment involving radiotherapy combined with chemotherapy. He informs her that the likelihood of survival with treatment is around 60 per cent at 5 years; without treatment it is less than 20 per cent. Louise decides that she could not tolerate the adverse effects following treatment, especially the nausea and vomiting, symptoms she has dreaded since childhood, and the fairly high likelihood of genitourinary complications, which she finds abhorrent. She rejects the treatment after a full discussion, where she clearly understands the consequences of not having treatment. She accepts the information as accurately representing the current state of knowledge concerning the treatment and prognosis of her disease. She is able to use the information about her illness and the side effects to generate consequences for her of having or not having the treatment. Although her life may be at stake, Louise cannot be treated involuntarily.

Beth

Beth is a 47-year-old woman who has a 20-year history of schizophrenia. When ill, she has the delusion that she is related to various royal families and this leads her to make some bizarre claims. She gives away her most valuable possessions. She also neglects her physical care, to the point that her hair becomes so matted it cannot be combed out and her head needs to be clean-shaven. She has had over five admissions in the past 8 years, always following discontinuation of prescribed antipsychotic medication; this, despite the fact that the medication is quite effective in alleviating her symptoms. During her last admission, following a good recovery from her illness, medication was discussed. Beth accepted that she suffered from a serious mental health problem and that the diagnosis of schizophrenia was justified according to the symptoms that she suffered. She also accepted that the symptoms responded well to the prescribed medication. However, she decided that she did not want to take it on a continuing basis. She understood the consequences of not taking it—the likelihood of relapse, the severity of the symptoms, and the likelihood of readmission, probably on an involuntary treatment order. However, she said that she was a very lonely person whose sole social activity was membership of a weekly sewing group, where she excelled in fine embroidery, something she was proud of since her teens. All the antipsychotic medication she had tried—at least four different drugs—because of their side effects, most notably a tremor of her hands, made it difficult for her to sew. She said she valued the social interaction and her achievements in embroidery more than remaining symptom-free, and indeed to avoiding hospital admissions. Under the Mental Health Act, Beth could nevertheless be lawfully placed on an involuntary treatment order, in this case a community treatment order—she had a mental disorder and treatment was clearly, from a clinical point of view, in the interests of her health and safety. Such an order would aim to ensure that she takes medication to prevent further relapses of her illness and thus prevent the likely consequent harms.

A patient with a 'physical disorder', like Louise, may refuse treatment even if the disease is life-threatening. Her decision will be respected, unless it can be shown that she lacks decision-making capacity. As we saw in Chapter 4, UK courts and other common-law jurisdictions in Western countries now set a very high value on the 'autonomy' of the individual. I accept that the idea of 'autonomy' is complex philosophically and may carry a variety of meanings. I will discuss the concept in greater detail later. For the moment, I will take it to mean the qualities of self-determination, self-governance, and living according to one's own conception of the good life. Respect for the autonomy of individuals is closely linked with the notion of respect for the dignity of others and the idea that others should be treated as an 'end' and never simply as a 'means' to an end. We generally accept that there are certain conditions that must be met for autonomous actions, including the kinds of abilities, described earlier under the notion of decision-making capacity—understanding, being able to use and weigh relevant information, and so on. It is also accepted that such actions should be made with freedom from duress, manipulation, and coercion. A social dimension to decision-making is important. Discussion with others may contribute greatly to our decision-making, but at the end of the day, one would expect an autonomous decision to be 'owned' by the decision-maker. Though not without controversy on some points, I think this account would be accepted by most people, certainly in 'Western' societies.

A person thus has an absolute right to refuse to consent to medical treatment for a physical disorder even where the decision may lead to a grave outcome. Paternalistic interventions in medicine (with the notable exception of psychiatry) that override the individual's wishes are only allowed when a patient lacks the mental capacity to make treatment decisions for himself or herself, and the treatment intervention is in the person's best interests'. It should be apparent from the earlier discussion of capacity and best interests that they pay substantial regard to the autonomy of the person in the sense I have outlined. They give serious attention to a person's right to self-determination and to make choices according to their idea of the good life and their personal values that support it. When decision-making capacity is absent, a best interests determination gives regard to the person's values and beliefs. What is best for the person is seen from the person's perspective, not from that of the clinician—it is not what the clinician thinks is best for the patient or what the clinician imagines he or she would choose if they were in the patient's shoes.

A fundamental failure to respect autonomy

In contrast to the key role of impairment in decision-making capacity for patients with a 'physical disorder', there is usually no legal role for capacity in the detention of, and initiation of involuntary psychiatric treatment for, those with 'mental disorder'. Instead of a functional criterion—whether the patient can make a treatment decision—we have here a status criterion—that the person has been given a diagnosis of a 'mental disorder'. There is nothing about such a status that has a necessary connection with autonomy or self-determination. There is no obligation to explore why the patient is rejecting a proposed treatment and to determine whether the patient's decision is deserving of respect in the light of, for example, their deeply held beliefs and values.

The further justification in the case of mental illness is that the treatment is in the interests of the health or safety of the person. (I shall come to the protection of others in a moment.) From whose perspective should this judgement be made? There is no requirement that it should pay serious regard to the patient's perspective. It is generally taken to be a judgement made by clinicians according to what they think is best for the patient. I am not saying that all clinicians in such situations totally ignore the patient's reasons for rejecting treatment or the patient's views about what is in their best interests. However, the tendency is to dedicate to it a limited regard, especially as the law places the clinician under no explicit obligation to take the patient's personal goals and values into account.

We see thus a vast gulf between the principles governing the detention and involuntary treatment of those with a mental disorder compared to those with a physical disorder—between psychiatric care and the rest of medicine. Why is this so? How is it that such different principles have evolved? The most likely reason is that there is an underlying assumption in mental health care and law that 'mental disorder' necessarily entails some kind of mental incapacity or incompetence. Thus a direct question about decision-making capacity does not need to be asked; the beliefs and values espoused by a person with a 'disordered' or 'diseased' mind, it is assumed, are not to be taken too seriously. A number of people I have discussed this with have talked about 'the organ of thought' itself being disordered, making anything like rationality, at best, suspect. However, we know from excellent research studies in my own hospital as well as in the United States that decision-making capacity is not necessarily impaired. Even in patients who are in a state of relapse and are at their most ill, that is, those who are admitted to a psychiatric hospital, around half retain decision-making capacity.[3,4]

In previous chapters, I outlined the different histories of treatment without consent in mental health law versus the law applying to patients in the rest of medicine. Mental health law has shown no evolution in its fundamentals over the past 200 years or so. Changes have occurred in the procedures or mechanics—for example, in certification, authorization, review, and appeal processes—but the criteria for compulsion have remained essentially unchanged. An underlying paternalism has continued largely unchallenged. On the other hand, we have seen a marked evolution in the concept of consent in the rest of medicine, especially over the past 40 years or so. Paternalism here has lost significant ground to patient autonomy. These different histories, I suggest, are explained by a persisting stereotype of people with mental disorders as being incompetent, and without agency or the capacity for self-determination. It is also testament to the fact that they have had no 'voice' in society—although recently that has started to change.

By failing to respect the autonomy of the person with a mental illness, by not presuming capacity unless there is reason for doubt, by assuming that mental disorder entails incapacity, and by enshrining these prejudices in legislation which applies uniquely to those with 'mental disorder', current mental health legislation discriminates against those with mental illness and serves to stigmatize them. They are considered to be, in some way, less deserving of respect than others simply because they have been placed in a particular category of persons.

The protection of others criterion: an unconcern for fairness

Civil commitment law generally confounds the health interests of the patient and the protection of others.[5] The 'risk' criterion, almost mantra-like, couples the safety of the patient and the protection of other persons. If the person has a mental disorder (for which treatment is considered to be appropriate) and presents a risk to others, involuntary treatment can be initiated. However, a person's health interest (or safety) and the protection of others are quite separate ends; acting on the former empowers others to act when the patient cannot act in his or her best health interests. On the other hand, protection of others turns on the risk of harm. This risk, assuming for the moment that it can be accurately assessed, may not have much to do with the person's mental disorder, or with the person's capacity to make treatment decisions.

Where does the discrimination lie in relation to the 'protection of others'? People with mental disorders are unique in being liable to detention (albeit usually, but not always, in hospital) because they are assessed as presenting a risk of harm to others, but without having actually committed an offence. Everyone else in society must have committed an offence, or be strongly suspected of having committed one, before they can be detained—on remand in prison, for example.

The discrimination can be well illustrated diagrammatically as in Fig 5.1. The larger circle represents all persons in the community who at a particular time present a risk to others at a significant level. The smaller circle contains all persons in the community at a particular time who have a mental disorder. Those in the larger circle might include, for example, habitual spouse abusers, those with short tempers—especially when intoxicated or provoked—or those who drive recklessly. The important observation is that only those people in the area of overlap between the circles containing those with mental disorders and those who are judged 'risky' can be detained under civil commitment legislation on the basis of risk, not on the basis of an offence having been committed. Such detention of those with a mental disorder constitutes a form of 'preventive detention', to which most societies, in other contexts, have a strong aversion on civil liberty grounds.

Let's imagine that everyone in the larger circle presents an equal level of risk, one that is judged unacceptable—assuming that this can be accurately judged (which, in reality, as we have seen in Chapter 3, it cannot). Anyway,

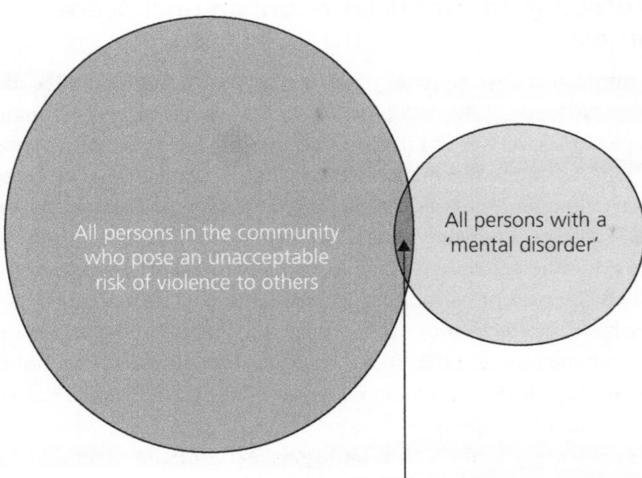

Fig. 5.1 Risk of violence, mental disorder, and liability to preventive detention.

let's assume for the sake of argument that it can. Why, as is commonly the case, should the person with a mental disorder in the overlap zone be more liable to be detained on the basis of that unacceptable risk than the person without a mental disorder? The principle of fairness, or justice, would demand that all of those presenting an equal level of risk to others (that is, all those in the larger circle in Fig. 5.1) should be equally liable to detention. If preventive detention is to be allowed for those with a mental disorder solely on account of their risk to others, if we are to avoid discrimination, so should it be for all of us. This of course amounts to a generic dangerousness or preventive detention provision against which many will recoil. But the principle of non-discrimination requires that either we have generic dangerousness legislation applicable to all of us, or that we have no preventive detention for anyone, including those with a mental disorder. Under a generic form of legislation, once having exceeded the acceptable threshold of 'risk', an intervention would occur; this might be psychiatric treatment, if appropriate, for those with a mental disorder, or other interventions including a custodial sentence for those—who will form the great majority—who are not.

Why has this discriminatory situation in relation to the protection of others arisen, and why is it so very rarely challenged? Again I suggest that a culturally rooted stereotype of people with mental illness is at work. It is marked by a deeply embedded assumption that dangerousness is intrinsic to, is part and parcel, of mental illness.

An examination of the circles in Fig. 5.1 points to another source of disquiet. There is sometimes a temptation for societies to expand the 'mental disorder' circle to include people with various behaviours that are seen as a threat to the social order. I gave an example in Chapter 3—government proposals in England in the mid 1990s under which the adoption of a new, state-defined diagnosis ('dangerous severe personality disorder'), coupled with an imputation of risk, was proposed to be sufficient to detain someone, even in the absence of a previous violent offence or the possibility of effective treatment.

It should be clear that people who enter the category of having a mental disorder do not receive the protections from preventive detention that the rest of us do. In a risk-averse society or in a society where important institutions see themselves under threat, the potential for broadening the scope of 'mental disorder' and 'risk' is troubling.

In Chapter 4, I discussed the problem of the level of 'risk' that might be unacceptable in a community as opposed to a hospital setting. The threshold for implementing a community treatment order on the basis of an unacceptable risk—in effect, the risk (of relapse) of a future risk (violence)—can easily drop. In Australia in 2011–2012, 13 per cent of all mental health community service contacts were with patients on a community involuntary treatment order. About a third of contacts with patients with schizophrenia were with patients on an order.[6] Before the introduction of community treatment orders there were, of course, none. The number of hospital treatment orders has not declined.

Some facts about violence and mental illness

Many people when thinking about appropriate laws believe that an association between mental disorder and violence makes mental illness not equivalent to physical illness. The dangers posed by the mentally ill, it is supposed, justify and demand that society be protected through special measures.

At this point I would like to digress slightly and make some comments on the relationship between mental illness and violence. 'Dangerousness' may be a consequence of having a mental illness in a small minority of patients. The risk, in the absence of alcohol or substance misuse, or of an 'antisocial personality'—that is, someone who has a propensity to commit antisocial acts associated with a character that is more 'bad' than 'mad'—is modestly, if at all, raised.[7,8] People with severe mental disorder, those with a psychosis or major disturbances of mood, perpetrate only a small fraction of serious violence in our society, around 2 per cent.[9] Furthermore, violence is no more predictable in those with a mental illness than in those without. The predictors of violence, in so far as it can be predicted, are essentially the same for those with a mental disorder as for those without. Even if violence were significantly more common in those with a mental illness than those without, it would still be unjust to fail to assess and manage risk in the same way for all.

But my experience has shown that many will retort when offered these statistics that there is nonetheless an important difference. Surely the propensity for violence is 'treatable' and thus more preventable in those with a mental illness. I doubt that many 'mentally disordered offenders' who have been in high secure hospitals such as Broadmoor in England for 5, 10, or 20 years would agree. Indeed, it is quite possible that psychological or group interventions aimed at reducing violence in violent persons who are not mentally ill, such as spouse abusers or heavy drinkers, may be more effective than interventions for violence in those who are mentally ill. Examples of such interventions might be 'anger management' training or interventions aimed at preventing binge drinking in non-dependent but heavy drinkers. Since dangerous people who do not have a mental illness vastly outnumber those who have a mental illness, interventions directed at reducing violence in the former will likely be far more effective in reducing the overall level of violence in the community than can be achieved by targeting the latter. If the success rate of an intervention is, for argument's sake, say, 10 per cent in both groups, one-tenth of 98 per cent is much bigger than one-tenth of 2 per cent!

If protection of the public is the aim, it is clear where the effort should be directed. Of course, this would require generic dangerousness legislation. All those who represent a risk to others that exceeds a threshold of what can be tolerated would be apprehended. That would be the first step. The second step would involve a court deciding on the best disposal of each case. If the person has a mental disorder, this might be a treatment order; we shall see later when this would be appropriate. If the person does not have a mental disorder, this might be a psychological intervention aimed at risk reduction, or if no intervention is possible, a custodial sentence. But, as I said earlier, many recoil at the idea of preventive detention—except, it appears, for those with a mental disorder, a group whose rights are easily discounted. Justice demands that all people who are equally risky should be treated equally, and be equally subject to preventive measures that a society may deem appropriate.

The anomalous position of mental illness

Let's hark back to patient P whose case was presented at the beginning of this chapter. She was on a compulsory order for the treatment of schizophrenia, but was judged to have decision-making capacity in relation to her gangrenous foot. If the Mental Capacity Act rules had been applied to her mental disorder, would she have been deemed to have capacity? We don't know, of course. But let's turn the question on its head. What would have happened if the Mental Health Act principles had been applied to her physical illness? If they had been applied to the question of the proposed surgery, I think it is almost certain that a compulsory order would have been made. The civil commitment type criteria were clearly met—the patient had a 'physical disorder' for which there was an appropriate treatment, there was a very substantial risk to her health as a result, and, as one of the experts said, 'any surgeon in the land' would have recommended amputation. How many of us would accept a framework where a doctor or a clinical team decides for us when we should have a treatment without needing to take into account our capacity and a right to make treatment choices for ourselves, made in the light of our personal life goals and values? Not very many, if any, I suspect.

At this point I draw your attention to another inconsistency.[10] While decision-making capacity plays virtually no role in judgments about involuntary *treatment* for people with a mental illness, when it comes to consent to participation in *research*, decision-making capacity and informed consent apply equally for patients with and without mental disorders. Why should there be such a difference?

I hope it is now clear that conventional mental health legislation, as adopted in most jurisdictions, discriminates unfairly against people with mental disorders. It reflects and reinforces stigmatizing stereotypes. Autonomy (or the right to self-determination) is not respected; preventive detention is singularly applied to this group. The 'two-track' approach, one set of rules for the mentally disordered and another for the rest of medicine, is inconsistent with the principles of health care ethics and with basic notions of human rights, especially freedom from unnecessary discrimination in the law. Some other form of legislation is thus required. Chapter 6 will present a framework that is non-discriminatory.

References

1. **Grisso T, Appelbaum PS.** *Assessing Competence to Consent to Treatment: A Guide for Physicians and Other Health Professionals.* New York: Oxford University Press, 1998.
2. **Szmukler G.** *How Mental Health Law Discriminates Unfairly Against People with Mental Illness.* Gresham College Public Lecture, 15 November 2010. http://www.gresham.ac.uk/professors-and-speakers/professor-george-szmukler
3. **Owen GS, Richardson G, David AS, Szmukler G, Hayward P, Hotopf M.** Mental capacity to make decisions on treatment in people admitted to psychiatric hospitals: cross sectional study. *British Medical Journal* 2008; 337:a448.
4. **Grisso T, Appelbaum PS.** The MacArthur Treatment Competence Study. III: abilities of patients to consent to psychiatric and medical treatments. *Law and Human Behavior* 1995; **19**:149–174.
5. **Campbell T, Heginbotham C.** *Mental Illness: Prejudice, Discrimination and the Law.* Aldershot: Dartmouth Publishing Company, 1991.
6. **Australian Institute of Health and Welfare.** *Mental Health Services in Australia.* Canberra: AIHW, 2014.
7. **Coid J, Yang M, Roberts A,** et al. Violence and psychiatric morbidity in a national household population—a report from the British Household Survey. *American Journal of Epidemiology* 2006; **164**:1199–1208.

8. **Elbogen EB, Johnson SC.** The intricate link between violence and mental disorder: results from the National Epidemiologic Survey on Alcohol and Related Conditions. *Archives of General Psychiatry* 2009; **66**:152–161.
9. **Flynn S, Rodway C, Appleby L, Shaw J.** Serious violence by people with mental illness: national clinical survey. *Journal of Interpersonal Violence* 2014; **29**:1438–1458.
10. **Szmukler G, Hotopf M.** Double standard on capacity and consent? *American Journal of Psychiatry* 2001; **158**:148–149.

Part II

A solution

Chapter 6

A law that does not discriminate against people with mental illness

We have seen how civil commitment under mental health law discriminates against people with a mental illness. Such law fails to respect the person's autonomy or right to self-determination in the same way as it does for those with a non-psychiatric illness. The 'mental disorder status plus risk' formula for those with a mental illness finds no place for consideration of whether the person has decision-making capacity and whether non-consensual treatment would be in the person's best interests, as is the case for those with a non-psychiatric illness.

In the early 1990s, I began to think about a framework that would not discriminate against my patients. Campbell and Heginbotham in their revealing book, *Mental Illness: Prejudice, Discrimination and the Law,*[1] made a crucial point:

> '… there is no justification for dealing with persons with mental illnesses according to rules and procedures which are not in principle prepared to apply to all citizens. Whatever interest society has in protecting people from themselves or from others cannot be justly served by institutionalizing social prejudices around the protean concept of mental illness, or its even more amorphous administrative umbrella concept, 'mental disorder'.[1,p55]

The idea followed of tackling discrimination against people with mental disorders by not making psychiatric treatment the subject of special legislation, and, instead, by applying the same principles concerning involuntary treatment across all fields of medicine. An important point made by Campbell and Heginbotham is that if a law is generic, that is, it applies to those of us who do not have a mental illness as much as those who do, we will take more care in ensuring it is carefully drawn and implemented. As we have now seen, the rights of persons with a mental illness are easily discounted.

By the early 1990s, this principle of a generic framework seemed quite clearly correct, and a psychiatrist colleague, Dr Frank Holloway, and I developed an outline schema that we believed could work, from a clinical point of view at least.[2] We presented this approach in various fora with a degree of success in interesting our colleagues, though the majority remained sceptical. Most were somewhat taken aback by the nature of our criticisms of mental health law and by the kind of regime that we were proposing in its stead. Thinking that has been so deeply embedded in our profession for so long cannot be easily challenged. In fact, I applaud my colleagues' general conservatism, especially in the light of past enthusiasms for treatments peppering the history of psychiatry that turned out to be non-effective and often harmful. I shall discuss later some of their criticisms of our proposals.

At talks that I gave at various mental health service users' fora, the ideas were met with greater enthusiasm. The themes of distress and humiliation associated with laws and practices that failed to respect patient autonomy nearly always came to the fore in discussions about involuntary treatment. There was virtually unanimous support for something better. In 2003, I had the good fortune to meet John Dawson, a professor of mental health law at the University of Otago in New Zealand. I had arranged for him to give a seminar at the UK Institute of Psychiatry on community treatment orders, a subject that he had researched thoroughly. We later met for a coffee, where I expressed my serious misgivings about the grounds for community treatment orders. The discussion moved on to discrimination and how impaired decision-making capacity might work as a basis for involuntary treatment in psychiatry. There followed further discussions that were invaluable. John brought the rigour of a legal mind—quite an uncompromising one at that—to the clinical–philosophical schema I had been elaborating.

About 6 months later we concluded, thanks to email making the 12,000 miles separating us practically irrelevant, that we had reached a point where the clinical and legal had met sufficiently for us to produce a proposal for a new legal framework aimed at eliminating the discrimination that was so troubling. We committed our thoughts to a paper that was published in the *British Journal of Psychiatry* in 2006 that has been quite influential—'Fusion of mental health and incapacity legislation'.[3] The introduction was as follows:

> Why should separate statutes govern the involuntary treatment of 'physical' and 'mental' illness? Why not bring all involuntary treatment under a single statutory scheme? The principal justification for all treatment

> without consent could then be incapacity to make necessary treatment decisions. . . . Its development was hinted at in the UK law reform process . . . even as proposals for new incapacity and reformed mental health legislation were developed, simultaneously, on largely separate paths. Each regime has its particular strengths. In this special article we advocate fusion of the two schemes into a comprehensive involuntary treatment statute.[i]

At this point, I need to prime the reader concerning how this part of the story, a proposal for a framework for non-consensual treatment that is not discriminatory, will unfold. I will first give an account of what I might now call the 'first formulation' of the 'Fusion Law' proposal. Following a number of presentations at conferences, seminars, and lectures, it became clear there were a number of critical questions that needed to be addressed more thoroughly. At the top of the list were questions about what was meant by two key notions: the 'capacity' to make treatment decisions and 'best interests'; and how and by whom they should be assessed. 'Won't a person who disagrees with the recommendations of their doctor be labelled as lacking capacity?' was a common concern. Chapter 7, 'On being able to make decisions and making decisions for others', will give an account of how I believe these challenges can be met. The role of a person's beliefs and values and their 'interpretation' is given a major part, one that is certainly much larger than in standard accounts of decision-making capacity and best interests. At around the same time, the United Nations was working on the production of a new convention that would spell out the 'rights of persons with disabilities'. This placed huge emphasis on persons with disabilities' autonomy and all rights to be enjoyed 'on an equal basis with others'. The implications of this convention for persons with mental disabilities are profound and challenge the validity, under any circumstances, of making decisions *for* other people ('substitute decision-making') as opposed to supporting them to make decisions *for themselves.* We are enjoined by the convention to 'respect the rights, will and preferences' of people with disabilities. This includes people with mental health disabilities. Chapter 8 will describe how some elements of the 'fusion proposal' can be reformulated to meet the challenges posed by the convention. Bear in mind that both the 'fusion proposal' and the 'disability convention' are animated by the same aim—eliminating discrimination against persons with mental health disabilities.

---

[i] Reproduced from Dawson J and Szmukler G., 'Fusion of mental health and incapacity legislation', *British Journal of Psychiatry*, 188, 2006, pp. 504–509.

A single, generic law: the 'fusion' proposal

The simplest way of avoiding the unfair discrimination against people with a mental illness manifest in mental health law compared with that covering general medicine would be to adopt a single, generic law governing treatment without consent that covers all patients, in all specialities, in all settings—medical, surgical, psychiatric, nursing and care homes, or indeed, anywhere in the community.

On what foundations can such a law be built? John Dawson and I proposed that the approach should be based squarely on decision-making capacity and best interests. Given the value placed on autonomy and self-determination in our society, we regarded an impairment of the ability to decide for oneself as the soundest justification for proceeding to a consideration of whether treatment without consent might be warranted.

But a capacity–best interests law on its own, like the Mental Capacity Act, would not suffice. Our proposal builds on the strengths of the two existing regimes that I have discussed, including the one I have so severely slated—civil commitment under the usual mental health law. That is why we have termed it a 'fusion' law. The strength of capacity-based law, such as the Mental Capacity Act, in giving due weight to the patient's autonomy when capacity is retained is counterbalanced by a number of weaknesses. These lie in the lack of sufficient attention to powers governing forced treatment and detention in hospital. The Mental Capacity Act, for example, deals only briefly with the use of force. 'Restraint' can be used when it is judged to be necessary to prevent harm to the person who lacks capacity. The restraint must also be a proportionate response to the likelihood of the person suffering harm and the seriousness of the harm. As we shall see later, this must not amount to a 'deprivation of liberty'. Detention and the use of force are exactly those areas in which civil commitment schemes, such as the Mental Health Act, are strong. The use of force, and the detention and involuntary treatment of objecting patients, are clearly authorized and regulated by such legislation. Clearly stipulated are key issues including who can authorize detention and treatment; where; for how long; for what treatments; with what processes of review and appeal; and so on.

The lack of clarity concerning the use of force and detention in capacity-based legislation can pose a problem for the treatment of patients with 'physical disorders'. Patients who object to treatment but who do not have a 'mental disorder' as generally understood are not uncommonly placed under the Mental Health Act—inappropriately—because of a reluctance by clinicians to use force unless they can rely on clear statutory authority of the Mental Health Act kind. Here is an example from my own experience:

Use of force

I remember being called one night by a general practitioner to assess a patient for a compulsory order whose illness was bleeding 'oesophageal varices'. People who drink alcohol heavily for a long time may develop swollen veins in their oesophagus and these sometimes bleed profusely. The patient about whom I had been called had lost enough blood to affect his brain, making him confused and lacking in decision-making capacity. He refused to get into an ambulance and then, when the police were called, physically resisted leaving his home. The patient could have been forcefully taken by the police to a hospital in his 'best interests' under the common law at that time, but the police were reluctant to exercise the necessary degree of force without a clear authorization, such as an order under the Mental Health Act. In the end, given that the patient was now urgently in need of a transfusion, I agreed to a Mental Health Act order but stated he should be taken directly to a general hospital, not a psychiatric hospital.

In this case, the imperative for treatment was overwhelmingly clear. In other instances, when there is no such treatment imperative, some patients may not be treated at all, even though treatment would have been in their best interests. This may occur when the clinician does not probe too deeply into the question of whether the patient who is rejecting a treatment lacks decision-making capacity because if this were to be the case, there would be uncertainty about how exactly to proceed to treat the patient against their objection. Accepting the refusal as being made with capacity is a clearer course of action—after all, capacity must be presumed under legislation like the Mental Capacity Act, and rebutted if a non-consensual intervention is to be made.

We therefore advocated a legal regime that retains the strengths of both incapacity and mental health legislation, but still relies squarely on the inability of the person to make a significant care or treatment decision as a necessary, though not sufficient, justification for an intervention.

This scheme would govern the treatment without consent in any medical condition, thus avoiding the problematic distinction between 'physical' and 'mental' illness. Research carried out with my colleagues in London at the Maudsley Hospital, a psychiatric hospital, and on medical wards at King's College Hospital, has shown that a lack of decision-making capacity is as common in the general hospital as in the psychiatric hospital[4,5] and that it can be assessed reliably, especially by experienced clinicians with even a moderate degree of training.[6]

Key provisions of the 'fusion' proposal

I provide here an outline of the most important provisions of a Fusion Law developed with John Dawson and Rowena Daw, a lawyer with special expertise in discrimination law.[7] This résumé covers the underlying principles, the general provisions, the requirements for compulsory treatment, and the forensic provisions. I have attempted to reduce legal technical terms to a minimum.

In our initial formulations of the Fusion Law, we use the term 'capacity' to stand for 'decision-making capacity'. I have retained this term for this account of the fusion proposal though I now favour the term 'decision-making capability' as will be explained in the next chapter.

The principles

The following principles apply to the Fusion Law:

1. A person must be assumed to have capacity. A lack of capacity must be established.
2. A person is not to be treated as unable to make a decision unless all practicable steps to support the person to do so have been taken without success.
3. A person is not to be treated as unable to make a decision merely because the person makes an unwise decision.
4. Any act done for or on behalf of a person who lacks capacity must be in his or her best interests,
5. Before acting, regard must be given to whether the outcome sought can be as effectively achieved in a way that is less restrictive of the person's rights and freedom of action.

Scope of the law and definitions of 'capacity' and 'best interests'

The general provisions include a definition of 'capacity' and 'best interests', based to a large degree on those in the Mental Capacity Act. However, the definition of capacity that we offer is broader, explicitly including the ability to 'appreciate' the necessary information. A person may be able to use information for some purposes yet still not be able to 'appreciate' how the information is relevant to their personal predicament. (This is discussed further in Chapter 7 which deals in detail with the meaning of 'decision-making capacity'.)

In defining the scope of the Fusion Law, reference is made to persons with 'an impairment or disturbance in the functioning of the mind'. We do not use the term 'mental disorder', however, because this may be interpreted as referring only to 'psychiatric' disorders.

Scope of the Act

The Act applies to persons who because of 'an impairment or disturbance in the functioning of mind' lack the capacity at a critical time to make a decision relating to their care or treatment.

Note here that decisions are specific—a person may have the capacity to make one decision, but not another.

Definition of capacity

A person lacks capacity if he or she is unable to:

1. Understand the information relevant to the decision.
2. Retain that information.
3. Use, weigh, or appreciate that information in making the decision.
4. Communicate the decision (by any means).

Definition of best interests

1. In determining what is in the best interests of a person, the decision-maker must consider all the relevant circumstances. This includes whether it is likely that the person will at some time have capacity for the decision that needs to be made, and if so, when that might be.
2. As far as is reasonably practicable, the person must participate in making the decision. This includes attempts to improve the person's ability to participate, as fully as possible in the decision.
3. The decision-maker must consider, so far as is reasonably ascertainable: (a) the person's past and present wishes and feelings (and, in particular, any relevant written statement made by the person when they had capacity); (b) the beliefs and values that would be likely to influence the person's decision if he or she had capacity; and (c) any other factors that the person would be likely to consider if able to do so.
4. In determining what is in the person's best interests, the decision-maker must take into account, if practicable, the views of (a) anyone named by the person as someone to be consulted, (b) anyone engaged in caring for the person or interested in the person's welfare, or (c) any substitute decision-maker appointed by the person or appointed for the person by the Tribunal (to be specially constituted under the Fusion Law).

5. The principle of best interests applies to all decisions made on behalf of the person, unless otherwise specified.

If all of these factors were met, a decision might be in the person's best interests although it is not in accordance with the person's present expression of wishes and feelings, and although the person objects to the treatment.

A 'general authority' is established that permits people caring for a person who lacks capacity to perform certain routine acts (for example, maintaining hygiene) without requiring a specific authority under other provisions. A proportionate degree of restraint of the person in their best interests is permitted under this authority. Generally, where medication is to be administered over the person's objection, the involuntary treatment process, described next, should be initiated. Medication may only be administered using force under the 'general authority' if it is immediately necessary to prevent serious harm to the patient.

A general requirement for consultation concerning a person's best interests applies throughout the Fusion Law, but is supplemented in different circumstances by specific additional requirements.

Involuntary treatment

Before a person is placed under involuntary care and treatment over their *objection*, a set of conditions must be met. These are:

1. The person has an impairment or dysfunction of mind.
2. The person lacks capacity to make a decision about his or her care or treatment.
3. The person needs care or treatment in his or her best interests.
4. The person objects to the proposed care or treatment.
5. The proposed objective cannot be achieved in a less restrictive fashion.

If any of these conditions are no longer met, the person must be discharged from compulsory powers.

Illustrating the value of the 'fusion' approach, impaired capacity is a necessary condition, but the processes of emergency assessment and treatment, detention, the use of force, and compulsory treatment, are clearly regulated.

In *emergency circumstances*, a 'reasonable belief' that the person lacks capacity is sufficient to authorize an intervention. Suitably qualified professionals can then intervene, using similar powers to those provided by a civil commitment scheme: that is, powers of entry, detention of the person, transportation to assessment, use of reasonable force, and so on.

The patient then will enter a *staged assessment process*, during which immediately necessary treatment can be authorized. The emergency assessment would last only for 24 hours. A structured assessment of the person's capacity would take place within that time, and if an extension of the order were required, a second opinion would be necessary, and of course, consultation with all those who would be involved in the assessment of best interests. If there were agreement that further involuntary treatment were justified, a 'care plan' would be developed and shared with the patient and those involved in the best interests determination. Treatment could then continue for 28 days. If involuntary treatment were to continue beyond 28 days, authorization by a tribunal would be the next step. The care plan would include details of the treatment and include an analysis of the need for detention, the appropriate place of treatment—which might be in the community—and arrangements for continuing care.

Comprehensive review and accountability mechanisms would apply. All involuntary patients would have ready access to rights advice and to independent review of their status before a court or tribunal.

In the proposed scheme, involuntary treatment would be restricted to patients who lack capacity and for whom it is in their best interests. However, this would not preclude involuntary treatment for the *protection of others* in two sets of circumstances: (1) where treatment for the protection of others is in the patient's best interests, and (2) where in the course of providing treatment in the best interests of the patient, there arises a risk of harm to others. An example of the first might be where as a result of illness and its associated loss of capacity, the patient becomes aggressive towards a near relative, with whom he or she normally has a good relationship and who is the patient's main supporter, both of which he or she clearly values highly when well. These considerations would be important in a best interests assessment. The principle here would be that the interests and preferences of other people can be considered in so far as they affect the interests of the person without capacity. An example of where in the course of providing treatment in the best interests of the patient there arises a risk of harm to others would be one where measures need to be taken to prevent harm to other patients that might be caused by an aggressive patient whose best interests require treatment on an inpatient unit.

Offenders with an impairment of mental functioning

Some people, including many of my forensic psychiatry colleagues, have expressed concerns about the application of a capacity-based approach when it comes to people with a mental illness who have committed an offence. A major reason why the government in England did not accept an impaired capacity criterion when a new Mental Health Act was being planned in the late 1990s and early 2000s was a fear that the protection of the public would be compromised. As I have mentioned earlier, England has become perhaps the most risk-averse country in the world when it comes to attempts to exercise control over people who are deemed to present a risk to others. People with a mental disorder have been a special focus of attention.

The Fusion Law proposals for people who have committed an offence and who have an impairment or disturbance in the functioning of mind are set out later in this section. Note again that we do not talk about people with a 'mental disorder' as this might lead one to think about the provisions as only applying to people with a psychiatric disorder. Remember, the Fusion Law is generic—people with a disturbance of mental functioning arising from any illness may fall within its scope. Examples would be confusional states due to metabolic derangements associated with diabetes or an infection, adverse reaction to medication, a brain disorder such as epilepsy, or indeed a 'non-illness cause', such as overwhelming emotional turmoil.

In Chapter 5, I showed how people with a mental illness were treated unfairly when it came to preventive detention based on attributions of risk. Mentally ill offenders face another form of discrimination. In England, for example, if a serious offence has been committed, a very common disposal by the court is a 'hospital order'. If the offence is very serious, a 'restriction order' may be attached. The person will usually be sent to a medium- or high-security hospital without a time limit; discharge will occur when the clinicians believe it appropriate. When a 'restriction order' is in place, discharge cannot occur without the agreement of the Ministry of Justice. Usually in such cases, between leaving hospital and a full discharge, there is a lengthy period of 'conditional discharge'. Certain conditions must be followed by the patient—for example, taking medication, residing at a particular place, or avoiding illicit drugs. The person can be recalled to hospital if those conditions are breached. The patient can appeal to a tribunal against the detention or restriction (usually without success). The important point in relation to discrimination is that despite having committed the same offence, a person with a mental disorder may end up being detained (in hospital) for a much longer period—often very much longer—than a person without a mental disorder (in prison). The Fusion Law aims to avoid this unjust disparity.

The proposals for offenders are as follows:

First is a *general principle* that is basic to the Fusion Law: any offender with an impairment or disturbance of mental functioning who lacks capacity can be treated involuntarily in their best interests (as can any other patient without capacity). An offender with a mental impairment who *has* capacity can be treated in an appropriate health care facility only with their consent.

Placement of persons on *remand* would follow these principles, as would *transfers from prison to hospital* of prisoners later found to have a mental impairment for which treatment is available. Any sentence would continue to run; the person would return to prison either because recovery had occurred and hospitalization was no longer required or, in the case of a person with capacity, consent to treatment had been withdrawn.

Two options would be available for a person with a mental impairment who has been *convicted of a serious offence*:

1. The person could be sentenced to the usual period of imprisonment. However, if they were found to lack capacity and need treatment in their best interests, they could be transferred to hospital for the necessary care. If capacity is regained in hospital, the person has the choice of continuing treatment with consent; if not, the person would be transferred to prison for the remainder of their sentence. An offender with capacity and who has a mental impairment for which there is a treatment could also be transferred to hospital if they consented to the treatment. If they changed their mind, they would be returned to prison. Note here that the term of detention is commensurate with the seriousness of the offence and thus comparable to that of a person without a mental impairment. If at the end of the sentence period the person with a mental impairment still lacks capacity and treatment would be in the person's best interests, an ordinary civil order could then be made. At this point the person is in the same position as any non-forensic patient on an involuntary treatment order.
2. The second option for the court in the case of a person who has committed a serious offence is to place the person on a compulsory treatment order without a concurrent sentence. This would only apply to a person who lacks capacity and where treatment is in the person's best interests. The patient would then be subject to the usual terms of a civil order. The order would be terminated by the responsible clinician when the

necessary conditions were no longer met—for example, if the patient wanted to leave hospital after regaining capacity, discharge would be obligatory.

So far so good; I think the principles work well. However, we now reach a problem area, one where neither health law nor criminal law seems to be fit for purpose. These are instances where:

1. A person is '*unfit to plead*' (or to stand trial)—that is, their mental functioning is so impaired that they cannot participate in a fair trial—but where on a 'trial of the facts', it is clear that a serious offence has been committed; or,
2. A person has committed a serious offence, but at the time of the offence was so mentally impaired that the verdict is '*not guilty by reason of insanity*'. This plea is usually restricted to cases of homicide.

In both cases, although the person has committed a serious offence, because of their mental state either at the time of the trial or at the time of the offence, they cannot be fairly convicted and therefore, in most jurisdictions including the United Kingdom, imprisonment is not regarded as a valid option. Thus the only possibilities are acquittal by the court, some kind of community supervision order, or a mental health disposal, usually admission to a psychiatric unit, usually to a secure one. The last may turn into detention for a very long time; the order is usually indefinite and may last for decades.

How would the Fusion Law principles apply here? If the person lacks capacity and treatment is in their best interests, involuntary detention and treatment would be justified. If the person had capacity now, but was not guilty of the crime by reason of insanity at the time of the offence—or less likely, they were 'unfit to plead' but at the same time retained decision-making capacity for treatment—they could not be treated involuntarily under the Fusion Law principles. What if such a person, though with capacity, were deemed a clear risk to other people? Unless some kind of 'third way' were to be introduced—perhaps under a form of generic dangerousness legislation as discussed in Chapter 5—the only detention available would be in a psychiatric setting. We are then faced with an argument that, until a 'third way' is implemented, we should compromise in this single instance and allow detention and involuntary treatment of a person with capacity if:

- the person has committed a serious offence; and
- a serious impairment or disturbance in the functioning of mind has contributed significantly to the commission of that offence; and

- an effective treatment can be offered that could be expected to reduce the risk of that disorder's reoccurrence.

This is not a satisfactory solution from a capacity–best interests point of view. However, my colleagues and I reluctantly accepted it, we hope, as an interim measure until a better solution is found.

I will look at some of the fears concerning public protection arising from a capacity-based approach in Chapter 11 when I examine the practical implications of adopting the proposed Fusion Law framework.

'Deprivation of liberty': 'a gilded cage is still a cage'

The subjects of interest here are people who lack capacity and are residents in hospitals, nursing homes, or care homes where they are essentially under the control of staff but *do not object* to their treatment or attempt to leave. In terms of their liberty, how should we regard their status? This has turned out to be a very complicated problem with potentially enormous implications—legal as well as practical.

Until recently, people in this position were not regarded as needing any special legal protections. The general law relating to negligent care, abusive treatment, and so on, was thought sufficient. This changed after a case was brought by the foster-placement carers of an adult man with severe autism and intellectual disability against Bournewood Hospital, a hospital for people with such disabilities. The man, known as HL, was an 'informal' (or voluntary) patient, but for 3 months his carers were not allowed contact with him. The intention of staff was to keep HL in hospital. The carers asserted that HL was 'deprived of his liberty', even though he did not attempt to leave. The case eventually went through the court system in England up to the court of last resort in the United Kingdom (up until 2009), the Law Lords of the House of Lords. The Lords upheld the 'status quo'; that is, such cases were covered by the so-called necessity principle—people who lacked capacity and who did not object could be treated informally in their best interests, even if they were more or less under the control of those treating them. The complainants, however, took the case to the European Court of Human Rights.[8] This court ruled, contrary to the Lords, that the patient had been deprived of his liberty. Furthermore, this had not been the result of a procedure set down in law. As the United Kingdom is subject to the European Convention on Human Rights, which was incorporated into UK law as the Human Rights Act 1998, UK law must comply with the decisions of the European court. New law was required. 'Deprivation of liberty safeguards' were added in 2007 to the Mental Capacity Act. Since then, a virtual consensus of opinion, including that of a House of Lords Select Committee[9] in 2014, has criticized the safeguards as administratively burdensome and desperately in need of substantial revision.

To make matters even worse, 'mental illness exceptionalism' sows further confusion. If the reader is unable to easily follow what I am about to say, you are certainly not alone. Judges have provided different, indeed contradictory, interpretations in very similar cases. There is no point delving into too many details, but as it stands, in the case of patients in a psychiatric hospital, if the person objects to the treatment for their 'mental disorder', the Mental Health Act provisions for involuntary treatment must be used. If the patient does not object, but there is a 'deprivation of liberty'—we shall come back to what that now means in a moment—the 'deprivation of liberty safeguards' as incorporated by an amendment to the Mental Capacity Act after the HL case are appropriately applied. Outside a psychiatric hospital—in nursing or care homes, for example—all persons who are deprived of their liberty, whether they object or not, come under the 'deprivation of liberty safeguards'. To illustrate how confusing the deprivation of liberty safeguards are, the intellectual gymnastics required to determine which set of rules should apply when a person is on a compulsory order in hospital for the treatment of a 'mental disorder', but is at the same time refusing treatment for an unrelated physical disorder, leave most of us mentally exhausted. It appears that the same person cannot be on both types of order simultaneously, leaving one or other malady technically untreatable. In such cases, the Court of Protection can fortunately step in, and using certain powers (its 'inherent jurisdiction'), declare that the deprivation of liberty associated with the treatment of the physical disorder, where the person is already on a psychiatric order, to be lawful. Every case needs a separate hearing.

The definition of what constituted a 'deprivation of liberty' given by the European court was a blurred one. It stated, for example, that the difference between a 'deprivation' of liberty and a 'restriction' upon liberty is 'merely one of degree or intensity, and not one of nature or substance'. What degree or what intensity, and how are they to be measured?

An important case (known as *Cheshire West*) heard in the English Court of Appeal attempted to clarify what the concept meant:

> A 39 year old man with cerebral palsy and Down's Syndrome, who lacked capacity, lived in a staffed bungalow with other residents. One-to-one support enabled him to leave the house frequently for activities and visits. However, he was not allowed to leave on his own. The man had developed

> a habit of putting the pieces of his incontinence padding in his mouth and on occasions ingesting them. These had included faecal contents. In addition to the hygiene risk there was the added danger of choking. Physical restraint was sometimes required to remove the contents from his mouth. Eventually he was placed in a special 'all-body' suit to prevent his reaching the incontinence pads. (*Cheshire West and Chester Council v P* [2011] EWCA Civ 1257)

Taking into account the notions of the 'purpose' of the actions taken and the 'normality' of the man's situation, the Court of Appeal decided there was no deprivation of liberty. The reason given was that the man's circumstances, when compared with the life experienced by any other person with the same disabilities, were similar. The arrangements to which he was subjected had the purpose of serving his best interests and were 'normal' or to be expected for someone with his disability.

The *Cheshire West* case eventually went to the Supreme Court. (This court had replaced the House of Lords as the highest court in the United Kingdom and started to operate in 2009.) Another case (known as *MIG and MEG*) was also considered. The Court of Appeal had in this case also decided there was no deprivation of liberty:

> The case involved two sisters with intellectual disabilities who lacked capacity. One was placed with a foster mother, to whom by all accounts she was devoted. Although she had never attempted to leave, it was common ground that she would have been restrained had she ever tried to do so. The other was in a residential care home, where she was sometimes subject to physical restraint and given tranquillising medication. (*P and Q and Surrey County Council* [2011] EWCA Civ 190)

The Supreme Court in 2014 took an entirely different view to the narrow view taken by the Court of Appeal.[10] It decided that however beneficent the purpose, or however 'normal' the arrangement might be for a person with a disability, there was still a deprivation of liberty if the person was (1) 'not free to leave'; and (2) 'subject to continuous supervision and control'. As Lady Hale so memorably put it: 'A gilded cage is still a cage'. Furthermore, the focus was not to be on the person's ability to express a desire to leave, but on what those with control over their care arrangements would do if the person sought to leave. Nor was the person's lack of objection relevant.

The ramifications of the Supreme Court decision are enormous. The number of people who would now be seen as deprived of their liberty has expanded hugely. Apart from psychiatric and general hospitals, locations with people who might now fall within the category include all varieties of nursing or care homes, supported accommodation, shared lives accommodation, and even some domestic settings where the state provides special services.

At the time of writing, the Law Commission in England is examining these challenges and will offer recommendations for changes to the law applying to deprivations of liberty as defined by the Supreme Court. This is indeed a challenging task.

Finding a solution, I suggest, would be much easier if there were a single 'fusion' law applying to all persons who are deprived of their liberty, whatever the cause of their lack of decision-making capacity.

Deprivation of liberty and the Fusion Law

In our Fusion Law proposal, we attempted to develop a practicable approach to a deprivation of liberty, one that is based on what we regard as in any case representing 'good practice'. In keeping with the generic nature of the proposal, no differentiation would be made between different causes of an impairment of capacity, or between the type of hospital or care home. Our definition of a deprivation of liberty was not far off that of the Supreme Court—(1) the person would not be permitted to leave upon expressing a wish to do so or attempting to do so, and (2) effective control is exercised over the person's care and his or her freedom of movement is so confined as to amount to a deprivation of liberty. We recommended the following procedure:

1. A medical practitioner or approved health or social care professional would decide that the person lacks capacity and there is a deprivation of liberty that is required in the person's best interests.
2. The person would be registered as deprived of their liberty with the appropriate authority that oversees the institution.
3. The authority would appoint a responsible clinician who will be in charge of the care of the incapacitous person, and who will then prepare a written care plan.
4. The responsible clinician must consult the 'responsible person' previously nominated by the incapacitated person or appointed by an appropriate body, or if such person does not exist, the person's primary carer.

The deprivation would be reviewed after 28 days in the first instance. If the conditions continue to warrant a deprivation of liberty, those involved would be able to extend it for not more than 1 year. An 'independent advocate' should become involved at this point. At any time, the incapacitated person, the responsible person, the carer, or the advocate could appeal to the 'Tribunal' if they believed the deprivation of liberty was not warranted.

If the patient is to be given a treatment that might have serious consequences, a second medical opinion would be required. What treatments fall into this category would be listed in 'regulations' attached to the legislation.

Summary of the proposal

In this chapter, I have outlined a non-discriminatory, generic Fusion Law, covering all medical specialties in any setting, describing how people should be helped who have difficulties in making serious treatment decisions for themselves. Involuntary treatment would only be given to objecting patients who lack decision-making capacity and where the treatment is in their best interests. People with capacity would only be treated with their consent. Before making an involuntary treatment intervention, all reasonable efforts should be made to support the person in participating as much as is possible in making a decision and in determining their best interests. These principles have also been applied in the recently described context of a 'deprivation of liberty'.

I suggest that they will also work well in the forensic setting with offenders who have an impairment or disturbance of mental functioning. However, there would need to be a change in the nature of hospital orders for people with a mental impairment who have committed a serious offence; indeterminate hospital orders would cease to exist. A case can be made that people who have committed a serious offence but who are 'unfit to plead' or 'not guilty by reason of insanity' might under certain narrow circumstances be treated involuntarily despite retaining capacity—at least until a more satisfactory method of dealing, in general, with people deemed 'risky' is constructed. Such a method would need to be some form of generic preventive detention or supervision order that would not discriminate against those with a mental illness.

In Chapter 8, I will examine a new development in international law that challenges all existing justifications for involuntary treatment. In formulating the 'fusion' proposal we were only dimly aware of discussions about a new United Nations convention that might be relevant. This United Nations Convention on the Rights of Persons with Disabilities has made me think carefully about the Fusion Law proposal, about discrimination against persons with mental illness, and about what 'decision-making capacity' and 'best interests' might mean. These concepts will be examined in detail in Chapter 7.

In Chapter 11 and 12, I will come back to some practical issues that the 'fusion' proposal would have to face, including fears expressed by some critics that the public will not be adequately protected from 'dangerous mentally disordered people', or that people with a mental illness who have capacity and who reject treatment will find themselves in a damaging, non-therapeutic environment of a prison instead of a hospital.

References

1. **Campbell T, Heginbotham C.** *Mental Illness: Prejudice, Discrimination and the Law.* Aldershot: Dartmouth Publishing Company, 1991.
2. **Szmukler G, Holloway F.** Mental health legislation is now a harmful anachronism. *Psychiatric Bulletin* 1998; **22**:662–665.
3. **Dawson J, Szmukler G.** Fusion of mental health and incapacity legislation. *British Journal of Psychiatry* 2006; **188**:504–509.
4. **Raymont V, Bingley W, Buchanan A,** et al. Prevalence of mental incapacity in medical inpatients and associated risk factors: cross-sectional study. *Lancet* 2004; **364**:1421–1427.
5. **Cairns R, Maddock C, Buchanan A,** et al. Prevalence and predictors of mental incapacity in psychiatric in-patients. *British Journal of Psychiatry* 2005; **187**:379–385.
6. **Cairns R, Maddock C, Buchanan A,** et al. Reliability of mental capacity assessments in psychiatric in-patients. *British Journal of Psychiatry* 2005; **187**:372–378.
7. **Szmukler G, Daw R, Dawson J.** A model law fusing incapacity and mental health legislation & outline of the Model Law. *Journal of Mental Health Law* 2010; Special Issue Ed **20**:11–24; 101–128.
8. *HL v UK 45508/99* [2004] ECHR 471.
9. **House of Lords Select Committee on the Mental Capacity Act 2005.** *Mental Capacity Act 2005: Post-Legislative Scrutiny.* London: The Stationery Office, 2014.
10. **UK Supreme Court.** *Judgment. P v Cheshire West and Chester Council. P and Q v Surrey County Council.* [2014] UKSC 19; 2014. [An excellent discussion of the implications of this ruling can be found at the Mental Capacity Law and Policy website: http://www.mentalcapacitylawandpolicy.org.uk/cheshire-west-the-supreme-courts-right-hook/]

Chapter 7

On being able to make decisions and making decisions for others

In this chapter, I will expand on the account of decision-making capacity and best interests that I gave in Chapter 6. This becomes especially necessary when it comes to dealing with a range of difficult cases, ones where standard definitions, as in the Mental Capacity Act, seem to fall short. The analysis will take us into the ways in which we 'interpret' the beliefs and values of others and how we attempt to make sense of what might appear at first sight difficult to understand. 'Understandability', of an empathic or everyday kind, though often demeaned for not being 'objective', is a central concern in the practice of psychiatry. Furthermore, we are all of us in our normal lives virtuosos in this ability. When we come to consider, in Chapter 8, the challenges presented by the exacting demands for autonomy and choice in the recent United Nations Convention on the Rights of Persons with Disabilities, we will see how the method of 'interpretation' can facilitate their realization.

I am also going to make a change in terminology. There are a number of reasons for this. First, I shall be reformulating 'decision-making capacity', taking greater account of the role of a person's beliefs and values. Second, the important United Nations disability convention mentioned (that we shall consider in detail in Chapter 8) uses 'capacity' in the different sense of 'legal capacity' and I wish to avoid confusion with 'mental capacity'. Indeed, as we shall see, some authorities have argued that 'mental capacity', or at least some versions of it, should play no role in determining whether people should have their choices recognized or not. From now, unless I am referring specifically to legislation that uses the term 'capacity', I shall use the term 'decision-making capability' (or speak simply of the 'ability' to make treatment decisions). I shall continue to use the term 'best interests', but as the discussion progresses it shall become strongly qualified and give paramount importance to the beliefs and values of the person to whom it is applied.

An expanded notion of 'decision-making capability'

Decision-making capability and best interests in the Fusion Law proposal carry a heavy burden in justifying non-consensual interventions. Those notions thus need to be clear enough to meet this challenge. In medicine, we usually expect investigations to have a high degree of 'objectivity'. Many of us slip into expecting the same quality in a test of the ability to make decisions. However, the judgement is of a different kind. A standardized 'objective' test of 'cognitive' functioning (covering memory, attention, and concentration) has only a modest correlation with a person's ability to make a specific treatment decision at a particular time. As we shall see, assessing decision-making capability may need to involve an 'interpretation' of a person's thinking and experiences, an examination that focuses on an altogether higher level of mental functioning. Especially relevant may be the beliefs and values held by the person—what they take as true and what they take as important in guiding the kind of life they want for themselves. While the research evidence on the agreement between assessors of decision-making 'capacity' points to very good inter-rater reliability, especially when made by clinicians with a similar training, there will always be difficult cases.

In Chapters 5 and 6, I presented the commonly accepted elements that make up decision-making capacity, such as appear in the English Mental Capacity Act 2005 or those described in the seminal work of Grisso and Appelbaum: the ability to understand and retain information about the nature of the treatment, why it is being proposed, and the consequences of accepting it or not; the ability to 'appreciate' the relevance of the information to the person's predicament; and the ability to use and weigh the consequences of accepting or rejecting the proposed treatment in the light of what is important for him or her.

This kind of assessment has been criticized as being too 'cognitive': that is, based too much, or exclusively, on mental functions such as concentrating, remembering, understanding, or manipulating concepts. Thus, it is claimed, it fails to take account of the crucial role that beliefs, values, and emotions may play in decision-making. The research shows that the majority of patients with an impairment of decision-making capability tend to fail on the largely cognitive-type elements of the standard types of assessment (as, for example, in the Mental Capacity Act)—even those patients without the obvious impairment of intellect that occurs in advanced dementia or more severe intellectual disabilities. The person may, for example, be unable to concentrate sufficiently well to repeat in their own words the information they have just been given, despite repeated attempts—or they may be unable to communicate an unambiguous decision or make a settled choice between treatment versus no treatment. (Perhaps with more decision-making support, they might do better. We shall look at this later.) Nonetheless, there are many instances where the assessment requires more. In these, the patient's beliefs and values will demand attention.

Beyond a 'cognitive' or 'procedural' view

Most of us would agree that the assessment of decision-making capability should respect a person's beliefs and values—what is important to them and their life goals—and not reflect the beliefs and values of the assessor. To avoid such a supplanting of the patient's values, the aim has been to make the test of decision-making capability essentially 'procedural'. This involves tracking the processes used by the patient in arriving at a decision, without attempting to question the wisdom of the person's underlying values or goals. Doing so tends to restrict the examination to 'cognitive' abilities—how the person uses the relevant information in the light of the beliefs and values the person holds, which in themselves are not to be overridden by those of the assessor. Such a 'procedural' test has a praiseworthy aim; it stops an assessor from deeming a person to lack decision-making capability because they make what appears to the assessor to be a bizarre or unwise decision. If the decision-making process is intact, the patient's decision is to be respected.

Unfortunately, a procedural view does not take us as far as our intuitions lead us. Consider two examples:

Jack

After obtaining a good degree from Cambridge, Jack, now 52 years old, had achieved a senior position in the civil service. Although not regarded as a 'high flyer', he was considered a 'safe pair of hands' and had recently organized a restructuring of his department that resulted in considerable cost savings. This earned him considerable praise from the Permanent Secretary to the Minister. Shortly afterwards, he was criticized by one of his colleagues for not sharing his ideas and seeking credit only for himself. Jack was very troubled by this accusation and started to ruminate on its meaning. Two months later he told his wife, Mary, that he planned to resign his post. He said he now realized that he was a 'mediocrity' who had 'at last been found out'. Somehow he had managed to fool his superiors all these years by appearing to be competent, but it was 'all a sham'. Following his resignation, Jack planned to take on a job more 'fitting' for a person of his abilities—he would seek a job as a hospital porter, preferably in a hospice for the terminally ill. Mary had noticed that Jack had lost a lot of weight, was waking in the early hours of the morning, and had lost interest in his main passions—reading biographies and mysteries, and following the cricket. He barely spoke spontaneously to Mary and his two children, though he had previously been devoted to them and was always interested in what they were doing. He seemed to find no pleasure in anything and only saw the bleak side of any event—personal, family, or social. He continued to go to work, but as one of his colleagues and a friend told Mary, he was barely managing and some action was probably going to be taken soon by his superiors.

After much pressure from Mary, a reluctant Jack agreed to see a psychiatrist. The psychiatrist made a diagnosis of a 'depressive illness'. Jack undoubtedly had many of the textbook symptoms—low mood, poor concentration, loss of interest in things that were previously important to him, guilt, a negative view of the future, an inability to find pleasure in anything, poor sleep with early morning waking and—as Jack reluctantly admitted when questioned directly on the matter—thoughts that life was not worth living, though he 'had not seriously contemplated doing anything about it'. The psychiatrist gave Jack a detailed justification for making the diagnosis, recommended an antidepressant drug and described its main side effects, and strongly advised Jack not to hand in his resignation while in this depressed state as this might prove a decision he would sorely regret later. He said Jack should certainly be on sick-leave from work, to which Jack responded as follows:

'Doctor, I understand why you say I'm depressed; I do appear to have many of what you call the "symptoms" of depression. I accept what you say about the medication helping most people to overcome what you call "the illness". Perhaps I would be one of those people. But I see things quite differently and I know me a lot better than you do. I'm confronting the truth of who I really am. I now recognize that I don't amount to much. I've somehow gotten away with an act; I've fooled people that I'm competent, even clever sometimes. Now, I've been found out. My wife and a friend who works at the Ministry with me say I'm really good at what I do, but they're just saying it out of pity—which I don't deserve. My real challenge is to accept my failures and to battle through to some resolution that causes the minimum damage to people around me. I need to lower my sights and do the kind of job that my talents—or what little of them I have—merit. I need to try to do some good in the world to make up for the all the mistakes I've made in my job that might have badly affected the lives of thousands of people in this country. So even if the medication were to make me feel "better", it wouldn't be real. It's like having a few drinks and feeling falsely happy. It doesn't solve the real problems. If I can't live the life that is really me, what is the point of it all? If I take an easy way out now, will it help me to deal with my problems in the future? If I don't do it myself now, I'll never do it.'

Alice

Alice was 22 years old and a fourth-year medical student. The doctor at the student counselling service had made a diagnosis of anorexia nervosa and recommended to the medical school that Alice's studies should be suspended until she had made significant progress in recovering from her illness. Alice's weight had dropped over a period of a year or so from 55 kg to 38 kg. Alice's social life had become constrained, especially as she avoided invitations that might involve eating with others. Visits home had become tense, especially at meal times.

Since she was a little girl, Alice had wanted to be a doctor. Both parents were doctors. She loved using her father's stethoscope on her dolls and later on, as a teenager, on her younger sister and her friends. People who knew her often commented on what a caring person she was, and what a fine doctor she would make. She was a very conscientious and excellent student and easily managed to get a place at a top medical school. Alice continued to be an outstanding student in her first year and the first half of her second year. At that time she started to diet. She had just broken up with her first boyfriend, and felt that if she could lose a few pounds she would feel better. No one ever thought she was overweight.

Alice's dieting gradually intensified and became more preoccupying. She constantly felt that if she could lose a little more she'd be 'just right'. She managed to pass her second-year exams though in comparison to her previous results, she performed quite poorly. Early in her third year, she was forced to suspend her studies until she was well enough to return. No particular minimum weight was specified, but her doctor said it would have to be one that was commensurate with her periods returning, probably around 48 kg. (Below a certain weight menstruation ceases in anorexia nervosa.)

Alice's doctor and parents were becoming very concerned about Alice's failure to show improvement even though it was now half-way though her fourth year. Her doctor organized a family session attended by Alice and her parents, and a student counsellor who had been seeing Alice weekly. Her doctor again reiterated the facts of her illness. She was suffering from anorexia nervosa. The symptoms were absolutely typical—self-starvation with major weight loss, a 'fear of fatness', loss of menstrual periods, and excessive exercise. Fortunately, she did not induce vomiting or take laxatives to further her weight loss. If Alice did not eat more and gain weight she risked suffering from serious physical complications, and these might even lead to an early death. Inpatient treatment was recommended as outpatient treatment had failed to make an impact on her illness. The inpatient treatment would concentrate on increasing her food intake coupled with individual psychotherapy and general support from the nursing staff and occupational therapist. Alice's response was as follows:

'I can see that I have what you call "anorexia nervosa". But I don't feel it is an illness. I can see that my physical health has suffered to some degree and that there are risks to my future well-being. I do feel tired more easily nowadays, but I remain very active. The threat of hospitalization worries me. I hope you're not thinking about a compulsory admission. That would be totally humiliating—totally wrong. It would completely shatter my self-confidence, everything I've strived for. The point is that I have never felt so much in control of myself and my life as I do now. People are amazed at the way I have been able to lose weight. I've had many compliments about my success in the past. I'm a bit preoccupied with food but I can manage it OK. I'm now the way I want to be. If you say that if I stay like this, I won't be able to resume my medical studies—well I prefer to be the way I am. It protects me as well, I think, from having to worry about other things that used to play on my mind. They're not important any more. Some people might say I'm trying to avoid things that I shouldn't. But everyone has to resign themselves to the positives and negatives that are available to them.'

Both Jack and Alice would seem to meet what I call the standard decision-making capability criteria, in a 'procedural' sense at least—they understand and retain the relevant information; they can see its relevance to their predicament; they are able to reason with the information; and, they clearly communicate a choice. Their decision appears to be reasonable if one accepts their guiding beliefs or values. After all, diagnoses and treatments, especially psychiatric ones, can be controversial. Not accepting medical advice is not in itself evidence of an inability to take account of the facts given of one's condition. It may be the result of reflecting critically on the opinions offered and judging they fail to sit well with what we feel is going on.

Yet our intuitions in the cases of Jack and Alice suggest that there is something problematic about their decision-making. In some way it seems to have been undermined. Their beliefs or values seem to have become distorted or 'out of joint'. In cases such as these it appears that making judgements about the nature, validity, or 'authenticity' of the person's guiding beliefs or values cannot be avoided. So a key question in such instances is: when assessing decision-making capability, how might evaluative judgements about the person's beliefs, values, personal goals, and so on, be exercised, and what degree of 'objectivity' can be achieved? I say 'objectivity' because of the critical importance that assessors do not impose their own beliefs and values on a decision-maker who disagrees with what seems to the assessor to be a sensible, even compelling, treatment recommendation.

The question can be recast in terms of 'autonomy'—how far does the person's specific decision at a particular time have the property of being 'self-determined', 'self-governed', or of being 'owned' by the person. In their important book, *Deciding for Others: The Ethics of Surrogate Decision Making*, Buchanan and Brock in pointing to what this might mean stated: 'a competent decision-maker also requires a set of values or conception of what is good that is at least minimally consistent, stable and affirmed as his or her own'.[1] Clearly required then is that an evaluation of an unusual or apparently unwise treatment decision must go beyond a simple examination of the content of the decision and the immediate explanation offered by the person. A more complex judgement—what may be called an 'interpretation'—may be required. As we will see, the kind of interpretation I am talking about here is not the type of 'interpretation' that psychoanalysts make. It is not an attempt to uncover the unconscious wellsprings of a person's behaviour. It is instead an attempt to clarify what a person believes and values and to examine the way in which these beliefs and values hang together.

Decision-making capability and the role of 'interpretation'

How could one evaluate what one intuitively felt were distorted or 'pathological' beliefs and values without imposing one's own? This was a problem that had bothered me for years. I was fortunate, a few years ago, to come across a PhD dissertation, *Judging by a Different Standard? Examining the Role of Rationality in Assessments of Mental Capacity* by Natalie Banner, a philosopher who explored the application of the ideas of a well-known American philosopher, Donald Davidson, to thinking about decision-making capability.[2] By a wonderful coincidence, Natalie had just taken up a position at King's College London, my university. We soon got to talking and looked in detail at what Davidson's approach could offer in a clinical context. Our verdict was that it could offer a great deal.

At this point, I think it is helpful to go into the philosophy in a slightly formal way. Davidson's method is called 'Radical Interpretation'.[3,4] He asks how we could go about making sense of the speech and behaviour of a 'radically unfamiliar speaker'—someone about whom we have no previous knowledge concerning, for example, their language or culture. What is required for making an interpretation of what the person says or does, of acts that at first seem strange or unintelligible? I think it is quite obvious why that method would have applicability in attempting to understand (or interpret), for example, a person who is expressing apparently bizarre ideas that lie behind a decision that seems irrational.

A starting point, according to Davidson, is that the interpreter is entitled to make certain assumptions about what might be going on in the unfamiliar speaker's mind—about his or her language, beliefs, and values—because we share 'in-built' mental structures and functions that govern the relationships between the meanings of what people say, the beliefs they hold, and their actions. The interpreter uses this shared standard (or normativity) to frame his or her attempts to understand the speaker: as Davidson put it: 'interpretation depends on reading some of the norms of the interpreter into the actions and speech of those he interprets'. This must be so since without these norms that are built into our human mental apparatus, it would be impossible to understand anyone.

'Principle of Charity'

Davidson's account of these norms is known as the 'Principle of Charity'. It states that: 'we must assume that a speaker is by and large *consistent* and *correct* in his beliefs'. These conditions of consistency and correctness are termed 'coherence' and 'correspondence', respectively.

I believe that this principle offers a valuable starting point when we are confronted by someone, in our case, a patient, who appears to be making a strange or unintelligible decision. We start off by assuming that a person's beliefs, intentions, desires, actions, and so on hang together broadly as a more or less coherent whole, and they largely reflect what is true. (This assumption is close in some sense to the 'presumption' of capacity in the Mental Capacity Act.) An interpreter is thus guided by these norms of the Principle of Charity as a first step in trying to understand another person. The qualification of 'by and large' is important as it reflects the fact that an interpretation of a person's statement or an action, for example, may be imprecise and may change as one learns more about the person. The demands for 'correspondence' and 'coherence' allow some leeway. Our mentality is sometimes fairly messy; we may form beliefs on flimsy, even conflicting, evidence, and we may make decisions based on feelings more than reasons. Davidson's theory allows significant scope for such normal inconsistencies. What the standards of Charity do imply is that there must necessarily be a broad background of true and coherent beliefs in order for a speaker to be interpretable at all. Indeed, it is only against this larger mosaic of largely true and coherent beliefs, intelligible to an interpreter, that we are able to recognize an area of incoherence or false beliefs. We may begin to perceive jarring discords against a background of a more or less harmonious set of beliefs and values.

On this view, the mental realm is holistic. For example, rather than focusing on the content of a particular belief for identifying a significant mental disturbance, we need to examine the ways that belief fits with the person's other beliefs, values, wishes, and so on. Exploring the context of such beliefs—their history and their connectedness with other beliefs, values, wishes, and so on—will identify whether they broadly cohere. If they do, the conclusion would be drawn that they are thus capable of supporting, rather than undermining, decision-making capability. A decision that may appear strange at first, may become intelligible.

The assessment thus goes beyond the 'procedural'—of how information is managed without making judgements about the values that are pursued. Instead it takes the substantive content of a person's beliefs and values into account. Even so, this need not lead to a paternalistic usurping of the person's beliefs and values. The judgement is not arbitrary, but subject to norms that we share. This form of interpretation is based on the normative relational structure of our beliefs, values, and actions.

Interpretation in practice

On this account, it is clearly insufficient to rely exclusively on a context-independent, 'objective', standardized test or checklist for assessing decision-making capability. The kinds of questions an assessor ought to bear in mind are of a quite different nature. For example, they will explore the consistency of the person's decision-influencing beliefs with his or her broader worldview and other values; the extent to which such beliefs have a basis in the real world; or, whether they are amenable to revision, challenge, or a reasonably sustained dialogue. It is only if we recognize the relational nature of the beliefs and values that may surround a treatment decision that we are in a position to identify anomalies in coherence or reality-testing that might indicate an impairment of decision-making capability. While a neat prescription for how capacity judgements should be structured cannot be offered, there are nonetheless strong grounds for a wider scope of enquiry than the 'procedural' approach demands.

The type of assessment I am discussing here is most pertinent to the ability to 'use or weigh' component of capacity in the Mental Capacity Act or to 'appreciation' and 'reasoning' in the account given by Grisso and Appelbaum. The method finds its place especially when the standard criteria—understanding, appreciation, reasoning, communicating a choice—seem to be met, but where the decision is nonetheless puzzling.

Interpretation requires an active role for the interpreter in attributing meaning to the speaker. It might seem this presents a risk of unwarranted paternalism. However, it is better to appreciate such influences on our judgement, rather than maintaining the illusion it can be simply procedural. The norms guiding interpretation are the general constraints in attributing broad coherence and correspondence. As I will describe in a moment, there are some further safeguards that can be applied.

There is another potential worry. Davidson recognized an inherent 'indeterminacy' in interpretation. Perhaps a belief that thus far appears mistaken, or a value that thus far appears not coherent, may not remain so with further probing of the person's wider system of beliefs and values. This is important. However, in a real-world clinical encounter, a practical judgement needs to be made whether a person lacks the ability to make a decision carrying important consequences. The aim is to reach a point in the dialogue where it is reasonable to conclude whether or not there is a significant-enough breach in the make-up of the patient's beliefs and values to undermine the person's decision-making ability. A degree of 'objectivity' appropriate for this purpose is the goal.

I present a brief note at this point on safeguards. Understanding the principles of the approach outlined, although based on shared norms of interpretation, probably requires training that goes beyond simple interview skills. I suggest that a decision, unless in emergencies, should not be taken by a single person. The assessment needs to be tested by asking others whether the case for an impairment of decision-making capability is sufficiently convincing. Especially important here are those who know the person well. If there is disagreement, there should be recourse to a tribunal or court. Some have made the interesting suggestion, particularly in mental health care, that there should be a process of institutional oversight involving among others those who have experienced involuntary treatment. They propose that those previously affected should have a voice in deciding how evaluations should be interpreted.[5]

Let's now return to Jack and Alice. We don't yet have a full account of Jack or Alice's broader schemas of beliefs and values against which we might look for a possible break in coherence or correspondence. However, we can discern some pointers that account for early intuitions that something was awry.

Jack

His colleagues regarded Jack as a capable civil servant. He had a recent success that earned compliments. However, a critical remark seems to have triggered a drastic change in his self-esteem, his self-valuation. Having decided that he was an untalented 'mediocrity', Jack's personal values changed. He decided he should look for menial and self-effacing work aimed at serving others befitting a person of such little worth. He gradually cut himself off from his family, which could be seen as apparently ceasing to value in the same way those previously important relationships. After hearing Jack's response to the proposal of treatment, the psychiatrist and Mary probed for details concerning the context of the change in Jack's beliefs and values. They could not make sense of the change. If this is so, we can see that there has been a disruption in both 'correspondence' (reality-testing)—Jack could not offer any reason other than the colleague's critical remark for why he was a 'mediocrity'—and 'coherence'—his 'new' values were largely at variance with his previous, enduring commitments, for example, towards his family and to work of a kind that involved a high level of responsibility and challenge. Jack's 'over-valued' and false idea that he was a 'mediocrity' was a partial explanation for the change in his personal goals, but for the large part the change was not understandable. A black mood, apparently arising from nowhere, distorted Jack's beliefs and values. A diagnosis of depression would certainly account for the change. One would thus conclude that Jack's decision-making capability concerning treatment for a depressive illness was impaired as a result of his adoption of new values that could be called 'pathological' or not 'authentic', as judged by his previous commitments. This, despite the fact that he might be seen as having capacity on a purely 'procedural' test—there was a certain logic behind his plans and new values if one we were to accept his belief that he was a 'mediocrity'.

Jack continued to deny any need for treatment.

Alice

Alice's case similarly illustrates a change in values that lacks coherence. Her previous commitment to becoming a doctor was enduring and powerful in animating her life choices. The replacement of that commitment, as well as her commitments to her family and friends, by the value of 'thinness' was understandable to a degree in terms of the sense of control over her life that Alice believed she had acquired. But how deep was Alice's new commitment? This question was explored in detail by Alice's counsellor. It became clear that Alice's sense of control was not as clear as she had imagined. In many key respects, Alice's self-starvation controlled her. It structured her life to the extent that it determined whom she would see and where—was it someone who might push her to eat more, or would she be exposed to circumstances where it would be expected she would eat? She found it difficult to explain why it should come down to a choice between becoming a doctor and being thin. Why couldn't she be a thin doctor? If she were truly in control, should she not be able to manage both? A sign that she was not really in control was the fact that her longstanding goal to become a doctor had been deposed by her drive for thinness. As the discussions on these themes progressed, an ambivalence about what were Alice's true values became increasingly apparent. She came to accept that she had lost the capacity to make a decision about treatment and now allowed herself to be persuaded into accepting admission to hospital for re-feeding.

The essence of the breakdown in coherence that I am describing is succinctly expressed by Claudius in *Hamlet*: 'poor Ophelia, Divided from herself and her fair judgment' (Act IV, scene 5). For both John and Alice, decision-making capability was undermined by such a 'division', by a disruption in the coherence of their 'true' beliefs and values. Let's now look at an instance where despite a strikingly unusual treatment decision, an assessment of the patient's values did not support a lack of decision-making capability. C's refusal of kidney dialysis, a life-saving treatment, was the subject of a hearing in the Court of Protection in England. I quote directly from the decision:

A life that 'sparkles'

C is a person to whom the epithet 'conventional' will never be applied. By her own account, the account of her eldest daughters and the account of her father, C has led a life characterized by impulsive and self-centred decision making without guilt or regret. C has had four marriages and a number of affairs and has, it is said, spent the money of her husbands and lovers recklessly before moving on when things got difficult or the money ran out. She has, by their account, been an entirely reluctant and at times completely indifferent mother to her three caring daughters. Her consumption of alcohol has been excessive and, at times, out of control. C is, as all who know her and C herself appears to agree, a person who seeks to live life entirely, and unapologetically on her own terms; that life revolving largely around her looks, men, material possessions and 'living the high life'. In particular, it is clear that during her life C has placed a significant premium on youth and beauty and on living a life that, in C's words, 'sparkles'.

With respect to youth and beauty, her daughter V states that ... upon being diagnosed with breast cancer in December 2014 when aged forty-nine ... C expressed the view that she was 'actually kind of glad because the timing was right' ... she did not want to discuss the benefits and risks associated with chemotherapy but was 'keen not to have any change in size or deficit that will affect her wearing a bikini'.

Following a diagnosis of cancer and an acrimonious breakdown of a long-term relationship, C went to a beach and took sixty paracetamol tablets with champagne. In summary, as a result of her paracetamol overdose C suffered an injury to her liver and an acute injury to her kidneys. Since admission to hospital C has, consequently, required renal replacement therapy ... [now] by intermittent haemodialysis for four hours three times per week. Generally, her doctors anticipated a recovery in due course. Dr L further records that C's kidney function has still yet to recover but anticipates an 85 to 95% chance of this occurring.

C's daughter's statement included:

[My mother's] reasons for trying to kill herself in September and for refusing dialysis now are strongly in keeping with both her personality and her long held values ... I believe that they are not only fully thought through, but also entirely in keeping with both her (unusual) value system and her (unusual) personality. Her unwillingness to consider 'a life she would find tolerable' is not a sign that she lacks capacity; it is a sign that what she would consider tolerable is different from what others might. She does not want any life that is on offer to her at this stage ... she doesn't want to 'live in a council flat', 'be poor' or 'be ugly' (which she equates with being old) ... 'Recovery' to her does not just relate to her kidney function, but to regaining her 'sparkle' ... to those who know her well, her entire identity has been built around being a self-described 'vivacious and sociable person who lives life to the full and enjoys having fun'.

The judge concluded that C had decision-making capability:

The decision C has reached to refuse dialysis can be characterised as an unwise one. That C considers that the prospect of growing old, the fear of living with fewer material possessions and the fear that she has lost, and will not regain, 'her sparkle' outweighs a prognosis that signals continued life will alarm and possibly horrify many ... C's decision is certainly one that does not accord with the expectations of many in society. Indeed, others in society may consider C's decision to be unreasonable, illogical or even immoral within the context of the sanctity accorded to life by society in general. None of this however is evidence of a lack of capacity. The court being satisfied that ... C has capacity to decide whether or not to accept treatment C is entitled to make her own decision on that question based on the things that are important to her, in keeping with her own personality and system of values ... As a capacitous individual C is, in respect of her own body and mind, sovereign. (*King's College Hospital NHS Foundation Trust and C* [2015] EWCOP 80)

'Understandability'

In the cases of James and Alice, there was a change in their values that was difficult to understand. The change seemed to entail a powerful psychological process that seemed to develop 'a life of its own': or as in the description of Ophelia, to divide them from themselves and their better judgement. The most important single book in my education as a psychiatrist is a very old one—Karl Jasper's *General Psychopathology* written in 1913, subsequently followed by a number of revised editions.[6] Jaspers started his career as a psychiatrist in Heidelberg, Germany, and wrote the first edition of this extraordinary book after only 4 years of clinical practice. He then shifted to philosophy, never to return to psychiatry. He drew an important distinction that has always acted as a key guide in my clinical practice—the difference between 'understanding' and 'explanation'. 'Understanding' is the grasping of meaningful connections in a person's mental life. How one psychic event emerges from another, Jaspers said, is understood by us directly, irreducibly, by empathy, that is, by imagining oneself in the shoes of another. We take into account the person's history, personality, and circumstances in trying to make sense of what the person says or does—to interpret them. 'Explanation', Jaspers claimed, was quite different. It follows the natural sciences, seeking law-like relationships between objective phenomena. 'Understanding' is not law-like; it is particular and non-generalizable.

What has this to do with psychiatry? Jaspers said that when, despite all our best efforts, we fail to 'understand' why a person says, believes, or does something important—that is, when that person becomes 'un-understandable'—we shift our mode of attempting to make sense of the person. We now seek an 'explanation'. The explanation will be at a different level: for example, it might be biological, and thus the scientific method rather than empathy becomes the appropriate approach to grappling with the experiences or behaviours that are no longer understandable. 'Mental illness', he argued, is demarcated precisely when a person's mental life has become 'un-understandable'. Understandable 'reactions', on the other hand—responses to taxing life events perhaps experienced in association with personal vulnerabilities—may cause distress and suffering, and may be seen as deserving help or treatment, but Jaspers would not regard them as constituting a 'mental illness'.

Davidson's Principle of Charity, of assuming that a person's beliefs, values, desires, actions, and so on hang together broadly as a more or less coherent whole, and that they largely reflect what is true, has an obvious kinship with Jaspers' approach that we start by assuming the person is understandable and attempt to empathize. Breaches in coherence or disruptions in reality-testing seem to translate well into Jasper's notion of 'un-understandability'. Both views, I suggest, are saying something very similar and fundamental about mental functioning and how we recognize it might be disturbed. They lead us to an approach for assessing not only whether a person has a mental illness of some kind—not our main concern at this point—but also to whether there is an undermining of their ability to make a decision about the need for care or treatment. There is a connection between mental illness and decision-making capability, though it is far from a one-to-one relationship. Many people with a psychosis—almost by definition a state of un-understandable experiences—may nevertheless see some of those experiences as unwanted and decide that treatment is necessary. Or they may become so distressed by their radically changed experience of the world that they will accept a treatment that might help them to cope better with their transformed reality.

Both Jack and Alice have experiences and beliefs that I suggest are not understandable. Both have experienced major changes in their values that I propose are not coherent with their previous values and commitments. Their new 'inauthentic' or 'pathological' values serve to undermine their decision-making capability.

Values can change

I am sure many readers will have thought about a potential difficulty: what about changes in values that we normally experience? Don't all major personal changes, almost by definition, involve a disruption of coherence in some sense? How would one distinguish a change that has the qualities of coherence from one that does not?

Major changes in a person's outlook and behaviour can indeed be coherent (or understandable). Most changes are fairly gradual and values evolve in an understandable way. Consider the following example:

> A senior civil servant, like Jack, who worked in another ministry, also decided that his work was not compatible with his values. His discomfort with what he was doing grew until he felt he could not continue and be true to himself in any real sense. He decided to apply for a position as a director of a charity that aimed, through a variety of projects, to improve the lives of people in

a number of low-income countries. The drop in salary was major. However, the man had become increasingly concerned about his department's role in undermining the position of certain marginalized groups in some countries. His strong religious beliefs in an obligation to offer help to the weak and the vulnerable were long established. He discussed his wish for a job change with his family, taking into account the effect it might have on their lives. Apart from the loss of income, he would be spending more time travelling, sometimes in countries that were not entirely stable.

No one expressed any concerns that this change in his life situation represented an illness of some kind or that his decision-making ability was impaired.

A well-known case springs to mind of a person who lost a massive amount of weight, like Alice, but again the underlying beliefs and values would be characterized as coherent. Many, myself included, regard Maria Callas as one of the greatest, if not the greatest, operatic soprano of the twentieth century (at least as far as nineteenth-century opera is concerned). An account of a drastic change she underwent at the age of 30, published in 2013 in the magazine *Limelight*,[7] is as follows:

> Callas began to lose weight – over 70 pounds [around 32 Kg] – after taking to heart Serafin's [a famous conductor] remarks about her figure. With a new ease about her body language came a hypnotic use of facial expression. (See the post-1953 photos of a woman who now likes being looked at by the camera.) Her new look inspired film director Luchino Visconti to move into opera for a series of productions with Callas at La Scala. (Ashman M. Maria Callas: the ultimate diva. *Limelight* Sept 2013.)

In Callas' case, although some claimed her voice was less magnificent after her weight loss, her new svelte figure enhanced her extraordinary stage presence and her immense power to move audiences. If Alice could become the slim doctor in the way that Callas had become the slim soprano, the issue of illness would probably not have arisen. In the former, her values had been usurped; in the case of the latter, they had been enhanced.

If the assessment of capacity, especially in difficult cases, involves more than a reductionist procedural approach, there are some important practical implications. I have already mentioned the need for some degree of special training. Since the skills required for interpretation of the kind I have been discussing are ones that we use in our everyday understanding of other people, this should not be too arduous. Second, a decision-making capability assessment may require substantial time. Repeated meetings with the person may be necessary, as well as observing their actions, and consulting with others who know them. Such procedures do not fit easily with time constraints imposed by emergency departments, for example. Nor do they comport well with trends in clinical practice to devise straightforward algorithms, checklists, or 'decision-aids' to assist, standardize, and speed-up clinical decision-making.

Rethinking 'best interests' in the light of interpretation

I am certainly not claiming that simply because a person like Jack or Alice has an impairment of decision-making capability, and has an illness for which there is a treatment, they should automatically qualify for involuntary treatment. Involuntary treatment would only be justified if it were in the 'best interests' of the person.

The guidance offered in the Mental Capacity Act is helpful in determining what might be in a person's best interests. Such guidance is appropriate since an exhaustive account of all possible factors that might need to be considered for any individual is impossible. The relevant circumstances to be taken into account will often be highly specific to the person whose 'best interests' are being assessed.

The guidance in the Mental Capacity Act was described in Chapter 5 and its adoption in the Fusion Law proposal was described in Chapter 6. In brief, the essential principles are as follows:

> The decision-maker should involve the person with impaired decision-making capability to the maximum degree that is feasible in the judgement of best interests
>
> The decision-maker must take into account the past and present wishes and feelings of the person, the beliefs and values that would have been likely to influence the person's decision if they had capacity, as well as any other factor that the person would be likely to have considered if they were able to do so.
>
> The decision-maker must consult, if practicable, a range of people—anyone previously nominated by the person who now lacks capacity, anyone caring for the person or who is interested in the person's welfare, and anyone appointed by the person or a court (or tribunal) as a substitute decision-maker.
>
> The least restrictive option must be chosen.

The principles aim to strike a balance between what has been called a 'substituted judgement'—where the substitute decision is the one it is believed that the person without capacity would have made if they had retained capacity—and 'best interests' in a narrower sense than that in the Mental Capacity Act—protecting the person's current well-being, not necessarily having special regard for the person's past or present wishes. In a 'substituted judgement', current preferences expressed by the person while not having capacity would be over-ruled by those expressed by the person when they had capacity (or are judged by the assessor to have been the likely preferences based on a consideration of the wishes, feelings, beliefs, or values of the person when they had capacity). In a more recent formulation of the guidance, the Victorian Law Reform Commission recommended in 2012 that 'legislation should require substitute decision-makers to exercise their powers in a manner that promotes the personal and social well-being of the represented person'.[8] They would do so 'when, as far as possible, they have paramount regard to making the judgments and decisions that the person would make themselves after due consideration if able to do so'.[8]

It would follow from my previous discussion of the role of beliefs and values and their possible distortion as indicating whether there is an impairment in decision-making capability that I would support the emphasis on 'paramount regard' being given to the decision the person would have made themselves if they had retained capacity. In cases where the person is likely to make a full or near-full recovery from their illness following treatment, the argument in favour is strong. We generally have good reason to assume that the person will wish to remain faithful to the values that have guided their life choices.

In fact, we begin to see here a *nexus* between decision-making capability and 'best interests'. It emerges that an analysis of decision-making capability based on the coherence of the person's beliefs and values and their possible disruption leads to a strong indication of what would be in the person's best interests: it would follow that *giving effect to the values to which the person has a deep commitment* would be in their best interests. If the person had retained capacity in the difficult predicament in which they find themselves, we can presume they would have acted according to these values—acting thus would have been a manifestation of the person's self-determination or autonomy. The demarcation between decision-making capability and 'best interests' thus begins to break down.

Problematic situations

Unfortunately, life can be more complicated than that. We will sometimes need to take into account the person's present wishes despite their lack of decision-making capability. Two sets of circumstances come to mind. The first is where a person with an illness from which they will *not* recover expresses a wish that is clearly contrary to a previously strongly held value.

Antecedent or present values?

An example arose when I visited my 99-year-old uncle in a Jewish nursing home in Australia. The food served there was strictly kosher, but a short walk from the nursing home was a delicatessen snack bar that served, among other items, attractive looking ham sandwiches. We discussed a difficult dilemma that had arisen concerning another resident. An observant orthodox Jew, now with quite severe dementia, who had never previously eaten ham, expressed a strong desire to have a ham sandwich. Attempts to thwart his wish resulted in him becoming very agitated. What should one do? Should we allow him to have it or not?

Having subsequently discussed this case with colleagues and others interested in capacity and best interests, I am impressed with the lack of agreement. Some argue that the demented person is now a different person to the person who was not demented. Why should the values of the 'previous person' determine the preferences of the 'new person'? Some argue that the decision should depend on the level of distress generated by a refusal. Others argue that people have an important interest in being remembered, even after their death, as having specific commitments that served to define who they were, and that have provided meaning and coherence to their lives. This memory could be damaged by the person being seen as having acted contrary to those commitments during the final chapter of the person's life: especially if these were the last memories people might retain. Presumably there would be a difference if the demented man were a former Chief Rabbi of Australia as opposed to an ordinary member of the community. I don't know how often such situations arise or how often the distress of a wish being thwarted is so difficult to manage. The best one can do, I suppose, is to decide on a case-by-case basis, to follow the best interests guidelines and attempt to find a solution on which there is reasonable agreement.

There is a variation on this theme that would argue for giving significant regard to a person's currently expressed preferences though they differ from those previously held. I am thinking here of people with a chronic mental disorder, like schizophrenia, whose personality and interests have changed over a number of years, and who now express and live by a set of beliefs and values that may be quite different to those they had before they became ill. If the 'new' set of beliefs and values were now stable, generally coherent, strongly endorsed by the person, and where the person's behaviour showed a strong commitment to those values, it might be reasonable to conclude that these were now the person's real or 'authentic' beliefs and values. Consider this case brought before the Court of Protection in England in 2015:

> The question was whether it would be lawful for doctors to amputate a 73-year-old man's severely infected leg. Without amputation he would shortly die. Since his 20s the man had a chronic mental illness, schizophrenia, as well as diabetes. Those who supported amputation argued that because of his mental illness, he could not reason adequately about the treatment. He had religious delusions, and described hearing angelic voices and that of the Virgin Mary. He said that he was not afraid of dying, that the angels had told him he was going to heaven. Furthermore, he couldn't face going to a nursing home. He thus refused the operation.
>
> The judge stated: 'Delusions arising from mental illness may rightly lead to a person's wishes and feelings being given less weight where that is appropriate. However, this cannot be the automatic consequence of the wishes and feelings having a religious component. Mr B's religious sentiments are extremely important to him, even though he does not follow an established religion'. And again: 'In some cases, of which this is an example, the wishes and feelings, beliefs and values of a person with a mental illness can be of such long standing that they are an inextricable part of the person that he is. In this situation, I do not find it helpful to see the person as if he were a person in good health who has been afflicted by illness. It is more real and more respectful to recognise him for who he is: a person with his own intrinsic beliefs and values'. (*Wye Valley NHS Trust v B* [2015] EWCOP 60)

In the light of this interpretation, as well as some other considerations such as the man's pride in his independence, the Hon Mr Justice Peter Jackson ruled that amputation was not in his best interests. In relation to the man's religious ideas, he made this very poignant comment:

> 'It is no more meaningful to think of Mr B without his illnesses and idiosyncratic beliefs than it is to speak of an unmusical Mozart.'

This succinctly sums up the case where a person with a long-standing illness develops a new set of enduring and generally coherent beliefs and values.

The second set of problematic circumstances concerns people with severe intellectual disabilities where it may be difficult to determine what their value commitments are. I am not an expert in this area, but from discussion with those who are, it appears that in the majority of cases, a clinician, working closely with those who know the person well, such as family or care workers, can build up a reasonable picture of what is important to the person, or at least what pleases or displeases them. This might suffice to justify an intervention if it were to give effect to what is thus ascertained as important to the person. If it is not possible to determine what is important to the person with a severe intellectual disability, one would then need to be guided by a general human rights approach.

Relevance to coercive interventions

More common in general medicine and mental health care are situations like those facing the psychiatrists who were treating Jack and Alice. Both patients were assessed as lacking decision-making capability. If we take the view that their best interests could be defined in terms of their authentic beliefs and values, we would probably conclude that they should have treatment. The proposed treatment is very likely to result in a full recovery in Jack's case, and may do so in Alice's case, but in any event she would be expected at least to be able to return to her studies. Recovery from anorexia nervosa can be slow. Would it then be justified to now treat them involuntarily?

The answer is 'no'. There is more to a best interests determination than the conclusion that the treatment would be entirely consistent with, and give effect to, the person's personal values and life goals—goals that are currently threatened by disruptive 'pathological' values. Recall the fourth element in the best interests guidance quoted earlier. Any intervention made in a person's best interests should be the least restrictive option consistent with achieving the desired outcome. Related to this issue is the question of what impact the involuntariness of the intervention would have on Jack, and how that would fit with his best interests; would his values, when well, support an involuntary intervention in these circumstances? But in any case, not all alternatives have been exhausted. Indeed, we have seen that Alice was persuaded to accept treatment after a series of meetings with her counsellor. A range of interventions might be appropriate in Jack's case. Further meetings—some perhaps including his family—aimed at exploring with him the consequences of his actions might be successful in changing his mind about treatment. One might consider other interventions that move in a more coercive direction. Involuntary treatment is not the only form of 'coercion'. I will consider these interventions in Chapter 9.

What one can conclude, I suggest—given that most of the requirements of a best interests determination have been satisfied—is that the psychiatrist, after discussion with the family and others concerned with Jack's welfare, is licensed to pursue the matter of treatment with Jack. How far the matter should be pursued will also depend on another factor which is implicit in the recognition that Jack must make what is clearly a serious decision—the significance of the harms he is experiencing and that would clearly further ensue if he were to continue to reject treatment. For example, resigning from his job would certainly be a serious step. The severity of the harms, I suggest, is closely related to the magnitude of the gap between Jack's authentic values and his new, 'pathological' values.

It is now necessary to introduce a new entrant into the debate about involuntary treatment and substitute decision-making. Chapter 8 will describe the recent Convention on the Rights of Persons with Disabilities adopted by the United Nations in 2006 that poses major challenges to existing practices and has the potential to be a real 'game-changer'.

But before moving on, I cannot resist concluding this chapter with some pithy remarks from the philosopher P.F. Strawson, rebuking those who, in their quest for 'objectivity', fail to appreciate the profoundly human aptitude manifest in the kind of interpretation discussed in this chapter. I found it in Jonathan Glover's *Alien Landscapes? Interpreting Disordered Minds*, a book that offers an in-depth treatment of the subject.[9] Strawson discussed two types of explanation, one in terms of scientific laws, the other:

> in terms of what is sometimes called, with apparently pejorative intent, 'folk psychology', i.e. the ordinary explanatory terms employed by diarists, novelists, biographers, historians, journalists and gossips, when they deliver their accounts of human behaviour and human experience – the terms employed by such simple folk as Shakespeare, Tolstoy, Proust and Henry James.[10,p56]

References

1. **Buchanan AE, Brock DW.** *Deciding for Others: The Ethics of Surrogate Decision Making.* Cambridge: Cambridge University Press, 1989.
2. **Banner NF.** *Judging by a Different Standard? Examining the Role of Rationality in Assessments of Mental Capacity.* [dissertation]. University of Central Lancashire, 2010. http://clok.uclan.ac.uk/1441/ [This led to further joint work with me: Banner N, Szmukler G. 'Radical intepretation' and the assessment of decision-making capacity. *Journal of Applied Philosophy* 2014; 30:379–374.]
3. **Davidson D.** Radical interpretation. *Dialectica* 1973; **27**:313–328.
4. **Davidson D.** Radical interpretation interpreted. *Philosophical Perspectives* 1994; 121–128.
5. **Freyenhagen F, O'Shea T.** Hidden substance: mental disorder as a challenge to normatively neutral accounts of autonomy. *International Journal of Law in Context* 2013; **9**:53–70.
6. **Jaspers K.** *General Psychopathology.* Manchester: Manchester University Press, 1963. [Translated from 1923 edition by K Hoenig, M Hamilton.]

7. **Ashman M.** Maria Callas: the ultimate diva. *Limelight.* September 2013. http://www.limelightmagazine.com.au/Article/358421%2Cmaria-callas-the-ultimate-diva.aspx
8. **Victorian Law Reform Commission.** *Guardianship* (Final Report 24). Melbourne: VLRC, 2012.
9. **Glover J.** *Alien Landscapes? Interpreting Disordered Minds.* Cambridge, MA: Harvard University Press, 2014.
10. **Strawson PF.** *Skepticism and Naturalism.* London: Methuen, 1985.

Chapter 8

A new United Nations 'disability' convention: 'respect for rights, will and preferences'

Recently, in a development of major significance, the rights of persons with 'disabilities' have been clearly spelt out through the Convention on the Rights of Persons with Disabilities adopted by the United Nations (UN) in 2006.[1] It came into force in 2008. When my colleagues and I started to think about the 'Fusion Law' proposal we were not aware of the discussions leading to the development of the Convention. However, in recent years it has become clear that the Convention presents serious challenges to a host of conventional practices in respect of people with disabilities. Does it damage the 'fusion' proposal? I believe the principles of the proposal retain their validity, as do most of the procedures. The Convention has forced me to think again about 'decision-making capability' and 'best interests'. Some of that thinking, particularly concerning the role of beliefs and values in decision-making, was discussed in Chapter 7. We will see that this formulation can fit well with the requirements of the Convention.

A 'paradigm shift'

The relevance of the Convention for our discussion follows its characterization of 'disability':

> Persons with disabilities include those who have long-term physical, mental, intellectual or sensory impairments which in interaction with various barriers may hinder their full and effective participation in society on an equal basis with others.[1]

This is not an exhaustive definition. However, it is accepted by almost all authorities that persons with a mental disorder which is long term and which is likely to result in the person being treated within the mental health system are to be included. The vast majority of those with a serious mental illness—for example, a psychosis, bipolar illness, severe depression, and autism—would fall into this category. So would people with dementia, intellectual disability, and neurological disorders with long-term impairments such as cerebral palsy, stroke, head injury, multiple sclerosis, Parkinson's disease, and so on.

Note also that the model of disability evident in the characterization quoted is what has been called a 'social model'. It is the level of accommodation made by a society that determines the degree to which an 'impairment' becomes a 'disability'. For example, if mobility aids such as elevators and wheelchair ramps are available in all public buildings, paraplegia ceases to be a hindrance in participating in activities in those places.

As we look at the rights particularized in the Convention, we will see why it has been said to mark a 'paradigm shift' in thinking about how our society should see people with disabilities. An example is the challenge to involuntary treatment—under any circumstances. Conventional civil commitment law becomes incompatible with the Convention.

I maintain that the Fusion Law is compliant with the Convention and I shall spell out the reasons why. However, some changes in emphasis in the Fusion Law are warranted, particularly placing greater weight on the nature of support for people who are having difficulty in making a serious health care decision. The Convention is claimed by some authorities to reject impairment of decision-making capacity and best interests as adequate justifications to support non-consensual treatment or social care interventions. If so, this is clearly a problem for the Fusion Law. The Convention itself does not mention the terms 'mental capacity' or 'best interests'. It speaks instead of 'respect for the rights, will and preferences' of the person as the beacon that must direct us as to how we should act when there is an important decision to be taken by the person who nevertheless cannot take it wholly independently. Some authorities argue that any form of 'substitute decision-making' is not compliant with the Convention. 'Substitute decision-making' refers to somebody making a decision on behalf of, or in the place of, and without the agreement of, a person who is supposed to lack the ability to make a decision for themselves. A large part of this chapter will be devoted to exploring the relationships that might exist between 'capacity' and 'best interests' on the one hand, particularly as these notions were developed in Chapter 7, and the notion of 'will and preferences' on the other. I will suggest there is an important tie-in that needs to be worked through.

What the Convention says

First, a few words about the general features of the Convention are in order. It is noteworthy that, for the first time ever in the creation of a UN Convention, there was formal, active involvement of disabled peoples' organizations in the drafting and negotiations behind the Convention. At the time of writing, the Convention has been signed by 160 states and ratified (or adopted by 'accession'[i]) by 164. By signing the Convention, states parties indicate their intention to take steps to be bound by the treaty at a later date. Signing also creates an obligation to refrain from acts that would defeat the object and purpose of the treaty. The next step is 'ratification'. Ratification signals the willingness of the State party to undertake the legal rights and obligations contained in the Convention.

The overall purpose of the Convention, stated in Article 1, is to

> promote, protect and ensure the full and equal enjoyment of all human rights and fundamental freedoms by all persons with disabilities, and to promote respect for their inherent dignity.[1]

Eliminating discrimination by ensuring that rights may be enjoyed by persons with disabilities 'on an equal basis with others' is a fundamental aim. Among the principles are respect for the inherent dignity, individual autonomy including the freedom to make one's own choices, and independence of persons; full and effective participation and inclusion in society; respect for difference and acceptance of persons with disabilities as part of human diversity and humanity; and equality of opportunity. Their relevance to the standing of persons with mental health disabilities is clear.

What rights are spelt out in the Convention? While it does not establish new human rights, the Convention does set out with much greater clarity the obligations on states parties to promote, protect, and ensure the rights of persons with disabilities. The Convention contains classic civil and political rights—such as the right to liberty, to integrity of the person, to freedom of expression, to privacy, to freedom from torture and inhuman treatment, to equal recognition before the law, and access to justice. It also includes economic, social, and cultural rights that have come to prominence more recently—including the right to home and family life, to education, and to health. Some of these rights have been framed so as to have particular bearing on people with disabilities—rights to non-discrimination, to independent living and community inclusion, to

---

i With 'accession', a state accepts the offer or the opportunity to become a party to a treaty. It has the same legal effect as 'ratification'.

work and employment, to participation in cultural life, and to be free from exploitation and abuse.

Signatory states are placed under obligations to modify or abolish existing discriminatory laws, regulations, and practices, as well as to provide programmes to support Convention rights. These include, for example, a duty to provide training on disability issues to those involved in the administration of justice; to provide programmes to recognize and combat exploitation; to provide community support services; to raise awareness of disability issues; and to combat discrimination.

The Convention establishes the UN Committee on the Rights of Persons with Disabilities, to which signatory States parties are to report periodically about their progress in its implementation. The Committee in turn publishes its observations and recommendations (called 'Concluding Observations') concerning this progress. The Convention requires governments to ensure that representatives of civil society, in particular persons with disabilities, are fully involved in this monitoring. States parties signing an 'Optional Protocol', 92 at the time of writing, recognize the competence of the Committee to examine complaints from individuals when local processes have become exhausted.

Depending on the jurisdiction, the Convention may or may not be automatically domesticated into law upon ratification. In many common-law countries (like the United Kingdom) it is incorporated into domestic law only when directly legislated. However, like any other international convention to which a state is party, it can be referred to by courts and be used to influence the interpretation of domestic law.

An 'authoritative' interpretation of a key issue

So far, so good. The position of people with mental illness or disabilities will be radically transformed for the better if those rights are to be put into practice. One hopes they will. There is, however, a significant challenge to the view I have presented concerning treatment without consent or against the objection of the person.

Both the Fusion Law approach and the Convention are in accord in aiming at eliminating discrimination against the same groups of people. Along with the general right to liberty, the Convention provides a further specification in Article 14 that 'the existence of a disability shall in no case justify a deprivation of liberty'. The Office of the UN High Commissioner for Human Rights has stated in 2009:

> [48.] ... Article 14, paragraph 1 (b) unambiguously states that 'the existence of a disability shall in no case justify a deprivation of liberty'. ... As a result, unlawful detention encompasses situations where the deprivation of liberty is grounded in the combination between a mental or intellectual disability and other elements such as dangerousness, or care and treatment. Since such measures are partly justified by the person's disability, they are to be considered discriminatory and in violation of the prohibition of deprivation of liberty on the grounds of disability, and the right to liberty on an equal basis with others prescribed by Article 14.[2]

On this account, 'mental disorder' or 'mental illness', even if it comprises only one of a number of necessary criteria for involuntary detention, makes that set of criteria inconsistent with Article 14.

Since then, the UN Committee on the Rights of Persons with Disabilities, charged with issuing authoritative interpretations of key articles in the Convention, has done so for Article 12, *General Comment on Article 12: Equal Recognition Before the Law* (2014).[3] This pivotal Article states that all persons enjoy 'legal capacity' in all aspects of life on an 'equal basis with others'. The Committee maintains that the right to 'legal capacity' encompasses both the ability to 'hold rights and duties (legal standing) and to exercise those rights and duties (legal agency)'. 'Legal capacity' is not defined in the Convention, though it is taken to mean the legal recognition of a range of acts such as the right to vote, to enter into contracts, to write a will, to marry, and so on. The General Comment interpretation also makes it clear that 'legal capacity' and 'mental capacity' are to be seen as distinct concepts. The former is a legal concept, the latter a psychological one.

Contrary to the virtually universal provisions in mental health and capacity law, the Committee states that the existence of an impairment (including a physical, mental, sensory, or psychosocial impairment) must never be grounds for denying legal capacity and the imposition of 'substitute decision-making'. For some people with disabilities, the exercise of that legal capacity will require support—sometimes a great deal of support. Its provision is a state party obligation under the Convention. We should recall here the social model of disability underlying the Convention. Support for those with an impairment in expressing their wishes—the impairment we are most interested in here—constitutes an accommodation that aims to forestall that impairment becoming a disability. It is the same idea as the role of mobility aids for those with paraplegia.

The Committee insists that the preservation of legal capacity means that we 'must respect the rights, will and preferences of persons with disabilities'. Interventions should never amount to 'substitute decision-making'.

The Committee takes the view that all persons retain legal capacity and that with the right level of support, people with disabilities will be able to express their will and preferences. The Committee rejects impaired 'mental capacity' as a basis for denial of legal capacity and rejects 'best interests', at least as it is conceptualized by the Committee, as a basis for substitute decision-making.

The Committee is serious about its interpretation. This is clear from its published 'Concluding Observations' following its examination of reports of progress from States parties in implementing the Convention. In the 40 or so published at the time of writing, the Committee has regularly concluded that states must take action to develop laws and policies to replace regimes of 'substitute decision-making' by 'supported decision-making' which respect the person's autonomy, will, and preferences.

The Committee also insists that the 'will and preference' paradigm must replace the 'best interests' paradigm to ensure that persons with disabilities enjoy the right to legal capacity on an equal basis with others.

While the Committee's accounts of 'substitute decision-making' and 'supported decision-making' appear clear enough, it has never provided an interpretation of exactly what is meant by 'respect for the rights, will and preferences' of persons with disabilities. In my view this has been a critical omission—especially so, in relation to situations where a person's will and preferences have radically changed. As we shall see, the notion (or notions) of 'will and preferences' can prove disconcertingly obscure or frankly contradictory.

How can the challenge be met?

As noted previously, the 'fusion' proposal and the UN Convention share a fundamental aim—the elimination of discrimination against persons with a disability, in this case, those with a mental health disability. You will recall that this was the original driver behind the 'fusion' proposal. Yet the interpretation by the Committee seems to be saying that a 'capacity' and 'best interests' approach is unacceptable and is a discriminatory basis for intervening in the life of a person with a disability.

What is clear—on the basis both of the interpretation of the UN High Commissioner on Human Rights as well as that of the Committee—is that any law that allows an interference with the rights of a person that is restricted to persons with a disability is discriminatory. Mental health legislation, virtually everywhere, transgresses this injunction. 'Mental disorder' in one form or another appears on the face of the legislation. No matter how many other criteria are specified—whether the law additionally only permits the person's detention or involuntary treatment in the interests of the person or to protect others—in thus singling out a particular group of people with a disability for special interference, such legislation breaches the Convention. The Committee has reiterated this position in its *Guidelines on Article 14 of the Convention on the Rights of Persons with Disabilities: The Right to Liberty and Security of Persons with Disabilities* published in 2015.

In this respect it seems well aligned with the 'fusion' proposal's emphasis on a generic law—one that applies to any person, whatever the cause of their impaired decision-making capability. Importantly from the point of view of the Convention, it applies equally to persons with or without a disability, as characterized in the Convention. The 'fusion' proposal is thus not discriminatory in this respect. But some will retort—perhaps it's not 'direct discrimination', but isn't it 'indirect discrimination'? The fact remains, they will quickly point out, that a disproportionate number of people with a mental health disability will have apparent problems with decision-making and thus be disproportionately liable to a non-consensual intervention. Isn't that 'indirect discrimination'? I will come back to this question in a moment, and explain why it is not.

'Respect for rights, will and preferences'

Article 12(4) of the Convention states that '... safeguards shall ensure that measures relating to the exercise of legal capacity respect the rights, will and preferences of the person ...'. As I have noted, in its interpretation of Article 12, the Committee did not offer a definition of 'will and preferences' though insisting that one must respect the 'rights, will and preferences' of people with disabilities.

What is meant by 'will'? Since it sounds very much like a philosophical idea, I turned to a number of eminent philosopher colleagues to inquire what philosophers have said it means. From these discussions and recommended reading I learnt very quickly that the meaning of 'will' was far from clear and indeed highly contested. In a recent book, *Action, Knowledge and Will* (2015),[4] John Hyman, traces the history of ideas of the 'will'. He notes the 'incomplete demise' of the 'modern theory of the will' that held sway from Descartes to the nineteenth century and which came under fierce attack in the twentieth century. The 'will' was conceived by Locke in the late seventeenth century, for example, as 'an act of the Mind, directing its thought to the production of any action, and thereby exerting its power to produce it'. The 'will' on this type of account sits with a kind of causal role between a desire and the act aimed at fulfilling the desire. An example of a twentieth-century attack on this concept of the 'will' is that of Wittgenstein, in his *Notebooks* and his *Philosophical Investigations*. In the latter (§611–§628), he maintained that an 'act of will is not the cause of the action, but is the action itself', and that voluntary action need not involve an 'act of volition'—it may involve 'no more than behaving in a familiar sort of way'—'I raise my arm without feeling surprised'. The willed act is one with the act of willing. Hyman concludes that in Wittgenstein's attempt to extricate the 'will' from the traps that can be laid by the way we use language, the act of 'willing' as such vanishes altogether.

In 2014, I was fortunate enough to be a participant in a series of workshops in London aimed at determining whether the Mental Capacity Act 2005 was compliant with the UN disability Convention. The workshops were organized jointly by the Essex Autonomy Project and the Ministry of Justice. The Essex Autonomy Project has done much valuable work on the meaning of 'autonomy', especially in connection with interventions aimed at assisting or protecting people with impaired autonomy. It is led by Wayne Martin, a philosopher, who has assembled an impressive multidisciplinary team that has engaged in discussions with a range of other academics as well as practitioners in medicine, law, social services, community support services, and other groups who deal with people with mental disorders, neurodegenerative disorders, intellectual disabilities, and impairments associated with brain damage. The workshops assembled over 20 experts in the field, drawn from the relevant disciplines. The conclusions have been published in an extremely useful report.[5] The subject of 'respect for rights, will and preferences' received much attention, as did the concepts of 'substitute decision-making' and 'discrimination'. Other areas were also covered, but for our purposes, the three I have mentioned are the most pertinent.

The workshop concluded that 'respect' for the rights, will and preferences cannot mean that one *must accede* to, or *agree to abide by*, the person's expressed will and preferences. This must be so because those three elements—rights, will, and preferences—may diverge. For example, to facilitate an act in accordance with a person's currently expressed 'preference', while purportedly supporting autonomy, may act in contradiction to a 'right'—for example, the right to enjoy freedom from exploitation, violence, and abuse, or the right to physical and mental integrity. Similarly, a person's 'will' and 'preference' may not point in the same direction. An example, discussed in the workshop would be: 'My *will* is to go to the dentist, but my *preference* is to go to the beach'. Or an example that is relevant to the case of Alice, the patient with anorexia nervosa who was described in Chapter 7: 'My *will* is to continue living, but my *preference* is to not eat'.

These examples point to significant differences between 'will' and 'preference' that I find persuasive.

A further problem with the requirement that one must respect the will and preference of a person is the fact that these might suddenly, and apparently inexplicably, change. Should we then respect the previously apparently well-established preference or the new preference?

I now return to the distinction between 'will' and 'preference'. This distinction seems to me consistent with some significant recent accounts of 'the will'. These share the idea of the 'will' as a kind of overseeing function that determines which desires should become intentions. They resemble in form an aspect of Kant's concept of the 'will', summarized by the philosopher J.B. Schneewind as follows:

> The will, then, as distinct from the ability to choose, is the capacity to transform felt urges or desires with causal force into motivating reasons for action with justifying validity. To possess a will is therefore also to be able to test desires to see whether or not they can be validated as reasons.[6]

Kant's idea of the 'will' forms part of a larger account including the choice of 'ends', but this is not relevant for our purposes. Some recent accounts of the 'will' have a similar general form. An example is that of Michael Bratman.[7] He sees the will as a higher-order, self-governing mechanism in which 'values' play a key role. Desires are subject to some kind of deliberation within higher-order, self-governing 'policies' or 'mandates' that extend reasonably coherently over time and that express commitments towards ends embodying a person's important values. Within this self-governing framework, desires justifying action have a 'reason-providing' quality through their relation to the 'will'. The accounts of Watson[8] and Hieronymi[9] seem to me to propose roughly similar notions of the 'will'.

From these accounts a fairly consistent distinction can be drawn between the 'will' as a higher-order function reflecting our values, as against our more immediate desires or inclinations (or 'preferences'). 'Will' and 'preferences', to a large extent, usually run together. It is when they diverge and a person needs to make a serious decision that a problem of interpretation may arise.

Thus 'will', I suggest, can be helpfully seen as being founded on a person's strongly held, deep, enduring, and reasonably coherent personal beliefs and values. In this sense, it is not the same as a present wish, desire, or 'preference'—even a strongly expressed present preference. This is an example discussed in the workshop[5]:

> Consider the case of a woman in labour who suffers from a very severe needle phobia. She is told that the baby is breech, and that the safest way

forward is to have a Caesarean Section. She is profoundly concerned for the health of her baby and herself and she consents to the procedure. In the language of moral philosophy: she *wills* that it take place. But upon being taken to theatre for the surgery she comes face-to-face with a needle. Sampling of the mother's blood is an essential part of the preparations for the C-Section. Upon seeing the needle she is overwhelmed with fear and very strongly expresses her *preference* that the nurse take the needle away. In such a situation, the medical staff face a dilemma. They can either honour the patient's will (the birth of a healthy baby by the safest means possible) or they can honour the patient's preference ('get that needle away from me'); they cannot do both.[ii]

The distinction may be even clearer in cases where a person has made an advance statement when he or she is their 'normal-self', anticipating a time in the future when they may not be able to express their 'will'. Consider the following cases:

Theresa

Theresa has an intellectual disability and also suffers from epilepsy. She lives in a supported group home. Following a fit she becomes confused for about an hour or so. During this confusion she has left the home and has ended up lost, on one occasion nearly hit by a car as she crossed a busy road, and on another, exploited by a stranger who took a pendant she loved. She made an advance statement that she should not be allowed out following a fit while still confused and for at least 1 hour. Following the next fit, she insisted on being allowed to go out while in such a confusional state.

Anne

Anne is a 23-year-old student at a prestigious school of drama. She has a bipolar illness. Her mother committed suicide during a depressive episode when Anne was 14, and she has other relatives with her illness. She lives with her father, a retired dentist. Anne's education has been badly affected by her illness, and she is determined to finish her drama course. Following recovery after a second involuntary admission she composed an advance statement based on her previous experiences of manic episodes: 'If I am unable to sleep for more than 3 hours on two consecutive nights; or, if I go wandering in town after midnight; or, if I say I am the resurrection of Sarah Bernhardt then I need to be treated—against my

[ii] Reproduced with permission from Martin W, Michalowski S, Jutten T, Burch W. *Achieving CRPD Compliance: An Essex Autonomy Project Position Paper.* University of Essex; 2015, p42.

will, if necessary. If I refuse, I accept I should be admitted on an order.' Unfortunately Anne relapsed 6 months later. Unable to sleep, flimsily dressed, she went out wandering around 2 am and was picked up by the police 4 hours later. She said she was a great actress. She refused any treatment intervention.

In these cases there is a clear divergence between the 'will' expressed in the advance statement, and the 'preference' expressed, as predicted, when the feared state of affairs arose.

If 'rights', 'will', and 'preferences' can diverge in this manner, what then are the implications for the meaning of 'substitute decision-making'? We need to go back to the fundamental aims of the Convention. The first 'General Principle' is:

> Respect for inherent dignity, individual autonomy including the freedom to make one's own choices, and independence of persons.[1]

The statement seems to point to a primary regard for the person's 'will' in the 'rights, will and preferences' triad as it has the strongest relationship to personal autonomy and the freedom to make 'one's own' choices—those giving expression to one's personal deep, 'real' or 'authentic' values. It ties in to some degree with the Mental Capacity Act formulation of best interests as requiring a consideration of both the past and present wishes and feelings of the person. The person's 'will', on the account I have given, thus reflects the person's deeply held value commitments. Harking back to the cases of Jack and Alice in Chapter 7, it is these commitments that I argued should be given predominance. The 'will' clearly expressed by Theresa and Anne in their advance statements, rather than their contemporaneous strong 'preferences', I propose, should also be given the greater weight. When it comes to the previously strictly orthodox Jewish care home resident with an irreversible dementia who wanted to eat a ham sandwich, as we saw in Chapter 7, one might be able to make a case based on a range of considerations that supporting the 'preference' for the sandwich could, in this particular individual's circumstances, outweigh the previously established 'will' to abstain absolutely from non-kosher food. Here the 'will' to eat only kosher might be interpreted by some as being that of a *different* person.

'Interpretation' and 'will and preferences'

I now draw your attention again to the account of decision-making capability and best interests that I gave in relation to the Fusion Law proposal in Chapter 7. I discussed the role of 'interpretation' in determining whether there was a lack of coherence between a person's deeply held beliefs and values—what I called the person's 'authentic' beliefs and values—and the person's currently expressed wishes that appeared at first sight to be seriously unwise or bizarre. If the authentic and the contemporaneous diverged significantly in terms of their coherence, this pointed to a possible impairment of decision-making capability. Best interests would on this account involve interventions attempting to give effect to the person's 'authentic' values. Following an analysis of the Convention along the lines I have just presented, we can now readily equate 'will' with the person's deep beliefs and values, and 'preferences' with the person's currently expressed wishes.

The formulations of 'decision-making capability' and 'best interests' as I have described them in the Fusion Law proposal could thus be recast in terms of 'will and preferences'. I have proposed an approach that takes account of the potential for problematic decisions in which a clash—or lack of coherence—between 'will' and 'preferences' may be evident. This is in line with the account of 'interpretation' presented in Chapter 7. If this equivalence is accepted, I am left somewhat unsure about which terms to now use. 'Capacity' and 'best interests' have longer usage but have different meanings in the minds of different people. ('Capacity' can also be confused with 'legal capacity' in the Convention.) 'Best interests' are understood by some as 'objective' best interests, aimed at enhancing the supposed well-being of the person who lacks capacity, without special regard to the person's beliefs and values. Others understand them as 'subjective' best interests, giving primacy to a person's beliefs and values. 'Will and preferences', to my knowledge, have not been given any definition by any authority in relation to the Convention. I believe the account I have just outlined is a reasonable one and is useful in clarifying the bases for decisions that are hard, at first sight, to understand. I will thus resolve the dilemma of terminology by referring to the reformulated approach in the 'fusion' proposal as a 'decision-making capability–will and preference' framework.

An Australian Law Reform Commission Report published in 2014 which examined '*Equality, Capacity and Disability in Commonwealth Laws*' offered an interesting view about the relationship between 'rights' versus 'will and preferences'[10]:

> The inclusion of 'rights' is the crucial safeguard. In cases where it is not possible to determine the will and preferences of the person, the default position must be to consider the human rights relevant to the situation as the guide for the decision to be made.[10,p3.53]

The UN Committee stated that where, after significant efforts have been made, it is not practicable to determine the will and preference of an individual, a 'best interpretation of will and preference' should be made. (Note here the use of the word 'interpretation' and how it relates to my usage of the term.) I imagine there will be cases where the Australian Law Reform Commission recommendation might prove applicable, and others where the UN Committee's 'best interpretation' might be more appropriate, especially where there are people who can provide fragments of relevant information about the person in difficulty.

Discrimination—direct and indirect

I now return to the question of discrimination. By making the Fusion Law generic and omitting reference to any group of persons with a disability, it is certainly not discriminatory on the 'face' of the proposal. I am inclined to argue that a short-term 'impairment or disturbance in the functioning of mind' in the Fusion Law does not qualify as a 'disability' in the sense required by the Convention. For example, it is conceptually distinct from a disability—it may occur equally following an acute head injury in a person with or without a disability. The range of rights described in the Convention does not appear to be particularly under threat for someone who is suffering concussion following a collision of heads in a football match. Furthermore, it is hard to think of an impairment of the ability to make decisions that is not related to some kind of impairment or disturbance in the functioning of mind. However, if it were accepted that the terms 'impairment or disturbance of mental functioning' were unacceptable, it would probably not make much difference to the Fusion Law if it were dropped. Nevertheless, whichever position on this point is adopted, a disproportionate number of people with disabilities—especially mental disabilities—will be judged to lack decision-making capability and become the subjects of a form of substituted decision-making. Isn't this discrimination?

Certainly this would constitute a 'disproportionate effect'. However, a disproportionate effect does not automatically qualify as discrimination—in such cases, 'indirect discrimination'. For example, a person with an intellectual disability is rarely accepted at a medical school for training as a doctor. Entry qualifications for medical training do not explicitly exclude people with an intellectual disability. There is no direct discrimination. However, the entry criteria, usually requiring first-rate examination scores in academic subjects, do have a disproportionate impact on people with an intellectual disability. Yet we do not claim that the entry requirements for medical training discriminate unfairly against people with an intellectual disability. Why?

It is generally accepted, in law at least, that disproportionate effect does not amount to indirect discrimination if the disproportionate effect has three attributes: it has a *legitimate aim*, the criteria leading to the effect are *objective*, and the criteria are *reasonable*.[5] (1) The '*aim*', in the instances that interest us, should be seen in the terms of the fundamental principles of the UN Convention or of the Fusion Law. The aim is essentially to ensure that people experiencing a serious difficulty in making an important decision are supported in acting autonomously, that is, according to their deeply held personal beliefs and values, or that those values are given effect through the facilitation of others until the person's autonomy is restored. (2) There has now been a substantial body of research on the standard criteria for 'decision-making capacity' as defined, for example, in the Mental Capacity Act or in the work of Grisso and Appelbaum.[11] The level of agreement between assessors, a key index of '*objectivity*', is high. A similar level of evidence does not exist in the minority of cases where the substantive content of a person's underlying beliefs and values enter the analysis. However, as I discussed in Chapter 7, 'interpretation' is based on mental structures that we share and that allow us to understand the relationships between beliefs, values, intentions, and so on. Furthermore, I have proposed that determinations need to involve more than one person and should always include people who know the person well. Mechanisms for appeal to a tribunal or court where there is disagreement further enhances the validity of the assessment. (3) When it comes to the question of '*reasonableness*' I can do no better than quote from the report from the Essex Autonomy Project workshop'[5]:

> In assessing the reasonableness of differential treatment, we are asking about the relationship between the basis of differential treatment and the aims it is intended to advance. Is the former a reasonable means to adopt in pursuit of the latter? In the case of the functional test for decision-making ability, the answer is yes. The crucial point is that autonomy is intrinsically related to decision-making ability: the former depends on the latter. A person who lacks the ability to make the decisions they face in a particular domain, even when support is provided, cannot accurately be described as acting autonomously in that domain; they lack the potential for self-legislating self-determination that lies at the core of the concept of autonomy. It is therefore reasonable to use a functional test of decision-making ability as a basis for differential treatment in advancing the aim of fostering and protecting individual autonomy, particularly when this aim may conflict with the equally legitimate aims of (inter alia) protecting a disabled person's right to life, or ensuring their protection and safety in situations of risk.[iii]

[iii] Reproduced with permission from Martin W, Michalowski S, Jutten T, Burch W. *Achieving CRPD Compliance: An Essex Autonomy Project Position Paper.* University of Essex; 2015, p22.

My conclusion is that the 'decision-making capability—will and preference' framework does not discriminate, neither directly nor indirectly.

The workshop report also made an important observation in this regard concerning the notion of 'legal capacity':

> The crucial point to remember is that the CRPD [the Convention] does *not* require states to recognise legal capacity in all disabled persons. It requires states to recognise the legal capacity of disabled persons *on an equal basis with others*. The same point applies to active legal capacity or legal agency. The CRPD does not require states to recognise active legal capacity in all disabled persons. It permits states to withhold recognition of active legal capacity from particular individuals (whether or not those persons are disabled) provided that the legal basis for doing so applies to all on an equal basis.[iv]

A person legally declared a bankrupt, whether the person has a disability or not, may be denied certain domains of legal capacity. For example, the right to be a director of a company or membership of a professional association of accountants can be withdrawn.

The Convention and the criminal justice system

There are long-standing legal provisions—the mental condition defences—that aim to protect vulnerable people from the risk of unfair convictions due to their inability to meaningfully engage with the trial process ('unfit to plead' or 'unfit to stand trial') or where they have committed an offence without being considered responsible or culpable ('not guilty by reason of insanity'). It is held in most jurisdictions that such people should not suffer criminal penalties.

Both the UN Commissioner on Human Rights and the Committee on the Rights of Persons with Disabilities have stated that criminal justice provisions concerning 'fitness to plead' and 'not guilty by reason of insanity' discriminate against people with mental health disabilities. In 2009, the former stated:

> [47] In the area of criminal law, recognition of the legal capacity of persons with disabilities requires abolishing a defence based on the negation of criminal responsibility because of the existence of a mental or

---

[iv] Reproduced with permission from Martin W, Michalowski S, Jutten T, Burch W. *Achieving CRPD Compliance: An Essex Autonomy Project Position Paper.* University of Essex; 2015, p23.

> intellectual disability. Instead disability-neutral doctrines on the subjective element of the crime should be applied, which take into consideration the situation of the individual defendant. Procedural accommodations both during the pretrial and trial phase of the proceedings might be required in accordance with article 13 of the Convention [the right to access to justice on an equal basis with others], and implementing norms must be adopted.[2]

In a similar vein, the Committee has stated that:

> [3] ... declarations of unfitness to stand trial and the detention of persons based on that declaration is contrary to Article 14 of the convention since it deprives the person of his or her right to due process and safeguards that are applicable to every defendant.[12]

An understandable source of their concerns is the deprivation of liberty that may follow from the mental condition defences. A psychiatric hospital disposal by the court is common and this is usually for an indefinite period. Commonly, the period of detention in hospital is considerably longer than the prison sentence would have been, had the person been found guilty of the offence in a normal trial. When discussing the Fusion Law proposal, I noted this problem and agreed that the current arrangements were unacceptable from an ethical point of view.

While the concerns of the Committee may have some justification, how the criminal justice procedures could be changed so as to comply with the insistence that the mental condition defences be abolished has, so far, not been clearly set out. Certain principles can be stated at a conceptual level. For example: (1) for accused persons with a disability facing trial, reasonable accommodations should be made to enable them to participate as fully as possible in the process; (2) culpability (*mens rea* or 'guilty mind') should be determined in a 'disability-neutral' manner, applicable to all defendants—perhaps on the basis of the person's beliefs when committing the offence and whether there was an intent to cause harm and, if there was, whether the person saw the harm as justified in the circumstances, for example, if subject to intolerable duress; (3) if a person with a disability is sentenced to imprisonment, reasonable accommodations should be made so as not to aggravate their condition. Even if such principles were to be accepted, the changes to the criminal justice system they would demand are far from clear.[13,14]

At the time of writing, law reform commissions in England, Northern Ireland, and Australia are reviewing 'unfitness' to plead or stand trial. All seem likely to retain a capacity-based element in their recommendations.

Supported decision-making

A valuable element in the disability Convention is the emphasis on decision-making support (or more accurately, support for the exercise of legal capacity). While this has been developed to a significant degree in services for people with intellectual disabilities and in some centres for people with dementia, it has not been a subject of special attention in most mental health services (or health services in general). This may be in part due to the stereotype of people with mental disorders as being essentially incompetent, and in part as a result of the relative ease of initiating involuntary treatment. When it comes to the admission process, as we will see in Chapter 10, little attention has been given to approaches that might reduce the likelihood of the need for compulsion. Events around the admission tend to be seen as preludes to treatment, not as its first phase—a critical phase at that, since the quality of the future relationship between the patient and the clinical team can be influenced to a large degree by the patient's experience of the admission process. In a large English study of patients admitted involuntarily, the patient's negative attitude to hospitalization during the first week of admission was strongly correlated with readmissions on an order and a negative attitude to services 1 year later.[15]

Support has a connection with a fairly recent concept in the autonomy literature, that of 'relational autonomy'. On this view, autonomy is not a quality that individuals possess in complete separation from others. Autonomy is achieved through relationships with others, for example, through various forms of support they offer. There is thus a clear relevance to disability. A person may be independently incapable of making a decision because of a difficulty in understanding some of the important information or through an inability to communicate clearly. I am reminded of a patient I saw some years ago:

Leonard

Leonard had a diagnosis of schizophrenia and had spent the last 15 years in a care home as he was unable to manage independently. He had no family or friends. I saw Leonard annually for review. I was immediately struck by the severity of what is termed 'thought disorder'; although Leonard's intonation, gestures, and facial expression were entirely unremarkable, I could make virtually no sense at all of what he was saying. The old textbooks gave this phenomenon the colourful name, 'word salad'. I suspect he had a brain lesion of some kind, though the neurologists found no clear evidence. What saved the day during the appointments was the assistance of the support worker from the care home who accompanied Leonard. She had known

> him for over 10 years. I would ask Leonard a question, even a simple one like 'how did you get here today', which despite his appearing being able to understand, resulted in responses that hardly made any sense. At this point the support worker began to step in and 'translate' what he was saying. At first I was sceptical that she really understood, but I was soon convinced. Leonard nodded his head in agreement while she recounted to me what he meant. On occasions I deliberately misheard and repeated inaccurately what the support worker had said. Leonard shook his head indicating I was mistaken.

This is a good example of at least one form of relational autonomy. Leonard's autonomy was enabled by means of the supportive actions of another. Important for me was the fact that Leonard was able to show that he 'owned' his responses and their underlying beliefs and values that he could not express independently. This 'moderate' view of relational autonomy continues to regard decision-making capability as essential to personal autonomy (or self-determination, or self-governance). However, it is only manifest in the right kind of supportive relationship.[16]

Relationships may be critical to autonomy at a deeper level. A helpful account is based on the idea of 'recognition'.[17] The claim is that full autonomy—in the sense of an effective capacity to shape one's own conception of a worthwhile life—is only possible under socially supportive conditions. Key here is the notion of social relations of 'recognition'. It is through our interactions with others, through their recognition of us, that we are able to develop and sustain our sense of 'agency'. The extent to which others recognize us as persons of value affects the way we value ourselves—self-interpretation is closely related to the interpretation of the self by others. Recognition plays an important role in nourishing and sustaining the attitudes of 'self-respect', 'self-trust', and 'self-esteem'. These qualities affect our capacity to exercise our autonomy—to experience ourselves as having values of our own that provide valid reasons for us to act on those values. The ability to make important decisions is consequently affected. Non-recognition may take a variety of forms—social marginalization or exclusion, oppression, stereotyping, humiliation, or denigration. A full account of relational autonomy, and thus of supported decision-making, should take into account this broader social context.

Supported decision-making may have a value beyond that of simply assisting people with impaired decision-making to express their will and preferences. The person with the help of supporters, especially those who have been given general guidance about what support involves, may be more likely to obtain information about a wider range of treatment options as well as about other agencies that can offer help to meet social and other needs the supported person might have. There is a potential shift from a purely protective role in preventing unwarranted involuntary admission—protecting the so-called negative rights that limit the state's intrusion on individual liberty—to providing a means of securing 'positive rights'—for example, access to the means of increasing community participation. I shall discuss the potential role of 'advance statements' or 'advance directives' in greater detail in later chapters, but note at this point that the discussion of treatment options with the clinical team and supporters when the person is reasonably well, noting the patient's will and preferences to be respected if there should be a relapse of the illness with a loss of decision-making capability, may serve to reduce the likelihood of involuntary treatment later. An advance directive could thus be considered a form of support for legal capacity.

The new emphasis on supported decision-making has started to stimulate the development of models for arranging support for people with decision-making difficulties.[18,19] At this stage they are in their infancy and research into what arrangements work best is badly needed. It is an entirely open question at present as to the appropriate degree of statutory regulation of issues such as whether there should be official registration of a person's supporter or supporters; the balance of informal (family and friends) and formal supporters (such as peer advocates or 'personal ombudsmen'); instructions concerning their role; mechanisms for monitoring the processes; and appeals to an administrative tribunal of some kind if there are concerns (for example, of undue influence). The effect on informal supporters of subjecting them to a degree of statutory regulation may be unhelpful in terms of a possible change in the nature of the relationship with the ill person, yet there need to be safeguards against abuses. The point has been well made that in the construction of support systems the voices of all the stakeholders should be heard, including, of course, those of persons with disabilities themselves.

An important concern is the exposure to abuse that people with disabilities may sometimes face when they pursue their will and preferences. The Victorian Law Reform Commission in its review of 'guardianship' law made an interesting recommendation—the creation of a new public wrong of abusing, neglecting, or exploiting a person with evident impaired decision-making ability, enforceable in civil or criminal law.[20] Indeed, one might ask, why should a 'vulnerable' person suffer restrictions, for example, in where they can safely go, in order to be protected from abuse from others? It seems more appropriate for the abuser to be the subject of restrictions. How possible this might prove remains to be seen.

Decision-making capability is not an all-or-none phenomenon

In 2010, the Law Commission of Ontario published an influential report by Michael Bach and Lana Kerzner with the title *A New Paradigm for Protecting Autonomy and the Right to Legal Capacity.*[21] I have since discussed with Michael Bach the applicability of the schema to people with mental illness as well as those with intellectual disabilities, the area with which he has been mainly involved. We agree that in principle it should be applicable.

The regime is more nuanced than the conventional categorization of people as having or not having decision-making capability. The authors proposed three ways in which people with disabilities could exercise legal capacity. (1) The first is where legal capacity is exercised independently, as measured by the conventional standards for decision-making, for example, as in the Mental Capacity Act or as proposed in the Fusion Law. This should be the presumption in all cases. (2) Others may not be able to act legally independently at some time because they lack the necessary decision-making abilities, and will require supported decision-making. Under this approach, people would access the assistance of support persons to turn their will and preferences into legally recognized acts. (3) The third way is termed 'facilitated decision making', and would be engaged when a person is unable to act legally independently and is without support persons able to translate the person's will and preferences into decisions. This might be because supporters are unavailable; or because interpretations of the person's will and preferences radically conflict; or the person is expressing wishes and taking actions contemporaneously that are known by others to be in direct conflict with what is known about that person's stable, long-standing, and expressed values and beliefs. 'Facilitation' would entail a person being appointed to mediate a decision-making dialogue with the person, his or her intimate support persons if available, and the professionals. The aim would be to arrive at the 'best interpretation of a person's will and preferences' that would be given effect via the facilitator. Such non-consensual interventions would only be justified after it is clear that a person cannot act independently, all efforts to provide support have failed, and that the person is suffering significant harms. Such interventions would require additional steps being taken to provide ongoing assistance so the person can re-establish their decision-making capability as soon as possible.

The Convention and the Fusion Law proposal

The 'fusion' proposal has the same intention in relation to treatment interventions for people with mental health disabilities as the UN Convention—to eliminate unfair discrimination and to ensure that people with mental health disabilities enjoy respect for their autonomy and self-determination on an equal basis with others. While the Convention still requires clarification of the meaning of 'will and preferences', a reasonable analysis suggests a parallel with the approach to the interpretation of beliefs and values that I outlined in Chapter 7. This involves an assessment of the 'coherence' between the person's present wishes (or 'preferences') with their deeply held values and commitments (or 'will'). Indeed, the Committee in its General Comment on Article 12 states:

> 18 ... Where, after significant efforts have been made, it is not practicable to determine the will and preferences of an individual, the 'best interpretation of will and preferences' must replace the 'best interests' determinations.[3]

The position taken by the UN Committee on the Rights of Persons with Disabilities that 'substitute decision-making' is not compliant with the Convention, I suggest, derives from a failure by the Committee thus far to fully analyse the meaning of 'will and preferences' and its implications. Of particular importance are situations where a person's preferences have radically changed.

The emphasis in the Convention on 'supported decision-making' is welcome and deserves a major research effort on how it can be best implemented in the context of mental health services. Probably the commonest complaint made by people with a mental illness who have been detained involuntarily is that no one listened to them. Even if this alone were mitigated by effective support arrangements, formal as well as informal, the effort will have been worthwhile. However, I am sure much more is to be gained. This leads us into a consideration of ways of reducing the need for coercive interventions in the first place. I will take this up in Chapter 10.

Up to this point our discussion has focused on involuntary detention and treatment. However, as shall become clear in Chapter 9, there are other measures that should be regarded as 'coercive'. These are best seen in a broader context of what I will call 'treatment pressures'.

References

1. **United Nations.** *Convention on the Rights of Persons with Disabilities.* United Nations, 2006. http://www.un.org/disabilities/documents/convention/convoptprot-e.pdf

2. **United Nations.** High Commissioner for Human Rights. *Annual Report to General Assembly.* A/HRC/10/49; United Nations, Office of the High Commissioner. 2009.
3. **Committee on Convention on the Rights of Persons with Disabilities.** *General Comment on Article 12: Equal Recognition Before the Law.* United Nations, 2014. https://documents-dds-ny.un.org/doc/UNDOC/GEN/G14/031/20/PDF/G1403120.pdf?OpenElement
4. **Hyman J.** *Action, Knowledge and Will.* Oxford: Oxford University Press, 2015.
5. **Martin W, Michalowski S, Jutten T, Burch W.** *Achieving CRPD Compliance: An Essex Autonomy Project Position Paper.* Colchester: University of Essex, 2015.
6. **Schneewind JB.** Kant on the will. In: Pink T, Stone MWF (Eds) *The Will and Human Action: From Antiquity to the Present Day.* London: Routledge, 2004; 154–172.
7. **Bratman M.** Valuing and the will. *Philosophical Perspectives: Action and Freedom* 2000; **14**:249–265.
8. **Watson G.** The work of the will. In: Stroud S, Tappolet C (Eds) *Weakness of Will and Practical Irrationality.* Oxford: Oxford University Press, 2003; 172–200.
9. **Hieronymi P.** The will as reason. *Philosophical Perspectives* 2009; **23**:201–222.
10. **Australian Law Reform Commission.** *Equality, Capacity and Disability in Commonwealth Laws* (ALRC Report 124). Sydney: ALRC; 2014.
11. **Grisso T, Appelbaum PS.** *Assessing Competence to Consent to Treatment: A Guide for Physicians and other Health Professionals.* New York: Oxford University Press, 1998.
12. **Committee on the Rights of Persons with Disabilities.** *Statement on Article 14 of the Convention on the Rights of Persons with Disabilities.* United Nations, Office of the High Commissioner, 2014. http://www.ohchr.org/EN/NewsEvents/Pages/DisplayNews.aspx?NewsID=15183
13. **Peay J.** Mental incapacity and criminal liability: redrawing the fault lines? *International Journal of Law and Psychiatry* 2015; **40**:25–35.
14. **Gooding P, O'Mahony C.** Laws on unfitness to stand trial and the UN Convention on the Rights of Persons with Disabilities: comparing reform in England, Wales, Northern Ireland and Australia. *International Journal of Law, Crime and Justice* 2016; **44**:122–145.
15. **Priebe S, Katsakou T, Amos M,** et al. Patients' views and readmissions 1 year after involuntary hospitalisation. *British Journal of Psychiatry* 2009; **194**:49–54.
16. **Martin W, Hickerson R.** Mental capacity and the applied phenomenology of judgement. *Phenomenology and Cognitive Science* 2013; **12**:195–214.
17. **Anderson J, Honneth A.** Autonomy, vulnerability, recognition, and justice. In: Christman J, Anderson J (Eds) *Autonomy and the Challenges*

to Liberalism: New Essays. Cambridge: Cambridge University Press, 2005; 127–149.

18. **Gooding P.** Supported decision-making: a rights-based disability concept and its implications for mental health law. *Psychiatry, Psychology and Law* 2013; **20**:431–451.
19. **Davidson G, Kelly B, Macdonald G**, et al. Supported decision making: a review of the international literature. *International Journal of Law and Psychiatry* 2015; **38**:61–67.
20. **Victorian Law Reform Commission.** *Guardianship. (Final Report 24).* Melbourne: VLRC, 2012.
21. **Bach M, Kerzner L.** *A New Paradigm for Protecting Autonomy and The Right to Legal Capacity.* Toronto, ON: Law Commission of Ontario, 2010.

Part III

'Coercion' viewed more broadly

Chapter 9

Treatment pressures and 'coercion'

As virtually every patient who has been admitted at some time to a psychiatric unit will tell you, there is much more to 'coercion' than involuntary treatment. An eminent American colleague, Paul Appelbaum, and I have put forward what we call a spectrum of 'treatment pressures'.[1] The spectrum forms a hierarchy comprising increasing levels of pressure that might be exerted on a person who is reluctant to accept or who rejects a proposed treatment that the clinician is convinced is important for the person's well-being. It is only at the top end that the term 'coercion' is warranted. The practical significance of the spectrum is that the greater the pressure to be applied on a person to accept treatment, the stronger must be the justification for exercising it.

A spectrum of 'treatment pressures'

In order to illustrate how the spectrum might work, we shall consider a patient under the care of a community mental health team (CMHT):

Daisy

Daisy is 32 years old and has been a patient under the care of her CMHT for 6 years. She has a diagnosis of schizophrenia and has had three admissions to the local psychiatric hospital, each time on a compulsory order. The last was a year ago.

When ill, Daisy has the belief that she has special powers to expel evil spirits from people's souls. This belief is held with conviction and against any evidence that is offered to the contrary—it is a delusion. In order to expel the spirits, Daisy performs certain quasi-religious rituals, one of which involves circling around the person to be saved with her arms outstretched. She also hears a number of 'voices', auditory hallucinations, which discuss her special powers and warn her that there are groups of evil conspirators who aim to thwart her activities. There are other changes as well when Daisy begins to become ill. She begins to neglect her hygiene and appearance. She stops brushing her hair, for example. Poor sleep, pacing restlessly around her flat, and weight loss are other features. At these times Daisy withdraws socially, cutting off contact with her mother and a close friend. She also stops paying the rent for her housing association flat and falls into arrears.

Daisy's father, an engineer of some kind, abandoned her mother when Daisy was 4 years old, and his whereabouts are unknown. Her mother works as a cleaner and has no other children. Daisy has one close friend, Vicky, a girl she has known since school. She sees her mother on Sundays for lunch, and Vicky and her husband every month or so. She loves playing with Vicky's little boy. Daisy was an average student at school, but was noted to have an artistic flair. She went on to train as a hairdresser and developed a good reputation among the clients of her 'studio' for being a creative stylist. Since becoming ill she has not been able to resume her career, finding the job too taxing, especially the social interactions.

Fortunately Daisy's illness responds quite well to treatment. The psychotic symptoms are well controlled by antipsychotic medication and support from her CMHT. She is currently on a fortnightly intramuscular injection of risperidone. She was started on depot injections because she was unreliable in taking oral medication. However, 3 months ago, given her stable condition over the previous year, her consultant had agreed that the dose would be decreased and that she would then resume oral medication at the lowest dose consistent with symptom control. Daisy also has a very good relationship with her community nurse, Tony, whom she has known for 5 years. He usually visits her every 2 weeks, has helped her with organizing repairs to her flat and dealing with her finances, and introduced her to a local art class to which she had become very attached. In fact, Daisy now wants to go to an art school, and has been encouraged to apply by the leader of the art class. He believes she is good enough. One of the reasons for Daisy being so keen on a reduction of her medication was to do with her painting. She complained that in addition to the medication making her feel like a 'zombie', it suppressed her creativity and made colours look 'less alive, sort of washed out'.

Unfortunately, Daisy also has another major illness—Grave's disease, a form of thyrotoxicosis, an over-active thyroid gland. The cause is an autoimmune reaction, where the body's immune defences attack the thyroid gland resulting in overproduction of thyroid hormones. This was diagnosed 2 years ago, during a period when Daisy was not experiencing any psychotic symptoms. She presented with severe weight loss, tiredness, tremor, irritability, and heart palpitations. Her community nurse, Tony, was instrumental in recognizing that these symptoms were not related to her mental illness—to which they could have easily been attributed—and took her to see her family doctor who immediately referred her to an endocrinologist.

> Daisy was treated with carbimazole tablets. These were discontinued after 18 months, when there was a 50 per cent chance of a remission. Sadly, this was not the case. Daisy quickly relapsed, and in fact became very ill with a severe recurrence of the thyrotoxic symptoms 9 months ago, for which she required hospitalization. She is now back on the medication. It has been proposed that she be treated with radioiodine which leads to the death of thyroid cells. The treatment would, however, probably leave her with an underactive thyroid gland and she would then need to take thyroid hormone for the rest of her life.

Those are the main background details. Daisy's situation started to change 3 months ago:

> As planned, the dose of the fortnightly intramuscular injection of risperidone had been reduced from 50 mg to 37.5 mg, and then to 25 mg. However, Tony noticed a few weeks later that Daisy was becoming unwell again. She had become gradually more withdrawn, and avoided seeing her mother and Vicky. Over the next few weeks, Daisy started thinking she might have a 'restoration' of her special spiritual powers. She admitted to Tony that those who conspired against her had started setting up 'mental tricks' to undermine her confidence. Daisy now refused her medication for both her mental illness and her thyrotoxicosis. If she could help others, she argued, she could expel the invasion of evil spirits from herself. She stopped paying rent, though still being in arrears, and ignored an agreement to pay these off according to a generous schedule negotiated with the housing association. Tony now noticed she had a tremor, looked tired and unkempt, and she had started to lose weight. Daisy said that she no longer intended to try for an art school even though she had started an application. Her spiritual mission was unarguably a more important vocation, she maintained.
>
> Tony became increasing concerned. After a discussion of the change in Daisy with the consultant psychiatrist, it was decided that Tony would visit later that day in an effort to get Daisy to resume her medication.

Tony's interventions trace the spectrum of treatment pressures that are employed commonly in psychiatric practice, but not infrequently in general medical care as well.

1. Persuasion

Tony tried to engage Daisy in a discussion of the pros and cons of resuming her medication. He suggested that her ideas about having a special mission were a sign that her illness was returning: had she not previously agreed, when well, that it was unrealistic? Problematic side effects were addressed;

he reiterated the promise that every effort would be made to keep the dose to a minimum. Perhaps a different drug could be tried that had fewer side effects or one with a different, more acceptable, side effect profile. Tony expressed concern that what was happening now was very similar to the sequence of events that had led to Daisy being admitted to hospital on three previous occasions, each time on a compulsory order. Furthermore, her other illness, Grave's disease, was now also becoming increasingly symptomatic. Daisy was reminded how ill she had become when the medication was previously stopped after 18 months of treatment to determine whether she was in remission.

Persuasion is the lowest level of pressure in our schema and the least problematic. It goes beyond a mere statement of the facts of the illness and treatment options. However, while aimed at a particular end, persuasion restricts itself to an appeal to reason (and to some degree to the emotions). The discussion with the patient revolves around an arguably realistic appraisal of the benefits and drawbacks of treatment. There is a respect for the patient's arguments and the treatment is discussed in the context of his or her value system. Persuasion can, however, involve substantial pressure if it is sustained and recurrent. An example would be if Tony were to visit Daisy every day to try to persuade her to accept treatment. If Daisy were to object to such visits and insist that Tony stop coming, efforts at persuasion would have to cease.

2. Interpersonal leverage

Daisy remained unmoved by Tony's attempts at persuasion. Tony reacted by becoming silent. He sighed and looked sad. He gazed distractedly at the floor. 'I'm really sorry you feel that way', he said. A limp handshake accompanied his departure. Perhaps they could talk about it some more next time.

Tony has known Daisy for 5 years and has been a dedicated, compassionate nurse. He has supported her during difficult times; he was instrumental in bringing her thyroid disease to the attention of doctors; he regularly accompanied her on visits to her family doctor; he had helped her with budgeting and obtaining debt relief; he had introduced her to the charitable organization running art classes; he had agreed to help her with her application to an art school; he had helped Daisy and her mother to improve their relationship by helping the mother to better understand Daisy's difficulties; and much else. Daisy has been grateful for his support. She has developed a significant degree of emotional attachment to, and even a degree of dependency on,

Tony. 'Interpersonal leverage' (or 'interpersonal pressure') can be exercised through this emotional bond. The patient may wish to please someone who has proved helpful, or react to signs of disappointment when a treatment suggestion is rejected. Perhaps Daisy might feel some threat of withdrawal of Tony's support, but this is certainly not what Tony intends.

3. Inducements (or offers)

Tony visited again the next day. He had recently met another patient's father who had a second-hand clothing store that specialized in very fashionable, high-quality labels. The man, grateful for the help his son had received and having learnt about the needs of patients with a mental illness, offered to help with second-hand clothing at a substantial discount. Tony knew how difficult it was for Daisy to buy the kind of 'flair' clothes that she loved. He said he would introduce Daisy to the shopkeeper, and said he was confident she could acquire articles at a price she could afford. However, there would be little point in doing so if she were to end up in hospital again. Recommencing her medication would avoid this unhappy event.

Although he did not mention it to Daisy, at his last mental health team meeting it was noted that another team was offering a payment to induce patients to take medication who were reluctant or who took it sporadically. There was sharp disagreement in the team about whether this would be appropriate in a case like Daisy's.

I shall consider 'inducements' together with 'threats' since they both have a particular form—as we shall see, they involve a *conditional proposition*.

4. Threats

Daisy did not change her stance on treatment. Meanwhile, her symptoms had become more worrying. She said she heard frequent references to her special mission on the television. 'Pretend workmen' who were engaged in road repairs nearby, she suspected, were there to spy on her. She had lost more weight and her tremor had become more evident. She complained of tiredness. The last symptoms were most likely due to her thyrotoxicosis. Tony, this time accompanied by the consultant, said that it was becoming more important for Daisy to have treatment; both her mental and physical state, he told her, were becoming seriously affected by illness. Daisy agreed that she was physically unwell but she was confident she could drive out 'the bad' by herself. She denied there was anything wrong with her mentally, apart from tiredness and the worries induced by people trying to undermine her. At this point Tony, backed up by the consultant, reluctantly said that if she did not agree to take her prescribed medication, they would have to arrange a 'Mental Health Act assessment'. (Tony had spoken to Daisy's mother beforehand, whom Daisy had refused to see. Her mother had agreed that involuntary treatment would be justified.) Her consultant would initiate the process and write the first medical recommendation for an involuntary treatment order. A social worker and a second doctor would also visit, the consultant said, and would very likely agree that involuntary treatment was now warranted in the interests of Daisy's health. At this point Daisy relented and agreed to accompany Tony and the consultant to the community team base to receive an intramuscular injection of her antipsychotic. She also agreed to immediately take a dose of carbimazole and to see the endocrinologist for an urgent examination to be immediately requested by the consultant.

Both inducements and threats are characterized by a particular kind of proposition—a conditional 'if … then' proposition. *If* the patient accepts treatment A, *then* the clinician will do X; or *if* the patient does not accept treatment A, the clinician will *then* do Y. But there is an important distinction to be made between propositions that offer an 'inducement', and those that represent a 'threat'.

Alan Wertheimer in his influential 1987 book *Coercion*,[2] and in a paper examining coercion in relation to mental health issues,[3] argues that *threats* 'coerce' but *offers* (or *inducements*) generally do not:

> The crux of the distinction between threats and offers is that A makes a threat when B will be 'worse off' than in some relevant base-line position if B does not accept A's proposal, but that A makes an offer when B will be 'no worse off' than in some relevant base-line position if B does not accept A's proposal.[3]

However, there is a question about what properly fixes the 'baseline'. Wertheimer argues for a 'moral baseline'. Here is an example to illustrate how it works:

Threat or offer?

A plastic surgeon will only perform a cosmetic operation on a patient with an unsightly physical disfigurement on condition of a payment of £5000. He is the only surgeon available who can perform this operation. Has he made a threat or an offer? Under a 'moral test', the key issue is whether the surgeon *ought* to operate for free—for example, under a totally free health care service where the patient has a *right* to a free operation of this kind. If so, the surgeon's proposition is a 'threat'. The patient is 'worse off' under this moral baseline if he does not agree to the proposition—he will not get the operation.

> On the other hand, if the patient is not entitled to a free cosmetic operation—where, for example, a health care system, excludes coverage for cosmetic surgery—then the surgeon's proposition is an 'offer'. There is in this case no moral requirement under this baseline for the surgeon to operate for free. If the patient does not agree to pay, he is no 'worse off' than if the surgeon's proposal had not been made. He has no *entitlement* to the operation.

A 'threat' thus anticipates making the recipient of the proposition worse off according to an accepted moral baseline, while an 'offer'—even if declined—does not. Baselines other than 'moral' have been proposed. For example, a 'legal' baseline has been suggested, that is, one determined by what the law requires. This is more easily defined than a 'moral' baseline, but has the disadvantage of relativity, being dependent on the law in a particular place and time. A 'statistical' baseline is also possible: whether the surgeon is making an offer or a threat will depend on what is 'normal' in their society. If he would normally operate for no payment, then his proposal is a threat. If not, it is an offer.

A threat makes a required action (an 'ought' action) conditional; the person threatened is threatened with the deprivation of a right, and thus would be made worse off. Threatening to remove a legal entitlement (for example, a housing benefit) makes the subject worse off if he or she does not accede. Daisy was threatened with a loss of her liberty, a fundamental right, if she refused treatment. People also have the right to choose whether to take medication or not. An offer of something which is not an entitlement but is in the nature of some extra assistance (for example, special discounts on desirable clothing as in Daisy's case) made on condition that the patient complies with the treatment would, if rejected, not make the patient worse off compared with the relevant moral baseline—what his or her position would have been if the offer had never been made. Daisy, for example, had no entitlement or right to a discount.

When I give talks on the subject of 'coercion', I have found that a good test of whether the audience has grasped the fairly subtle 'threat' versus 'offer' distinction concerns the conduct, in theory at least, of 'mental health courts' and 'drug courts', now fairly common, particularly in the United States. These involve a person with a mental disorder or a drug addiction who has committed an offence. In some courts, the judge may make the proposition that if the patient accepts supervised treatment, the expected custodial sentence for the offence committed will be waived.

Though quite a few people say this is a threat, it is in fact, technically, an offer. The 'baseline' here is the established sentence incurred by the offence. Rejection of the proposal of treatment makes the person no worse off: a custodial sentence would be imposed even if the offer had never been made. (I assume here that the term of the custodial sentence is not overstated by the judge in order to pressure the ill offender to agree to treatment. If it were, this would amount to a deception. I also assume that the terms of the treatment contract are accurately spelt out—including, for example, a right to withdraw, the restrictions on freedom imposed by the treatment plan, sanctions for non-compliance, and the duration of supervision. Furthermore that the conditions are understood and the person has the capability for making this decision—with appropriate support and counsel. I am personally unconvinced about the place of such courts: the provisos mentioned are difficult to meet in practice[4]; offers (or inducements), in general, as we shall see later are problematic in mental health care; and, under the 'fusion proposal', offenders with mental impairments could be dealt with effectively and less problematically without the need for such courts.)

5. Compulsion

At the top of the treatment pressures hierarchy is the use of compulsion. Both inpatient and community involuntary treatment orders have already been discussed.

The use of force is non-controversially 'coercive'. Thus the term 'coercion' is clearly applicable to 'compulsion' in the hierarchy just described. Following Wertheimer, I propose that the term 'coercion' also be applied to the use of 'threats', since the potential to render the person worse off generally represents the threat of the use of force. This usage of 'coercion' for compulsion and threats is consistent with common dictionary definitions of 'coercion': that it involves the use of force or the threat of its use.

'Subjective' versus 'objective' accounts of coercion

Some argue that what should count as 'coercive' is the perceived threat entailed by a proposal, regardless of the pre-proposal situation. They claim it is the coerced person's belief about what is the case that motivates their choice of action or non-action, rather than what may actually be the case. Michael Rhodes in his book *Coercion: A Nonevaluative Approach* maintains that 'perceived threat avoidance behaviour' is a necessary condition for coercion.[5] The context for such perceived threats requires further analysis. For example, was the perceived threat reasonably perceived as such? Were the 'coerced' person's actions reasonable in the light of the perceived threat? Unintentional coercion becomes a possibility. Rhodes gives the following example:

> A well-known mobster figure approaches a grocer and proposes to pay two dollars less than the marked price for a fruit basket. The grocer is uncertain whether the mobster is simply trying to bargain, making a genuine offer to buy, or whether there is an implicit threat and the risk of harm if he does not agree to the discount.[5, p47]

Such a situation has obvious relevance to mental health care where there is a stark power imbalance between clinician and patient. Will a failure to comply with a treatment 'offer' be followed by an unfavourable response from the clinician—for example, a less supportive report to a housing agency or a court? There is real value in these subjectivist accounts of 'coercion' for the clinical context. It is important for the clinician to ask himself or herself whether a patient mistakenly perceives what is intended as an 'offer' to be a 'threat'. However, an account like that of Wertheimer, based on a moral baseline, comports better with the framework that I will propose for justifying coercive interventions. Considering coercion from an 'objective' point of view makes such a framework more generalizable and thus more readily described in terms of morally relevant principles. Consideration of the situation from the patient's perspective, though, may point to issues that need to be explored and clarified with the patient—particularly when the patient perceives coercion in the absence of an intention to exercise it.

I shall return to threats and their relation to the notion of the 'coercive shadow' that I mentioned earlier in the book, in a moment.

Exploitation and 'unwelcome predictions'

There are two kinds of act that resemble coercion but do not meet the definition of coercion as set out—they involve neither threats nor compulsion. The first is 'exploitation'. Exploitation involves an offer that nevertheless takes unfair advantage of a person who is in a difficult predicament. Michael Rhodes considers the example of a homeless person in a cold climate who is offered a warm apartment but at a very high rent. The threat is a 'background threat,' and not of the landlord's doing. The key issue is the moral baseline. Exploitation, while often morally questionable, is not 'coercive'. Is it the person's 'right' in this example to be offered a room at a 'fair' rent? Most would say, no, it is not a 'right'. Further, exploitative offers, in some sense, expand possibilities for the recipient; if the offer is not accepted, the person is no worse off than he would have been if the offer had not been made. Both the exploiter and the person exploited can derive advantage from an exploitative offer (a warm room for the former, and a larger income for the latter). The harm lies in the exploiter taking *unfair advantage* of a person who is at a disadvantage. Exploitation thus involves an offer, but the context makes it morally unseemly or unacceptable.

The second situation that can be confused with coercion is what can be called an 'unwelcome prediction'. Tony telling Daisy that her stopping medication would result in an involuntary admission to hospital could be seen in two ways—as an unwelcome prediction, or as a threat. Much depends on the evidence supporting the prediction; for example, in Daisy's case, her history showed three highly similar instances in the past that resulted in a compulsory admission. Whether the clinician making the prediction will be an instigator of the event might also be relevant. A threat requires that the person making the threat has the power to see it through. I would not consider prediction of an unwelcome event, based on strong supporting facts, to be a threat, and thus it would be non-'coercive'. However, a clear line between the two interpretations may be difficult to draw in practice.

'Inducements' in the context of health care

From a purely conceptual point of view, the hierarchy of treatment pressures just outlined looks quite persuasive. I have argued for its relevance to health care. However, for some time I have had misgivings about the place of inducements and threats given the special context of health care, and especially mental health care.

In general, I think most people would agree that an inducement is less 'coercive' than a threat. We are regularly bombarded with inducements. For example, a bank may offer an interest-free period on a credit card debit as an inducement to move one's account to them. This would certainly be quite different to a threat aimed at achieving such a change—for example, a threat that if you declined to open an account with the bank, a detailed credit check would be instigated and changes to your credit rating would be imposed if previously unknown problems were to be to be uncovered.

However, inducements in a health care context can be problematic. An example is a proposal to offer a financial incentive to non-compliant or partially compliant patients with a psychosis to accept medication at the recommended dose. You will recall that this was discussed by Daisy's community mental health team. It is clearly an offer and thus it is not 'coercive'. The aim seems worthy—to improve the well-being of the patient. Yet there seems to be something not quite right about such an intervention. A survey of clinicians in the United Kingdom carried out by proponents of the approach revealed a widely held intuition that the practice is ethically problematic.[6] But why? Could a coercive intervention be preferable?

At first I found it quite difficult to put my finger on what was so troubling about the proposal. Now it appears quite clear. There are a number of reasons for such a practice being problematic.[7]

First, there is a difficulty with the nature of the transaction itself—an exchange of money for an agreement to take medication. Such an exchange is an example of 'commodification'.[8] The transaction involves an exchange of 'goods' that have very different kinds of value—money on the one hand, a means of preserving a person's health and well-being on the other. These values can be seen as 'incommensurable', that is, they are values that cannot be measured on a single metric or on the same scale or using the same 'coinage'. This is because one 'good'—health, well-being, human flourishing—lies in a higher, separate, domain than the other—money. Selling a child would be a stark example of an exchange of this kind. Such an exchange, were it to take place, corrupts or degrades the higher value—the value of a child. An exchange is corrupting when it ignores the differences between spheres of valuation and forces us to value all goods in the same way.

In paying patients to take medication, money could be seen as being exchanged for respect for the person—that is, there is a failure to respect a patient's decision about what is in his or her best interests (assuming for the moment that the patient has autonomous decision-making capability). Recall here the discussion about 'recognitional autonomy' in Chapter 8 in relation to supported decision-making. A denial of 'recognition' of the person's decision (or will) undermines the person's *agency* by undermining their self-respect or self-trust. There is at the same time another type of denigration—a corruption of the value of the treatment. It becomes an exchangeable commodity, measured on a money-based metric, rather than lying in a higher domain of value, that of fostering human well-being or flourishing.

Second, there may be a possibility of exploitation. It is the patient's vulnerability, psychological or material—often both—which would induce an acceptance of the offer. While the sums of money may seem small as far as most doctors or health service managers are concerned—for example, £15 each time the person accepts a depot injection of antipsychotic medication, usually fortnightly or monthly—for someone who is surviving on meagre social security benefits, it may be significant. As noted, in exploitation one party gains unfairly at the expense of the other (even though the one who is exploited may still derive some gain). Who gains unfairly here? A significant motive for financial inducements may be to reduce costs to the health service by preventing rehospitalization by preventing relapse. If it works, large savings could be made for a small financial outlay. Clinicians may also be rewarded in certain ways, including financial, by their employing health care institution for successfully reducing the number of admissions. An element of socially based discrimination may also enter here. Those patients who are less well-off are more likely to accept the offer of a financial inducement; and taking this line of thought further, a degree of stigma may come to be attached to those known to have accepted the offer.

Third, there is an issue concerning the 'fairness': why should non-treatment-adherent patients receive money, but prudent, treatment-adherent patients, not?

There is also a range of other problems of a practical nature: the patient–doctor relationship might change, with a richer discussion about the value of treatment being short-circuited by a financial inducement; ensuring that treatment adherence actually occurs might require injections rather than tablets, which may exclude a more effective treatment that is not available in an injectable form; it may not be possible in practice for payment to be terminated—why would a hard-up patient say that now they will be adherent even without the financial incentive; if it becomes known that reluctant patients will receive financial incentives, why would a hard-up patient, even if convinced about the value of the treatment, admit to an intention to take the medication?

In addition, a psychological phenomenon called 'crowding out' may operate when financial incentives are used to induce people to act in a certain way.[9] This may contribute to an undermining of personal agency in a way that differs from that I have just discussed. The phenomenon is one where 'intrinsic motivation' to act in a particular way—especially if the action normally has a strong voluntary commitment—is 'crowded out' by an 'extrinsic motivation' such as a financial incentive. 'Intrinsic motivation' refers to self-motivation for the achievement of an end valued by the person. The extrinsic motivator may be successful, in the short term at least, in inducing the behaviour. However, when the external reward, especially if seen as significantly controlling, is removed—when, for example, payment ceases—the behaviour diminishes. And here there is a key observation: the targeted behaviour diminishes to such an extent that it becomes less frequent than in cases where no extrinsic motivation was ever deployed. That is, there is a 'crowding out' of 'intrinsic motivation' by the 'extrinsic motivation'. The main negative effect of such rewards is said to depend on their undermining of self-regulation, an aspect of agency. As a consequence, people may take less responsibility for motivating themselves. Much controversy surrounds this phenomenon and under what conditions it might occur, especially outside experimental psychology laboratories where most of the research has thus far been done. However, it is worth keeping a close eye on future work in the field as it is clearly relevant to the long-term effects of financial incentives in health care.

Other problems with inducements may appear on the surface to be less troubling. An example, as in Daisy's case, is introducing the patient to a second-hand clothing store whose owner is sympathetic to people with a mental illness. Fairness is obviously one. Why should not all patients have such benefits or assistance? On what basis should some patients be offered inducements while others are not? Inducements that are general and not directly tied to the acceptance of treatment appear less problematic. The 'moral baseline', though, remains a critical issue. Its definition in this context would seem to require that a health service defines a patient's entitlements to various components of health care, but more than that, the help that can be offered in accessing other forms of care or assistance. Such 'entitlements' could be spelt out in a service's objectives or operational policies. Given the large variety of interventions offered by community mental health services, for example, and an ethos that prizes innovation and problem-solving, such a task could be daunting. Nonetheless, my analysis would indicate that it is highly desirable. A paradoxical consequence is that the greater the range of services and assistance offered, the greater the potential for coercive threats—withholding a service or type of assistance might mean the patient is 'worse off' under the moral baseline.

The self-agency problem, however, remains whatever the form of inducement, if it is clearly conditional on a person accepting treatment. The patient's agency is potentially undermined and there is always a degree of corruption of the value of the treatment. Its value is measured on a metric appropriate to commodities, not on its higher value in relation to health or human flourishing.

Having reflected further on these problematic aspects of inducements in mental health care, I am now inclined to place them outside the hierarchy of treatment pressures and to conclude that they have little or no place in treatment. In most everyday settings, offers may indeed be less coercive than threats. Many will be quick to point out that exposure to financial incentives is commonplace in many spheres of life in our market-orientated society. However, the particular context of health care—especially mental health care—requires special recognition. As we have seen, patients with mental health problems commonly experience a lack of respect in our society; often their values and preferences are not given recognition and they are seen as incompetent. Their agency is thus regularly undermined. Their confidence in their ability to act according to their own values may become shaky. Psychiatric treatments should aim to empower patients and strengthen their sense of agency, not undermine them. Inducements are likely to be undermining.

I alluded earlier to the possible relevance of the patient's decision-making capability when a financial inducement is being considered. In such cases it could be argued that the patient's agency is already undermined by their illness and that the lack of respect for the person's decision-making is thus less of a drawback. As the person has an impairment of decision-making capability, the next question becomes whether the intervention is in the person's best interests—does it concord with the person's deep or 'authentic' beliefs and values, or will and preferences? Perhaps one should not generalize, but it is difficult to see how an intervention that undermines a patient's agency and degrades the value of treatment can be consistent with supporting a person's values, or 'will' as we have defined it. Perhaps a strong argument for financial incentives being appropriate in a particular case can be made, but I remain somewhat sceptical.

'Threats' in the context of health care

Threats are usually seen as an unacceptable warp in the fabric of mental health care. They entail a troubling paradox: on the one hand, medical codes of practice generally condemn them as unacceptable; but on the other hand, they are apparently common, at least as perceived by patients. The Code of Practice (2015) accompanying the English and Wales Mental Health Act states:

> the threat of detention must not be used to induce a patient to consent to admission to hospital or to treatment (and is likely to invalidate any apparent consent). [10, chap. 40.17]

Though there are no statistics on the frequency of direct threats of admission to hospital if the patient should fail to accept treatment, studies that have asked whether 'voluntarily' admitted patients have felt 'coerced' into being in hospital find anywhere between 10 and 50 per cent saying they have. An example is a study conducted in London in 2005 in which I was one of the investigators. One-third of voluntary patients (that is, patients not on a compulsory treatment order) felt highly coerced, and two-thirds were not certain they were free to leave hospital.[11]

What can be done about this deeply disturbing situation? An explanation for the prohibition of threats is rarely made explicit. I can identify two critical concerns that may lie behind the injunction:

1. Threats may be made in 'bad faith', that is, involuntary treatment would not in fact be instigated by the clinician making the threat. It is made with the intention of pushing the patient to accept treatment 'voluntarily'.
2. The treatment though not truly 'voluntary' is not subject to any regulation, nor are there any specific protections for the patient (such as a right to a review or appeal).

These objections turn on a *lack of transparency*. It is likely that many patients, if it comes down to a bare choice, would see succumbing to a threat as preferable to a formal involuntary admission. Patients with whom I have worked as research colleagues have generally said so. The significant proportion of officially 'voluntary' patients who on direct questioning admit to having felt coerced into accepting such an admission points to an abhorrence of being legally detained on an involuntary order. Although the subjective experience of being threatened is undoubtedly distressing, it is unlikely that this would be worse than the subjective experience of forced admission and treatment. A threat, even if complied with, may offer the patient more freedoms than would a compulsory admission. For example, an admission may be avoided, as well as the stigma associated with being 'sectioned' or 'certified'; improvement may occur unexpectedly quickly—perhaps because of a change in the patient's social circumstances—prompting the clinician to remove the threat; even if an inpatient, it is perhaps more likely that the voluntary patient's preferences will be heard and respected than if they were on an involuntary order.

Can anything be done to deal with the objections? I have discussed this at some length with a philosopher colleague at King's College London, Tania Gergel, who has an interest in the philosophy of psychiatry and coercion. We have concluded that there are some possibilities. How acceptable they might be, we don't know. To our knowledge such ideas have not been proposed before, and they are offered here as a basis for further discussion, one that should centrally involve patients in the mental health system.

It seems to us that the term 'conditional treatment' may be a better descriptor than the word 'threat'. There is a range of existing conditional frameworks of which a community treatment order is one example: the person can remain in the community if they comply with the terms of the order; if they don't, they may be recalled to hospital.

A distinction needs to be drawn between threats that result in a patient accepting *conditional treatment in the community* as opposed to threats that result in a *conditional admission* to hospital. As we shall see, the former is less complex from a legal point of view. The latter would clearly involve a greater curtailment of liberty.

Conditional treatment in the community

We shall first examine the situation where a person is threatened with an involuntary admission to hospital if they do not accept treatment which can nevertheless be given in the community. An example would be a case such as Daisy's. She had discontinued her medication and had relapsed to the point where an involuntary order would be justified, but a prompt recommencement of medication would likely avoid the need for admission.

The following provisos might make such an intervention acceptable:

1. The clinician must record in the case notes that a threat has been made, the content of the threat, and state that the threat has been made in good faith (i.e. if the patient does not opt for the conditional treatment alternative to a Mental Health Act assessment, such an assessment will certainly be instigated; and that if such an assessment has been made and the assessors agree that an involuntary admission is warranted, that this will proceed). The fact that the patient has the decision-making capability to agree to 'conditional' treatment will also be recorded.
2. The clinician must notify the relevant local authority (for example, Mental Health Trust) that conditional treatment has been initiated, and the authority must register that this has occurred. Such data would be useful in monitoring the frequency of use of this measure and draw attention to potentially problematic variation between clinicians, departments, and services.
3. A care plan must be recorded in the patient's notes which must be discussed with the patient and the patient's representative (or carer).
4. The patient must have access to an independent advocate who is available to discuss the conditional treatment and its justifications with the clinician.

5. These conditions will need to be revisited after perhaps 2 weeks, and if conditional treatment is to be continued, regularly thereafter. There could be a time limit for such treatment.
6. When a point is reached where the option of involuntary treatment can no longer be justified, conditional treatment must be terminated. This follows from condition 1.

The patient can at any time refuse to go along with the conditional treatment. At this point, the clinician—having previously affirmed this action would be taken—must initiate a Mental Health Act assessment. The patient can then appeal under the terms of the (Mental) Health Act under which involuntary treatment has been authorized.

Confounding the problem of making threats transparent and adequately regulated is the wish of patients not to be treated under a formal legal order, on the one hand, and ensuring that the necessary procedures are adopted by clinicians, on the other. Guidelines or a code of practice may suffice for conditional treatment in the community. If the provisions were to be formalized in legislation, then conditional treatment might come to be seen in the popular imagination as being tantamount to being 'sectioned' or 'certified'.

Conditional treatment in hospital

When the choice offered to the patient is a 'voluntary' (conditional) admission as against an involuntary admission, measures such as those listed might not prove adequate in most places. A conditional 'voluntary' admission would probably be seen as amounting to a 'deprivation of liberty', for example, under the European Convention on Human Rights. A 'deprivation of liberty' here means confinement in the absence of a valid consent. If a conditional admission does constitute a deprivation of liberty, the procedures must be prescribed in law—that is, enacted in a statute. The patient would then be, in some sense, 'sectioned' or 'certified' under a (mental) health act.

As it is engendered by the understandable stigma associated with a legal treatment order, the conundrum could of course be mitigated if the stigma of such an order were neutralized. The Fusion Law proposal, by being generic and by widening involuntary treatment to include people with complications arising from 'physical disorders' and who do not have 'mental disorders', would be expected to reduce the stigma.

However, even in the absence of a Fusion Law, it might just be possible to argue that an admission under the constrained circumstances of a 'threat' of an involuntary admission does not necessarily amount to a 'deprivation of liberty'. Could a consent, under the threat of an involuntary admission, by a person with decision-making capability for such a decision—though not necessarily for a specific treatment—be nevertheless classed as a 'valid' consent? A necessary condition for a valid consent is that the consent is voluntary, not coerced. In one respect, the consent in the situation we are considering is clearly 'coerced'. But in another sense, might it still be 'valid'? The prospect of a 'conditional' admission might in fact be reasonably construed as an 'offer'. Remember that the difference between a 'threat' and an 'offer' depends on the 'moral baseline'. The moral baseline in this case could be considered to be an involuntary admission: this is what will automatically be initiated if the conditional proposition of a 'voluntary' admission is not accepted. The offer is an alternative—a 'conditional' admission. If the person says 'no' to the offer, they are no worse off than if the offer had not been made—the result will be an involuntary admission. (The situation is similar to that described earlier as obtaining in 'mental health courts', in theory at least, where following the commission of an offence the person can choose to accept an 'offer' of treatment thereby avoiding a custodial sentence. There is a similar kind of pressure exercised.) The 'conditional' admission offer could include a treatment plan, which might include, for example, conditions for periods of leave from the ward. There would have to be a time limit for such an admission. If restraint or force were to be necessary during the admission, then a formal compulsory treatment order would need to be instituted: such measures require statutory regulation.

I don't know whether the line of argument presented would stand up to legal scrutiny. Could a conditional admission be acceptable without a formal legal process? Probably not. If it were accepted, then the conditions 1 to 6 listed earlier for the community alternative might, with additions, form the basis for safeguards.

A further element of justification for a conditional admission might come from a type of 'self-binding' advance statement, made by the patient when well, that would favour such an admission in preference to a conventional involuntary admission.[12] Advance statements generally cannot order specific treatments, but they express patient preferences that can carry considerable weight in determinations of the person's 'best interests' or 'will and preferences'. (Advance statements are discussed in detail in Chapter 10.)

Like some of the complex issues we explored in relation to inducements, whether a place exists for threats in health care, especially mental health care, needs discussion. In any discussion, special regard must be paid to the views of people who are most likely to be subject to these forms of treatment pressure. It is possible patients may wish to avoid any situation that involves a 'formal' process, even a non-statutory 'conditional' one. A person may accept treatment against their true wishes in order to forestall even the prospect of a conditional choice being raised in the first place.

Justifying treatment pressures and coercion

Apart from the use of compulsion, where it is covered by legislation, I know of no framework in general use that provides a structure or guide for thinking about whether a treatment pressure, in a particular case, is justified or not. I have set out the treatment pressures in the form of a hierarchy, and suggested earlier that as one ascends the hierarchy, the stronger must be the justification for using the particular measure. I have expressed doubts about the place of inducements in mental health care. Threats, whether overt or covert, are clearly common in practice, even though many codes of practice say they should not be used. I have put forward some ideas for making threats acceptable by making them transparent and by introducing safeguards. Whether this would be acceptable to patients remains to be determined.

What framework could be used to help us determine whether a particular measure is justified for a particular person in a particular situation? I suggest that the 'decision-making capability–will and preferences' framework discussed in relation to the use of compulsion is equally applicable across the entire range of treatment pressures. In each case where an intervention on the hierarchy is being posited, the first question to be asked is whether the person has an impairment of their decision-making capability. The determination of an impairment may be based on the 'standard' criteria—understanding and retention of relevant information, ability to use and weigh it, and ability to communicate a decision—or, in more complex cases, based on the coherence of currently expressed preferences with those that are 'authentic', true or to which the person has shown a deep commitment in the past, a judgement that requires interpretation. If there is no evidence of an impairment, decision-making capability is to be presumed and treatment pressures are unjustified (apart, perhaps, for what might blur into 'persuasion'—that is, discussion that is aimed at ensuring that the relevant information has been understood and used by the person). If there were an impairment of decision-making capability, then the question of whether there was an intervention would give effect to the person's 'authentic' values (or 'will') would be considered. Relevant here would be the harms to the person—already present or clearly imminent—arising from the divergence between their authentic values (or will) and their present preferences. The more coercive the intervention, the stronger the threat to the person's authentic values, will, or preferences would need to be.

Sometimes deciding whether a threat would or wouldn't be justified may be difficult. In Daisy's case, after a careful discussion of her predicament and the lack of coherence between her refusal of treatment and her previously expressed values, the clinical team were in agreement that it was justified at this point. The value of a framework such as the one being proposed is that it provides a basis for discussion by the clinical team. Decisions, particularly at the coercive end of the spectrum, I suggest, should not be made by a single person. One of the major advantages of a multidisciplinary team is the range of perspectives and values that can be brought to bear on making clinical–ethical decisions of the kinds we have been considering.

Of course, it would be far preferable if we could avoid the need for coercive interventions in the first place. Are there clinical methods that are effective in achieving this? Surprisingly little research has been done to answer this question. What we do know, I review in Chapter 10.

References

1. **Szmukler G, Appelbaum P.** Treatment pressures, leverage, coercion and compulsion in mental health care. *Journal of Mental Health* 2008; **17**:233–244.
2. **Wertheimer A.** *Coercion*. Princeton, NJ: Princeton University Press, 1987.
3. **Wertheimer A.** A philosophical examination of coercion for mental health issues. *Behavioral Sciences and the Law* 1993; **11**:239–258.
4. **Seltzer T.** Mental health courts: a misguided attempt to address the criminal justice system's unfair treatment of people with mental illnesses. *Psychology, Public Policy, and Law* 2005; **11**:570–586.
5. **Rhodes MR.** *Coercion: A Nonevaluative Approach*. Value Inquiry Book Series. Amsterdam: Rodopi, 2000.
6. **Claassen D.** Financial incentives for antipsychotic depot medication: ethical issues. *Journal of Medical Ethics* 2007; **33**:189–193.
7. **Szmukler G.** Financial incentives for patients in the treatment of psychosis. *Journal of Medical Ethics* 2009; **35**:224–228.
8. **Sandel MJ.** *What Money Can't Buy: The Moral Limits of Markets*. London: Penguin, 2012.
9. **Deci EL, Koestner R, Ryan RM.** A meta-analytic review of experiments examining the effects of extrinsic rewards on intrinsic motivation. *Psychological Bulletin* 1999; **125**:627.

10. **Department of Health.** *Code of Practice: Mental Health Act 1983.* London: The Stationery Office, 2015.

11. **Bindman J, Reid Y, Szmukler G, Tiller J, Thornicroft G, Leese M.** Perceived coercion at admission to psychiatric hospital and engagement with follow-up--a cohort study. *Social Psychiatry and Psychiatric Epidemiology* 2005; **40**:160–166.

12. **Gergel T, Owen G.** Fluctuating capacity and advance decision-making in bipolar affective disorder: self-binding directives and self-determination. *International Journal of Law and Psychiatry* 2015; **40**:92–101

Chapter 10

Can we reduce the need for coercive interventions?

Sadly, this will not be a very long chapter. We know quite a lot about the experiences of patients who have been subject to involuntary treatment, but there has been very little research about how this knowledge could be put into practice. I will focus mainly on coercive interventions in mental health care.

It is important to bear in mind some important findings concerning patients' views of involuntary treatment. In a large English study involving 1570 involuntarily admitted patients, only 40 per cent of patients interviewed 1 year later believed compulsion was justified.[1] In a smaller subset who were interviewed more intensively, of those who said that compulsion was wrong, two-thirds nevertheless said they were unwell at the time and the vast majority said they needed treatment—but non-coercive treatment. Nearly all the patients interviewed in this part of the study, whether they thought the involuntary admission was right or wrong, described:

> various experiences, including not receiving sufficient information, not being involved in treatment decisions, perceiving professionals as having power over patients, and experiencing coercive measures contributing to the patients feeling out of control during their hospitalization.[2,p72]

An important concern expressed by many patients was the long-term, wider impact of involuntary hospitalization on their lives—on their independence, on their sense of themselves as autonomous individuals, on their social position, and on the likelihood that once having been 'sectioned' such an event would happen again more easily. An important finding was that those patients who were least satisfied with their treatment experience in the first week of admission were more likely to be readmitted on a compulsory order within the 12 months of follow-up.[1]

Having a 'voice' and 'procedural justice'

Here are some comments made to me by a very perceptive and high-achieving person on her experiences of involuntary detention:

> Three of them came to see me. The social worker was really quite flippant. She didn't seem to care. She just wanted to get it over with as soon as possible. The psychiatrist didn't really talk to me. He was more worried about whether there was a bed for me in the hospital. They'd obviously made up their minds even before they spoke to me.
>
> I've been 'sectioned' lots of times. Usually when they come to do it they really don't think you're worth talking to. They don't elaborate on the reasons why you need to be sectioned. They don't treat you like an adult. They don't appreciate how heavy it is for me—it's just routine for them. The last time I was going to be sectioned it was different though. I knew the social worker from before. She had a dialogue with me—it was unique. I was wanting to leave the hospital but, because of her, I decided to stay.

One of the key research findings on patients' attitudes to involuntary treatment is the correlation between 'not having a voice' or 'not being listened to' and feeling 'coerced'.[3] An in-depth investigation of patients' experience of coercion was conducted in the United States by the MacArthur Research Network on Mental Health and the Law.[4] This generously funded network under the direction of John Monahan comprised an expert multidisciplinary team. Their coercion project involved interviews concerning the admission process with over 400 patients as well as involved family members and clinicians.

The key results were as follows: a patient's formal legal status on admission, whether involuntary or voluntary was an imperfect guide to whether he or she experienced being coerced into admission. A significant minority of 'voluntary' patients experienced significant coercion, and a significant minority of 'involuntary' patients believed that they had freely chosen to be admitted. Patients' accounts of their hospitalization experiences tended not to change, even after their discharge. However, some later did change their views about whether their admission was necessary; about 50 per cent said it was needed, and 50 per cent said it was not.

How coerced the patients felt on admission to hospital depended on the nature of the 'pressures' exerted on them. 'Negative' pressures—such as threats and force—increased perceived coercion, while 'positive pressures' such as persuasion and inducements did not. Lower levels of coercion were associated with 'beliefs that others acted out of genuine concern, treated the patient respectfully and in good faith, and afforded the patient a chance to tell his or her side of the story'. The patients' perception of the justice of the process was important.

Thus the degree of coercion experienced was strongly associated with the degree to which the admission process followed what the researchers called 'procedural justice'; that is, patients being allowed a 'voice', and being treated with respect, concern, and good faith.

It comes as a surprise, then, that there has been virtually no research on whether it would make a difference to the frequency of the use and perception of coercion if staff involved in admissions were trained in 'procedural justice' methods. I know of no relevant study. A randomized controlled study with consecutive admissions being randomly allocated to 'procedural justice' versus standard treatment would probably not be possible—it would be difficult to deny 'procedural justice' to the control group. A study of coercion before and after introducing a 'procedural justice' emphasis project might provide some useful evidence as a starter. A later approach might be to use what is called a 'cluster randomized' study where some clinical teams are trained, and compared to those not trained, but that type of research design requires a large number of clinical teams. Nevertheless, the potential impact of a procedural justice approach in the admission process on coercion—in both its objective and subjective forms—surely demands examination.

A related idea is that patients are likely to be, and feel, less coerced if they are able to play a more active role in making treatment choices. The trend for service users' increased involvement in determining the shape and nature of services may be helpful in this regard but, again, the effect on coercion has not been studied.

However, there are methods that empower patients to make choices that have been researched.

'Advance statements' and 'psychiatric advance directives'

An 'advance statement' allows a person, when well, to state treatment preferences in anticipation of a time in the future when, as a result of the effects of an illness, he or she may not be capable of making treatment decisions. The anticipated loss of decision-making capability in mental health care usually occurs during a crisis due to a relapse of illness or during a time of especially disturbing events. An important aim of an advance statement is to give the person substantial influence over his or her treatment at such a time and thus to reduce the need for coercive measures.

Advance statements in psychiatry vary along a number of dimensions: whether the process for arranging the 'advance statement' is patient or service-provider led; whether the stated preferences are legally binding or not; and whether its construction is facilitated by a person independent of the clinical team. At least three major types of advance statement have been used in mental health care: 'crisis cards', 'joint crisis plans', and 'psychiatric advance directives'.

Crisis cards

In a 'crisis card', patients state their treatment wishes or nominate a person who should be familiar with their preferences, but there is little or no discussion with their clinical team. It is entirely 'consumer' led. In some jurisdictions, for example, under the Mental Capacity Act 2005 in England and Wales, stated treatment refusals now have legal force, but they can be overridden if the person is placed on an involuntary treatment order. The uptake of 'crisis cards' has been very limited.

Joint crisis plans

This is the type of advance statement with which I have been mainly involved. In contrast to 'crisis cards', the 'joint crisis plan' is the product of a semi-structured discussion between the patient (usually accompanied by a relative, friend, or advocate) and the clinical team (usually the psychiatrist and case manager) that aims to reach an agreement on what measures should be taken if a relapse should occur in the future. A critical element in the method is the involvement of a facilitator, independent of the clinical team, who ensures that the patient's 'voice' is heard. A 'joint crisis plan' is not generally legally binding (although as noted earlier, specific treatment refusals—but not treatment requests—may have legal force in some jurisdictions, though they, in turn, may be overridden by a compulsory treatment order). The clinical team makes it explicit that while it will do its best to comply with the preferences and terms agreed in the 'joint crisis plan', it cannot guarantee to do so in all respects. An example might be a crisis occurring in the middle of the night or at a distant location where those involved may not be aware of the plan.

While the 'joint crisis plan' is 'service-provider' initiated, it aims to achieve an advance agreement in which the patient has played at least an equal role. Indeed, in our work, what finally appears in the 'joint crisis plan', including the exact wording, is determined by the patient (though agreed by the clinician).

Our type of 'joint crisis plan' usually comprises much more than a statement of the patient's treatment preferences or refusals in the event of a relapse or crisis. For instance, it may include details of the current treatment plan (including medication and dosages); early signs of relapse; what has proven helpful in the past in arresting a relapse; what treatments have proven successful (or unsuccessful) when relapse has become established; who should be contacted to help; what symptoms or behaviours would indicate that admission would now be the right step; adverse drug effects or allergies; and practical issues that need attention, for example, who will make sure the patient's home is secure in the event of hospitalization, who will look after pets or plants, cancel milk deliveries, and so on. The specificity of content in a 'joint crisis plan', based on a careful analysis of past illness episodes, is an important advantage since relapse in most people tends to occur in a rather stereotyped manner.

This is what a 'joint crisis plan' might look like:

Crisis plan

If I appear to be experiencing 'mental health' difficulties that require decisions to be taken either against my wishes or in the absence of my agreement then I request that my sister, Mrs Jane Stuart, be contacted immediately, be informed of what is happening, and requested to attend as a matter of urgency. She has agreed to this.

My current care and treatment plan

My mental health problem or diagnosis: I have a diagnosis of schizophrenia.

Physical illnesses and allergies: I am allergic to penicillin; I am a diabetic and take metformin PR 2000 mg daily.

My current care plan: I see my care-coordinator, Percy Jones, every 2 weeks, and my consultant, Dr Peter Smith, every month.

Current medication: I take clozapine 500 mg daily.

Circumstances that may lead to me becoming unwell or have done in the past: Not getting enough sleep, stopping my medication, arguments with my sister.

What happens when I first start to become unwell: I become suspicious of people and jump to conclusions about their intentions. I sleep badly. When I start to hear voices—even though I don't believe they're voices at the time—then I am definitely ill and need treatment.

Treatments or other things that have, or have not, been helpful during crises or relapses in the past: My sister has a calming influence on me. It is better if I don't see my mother when I am in a bad state as she gets too distressed and it makes me feel worse.

Care in a crisis

What I would like to be done when I first start to become unwell: I shouldn't be left alone for too long as I get more paranoid when I feel isolated. If possible, I would like to stay with my sister for a few days.

Preferred treatment or social care during a crisis or relapse: Lorazepam (even IM) helps to calm me until my clozapine is re-established (if I have stopped it or missed doses). I am happy for the Home Treatment Team to see me, but I would like to be warned when they are coming.

Specific refusals regarding treatment during a crisis or relapse: I don't want haloperidol as its side effects are intolerable.

Circumstances in which I would wish to be admitted to hospital for treatment: When I stop answering my phone; when the voices say I'm a target of MI5; when I start accusing the neighbours of spying on me; when I won't eat any food I haven't prepared myself.

Practical help in a crisis: If I am admitted to hospital I would like my sister or mother to check that my flat is secure and to dispose of all perishable food. Please ask them to also bring me my iPod to hospital if it's still at home, and my Bible.

Agencies or people that have copies of this agreement: A record in my case notes and on the electronic records system for hospital staff; my GP; my sister (Jane Stuart); accident & emergency department at my general hospital.

With colleagues at the UK Institute of Psychiatry, Graham Thornicroft, Kim Sutherby, Claire Henderson, and Diana Rose, I have been an investigator in a series of studies looking at the feasibility and effectiveness of 'joint crisis plans'. Considerable time was spent working with patients to develop the best way of implementing the intervention. We showed it was feasible and found that patients formulating joint crisis plans said the way the agreements with the clinicians were made did not make them feel pressured to conform with what the clinicians wanted. When interviewed alone afterwards by an independent researcher, the vast majority of patients said they felt more in control of their mental health problems as a result of making the plan, and that they would recommend the intervention to others.

Two randomized controlled trials followed. The first involved 160 patients from eight community mental health teams in South-east England who had a diagnosis of a psychotic illness or bipolar disorder, and who had had at least one admission in the previous 2 years.[5] Almost 40 per cent of patients who were eligible took up the opportunity to complete a 'joint crisis plan'. We found that compulsory admissions over a 15-month period were halved compared to the control group who did not make a crisis plan (13 per cent versus 27 per cent). Given the success of this trial, we gained funding from the Medical Research Council for a larger trial—indeed a huge trial for a complex intervention of this kind—this time involving 64 mental health teams from Birmingham, Manchester, and Preston, as well as London.[6] Five hundred and sixty-nine patients participated. To our disappointment, we failed to replicate the finding of a reduction in the use of compulsion for those who had made a 'joint crisis plan'. We believe this was because of the lesser degree of 'buy-in' from clinicians this time. There was less enthusiasm to be part of the research project. Nonetheless the patients were again positive about the intervention.

There has also been another small randomized controlled trial of joint crisis plans for patients who repeatedly self-harm.[7] There was no difference in the rates of self-harming on follow-up, but 85 per cent of the patients said they would recommend the intervention to others. These positive endorsements perhaps suggest that what was important was the opportunity to voice their preferences and for the patients to feel respected.

A smaller study from the Netherlands showed a reduction in court-ordered involuntary hospitalizations for patients with a crisis plan.[8]

Thus a clear conclusion concerning the impact of 'joint crisis plans' on involuntary admissions is not entirely possible at present, though a recent meta-analysis points to their effectiveness.[9] Looking at the studies in which I was involved suggests that they may be effective, but only if clinical teams implement them appropriately. A striking observation in our studies was the frequency of readmissions. In our large multicentre study described earlier, approximately 20 per cent of patients were readmitted on a compulsory order within 18 months, with a further 10 per cent or so on a voluntary basis.

Psychiatric advance directives

Advance directives are in principle legally binding. The directives may be of three kinds: first, specified treatments that are refused or requested; second, statements about personal values, attitudes, or general preferences that may be used as a guide to those making decisions about treatment for the patient; and third, nomination of a person to act a 'substitute' or 'proxy' decision-maker. A psychiatric advance directive assumes that the patient had decision-making capability when it was made, and that the circumstances in which the psychiatric advance directive is triggered are those that were anticipated.

Medical advance directives have legal force in the United States. However, while specific psychiatric advance directive legislation enacted in some 25 states makes them ostensibly legally binding, there is some uncertainty about circumstances in which psychiatric advance directives may be overridden. Civil commitment legislation may do so if it specifically authorizes involuntary treatment. In some cases the directive may be overridden if it conflicts with 'generally accepted community practice standards', or if it conflicts with emergency treatment. However, if a separate decision concerning consent is required before involuntary treatment can be imposed on a patient following detention in hospital (the detention being based on 'disorder' and 'risk' criteria), then a psychiatric advance directive may prevail. The significant case here is *Hargrave v Vermont*, heard by the United States Court of Appeals, Second Circuit, which upheld an advance directive refusing all medication for a psychosis on the grounds that failure to do so would amount to discrimination against persons with a mental disorder. The court ruled that if advance directives for those with other disorders cannot be overridden, it should also be so for those with a mental disorder.

It is noteworthy that the evidence from the United States on psychiatric advance directives to date shows that refusal of all treatment alternatives is rare. I will look at issues relating to the implementation of advance directives in further detail in Chapter 12.

A variant of the psychiatric advance directive, termed a 'facilitated' psychiatric advance directive, has been introduced following research showing that despite an apparently widespread appeal of psychiatric advance directives to many patients, few actually made one. Difficulties in understanding the meaning and implications of a psychiatric advance directive and the practical complexities in making one are deterrents. In a facilitated psychiatric advance directive, an attempt is made to overcome these obstacles by making available a trained facilitator who explains what a psychiatric advance directive involves and, if the patient chooses to opt for one, assists with its completion. The service provider may also be asked to become involved in its planning.

A randomized controlled study in the United States of facilitated psychiatric advance directives[10] has indeed shown that facilitation results in a huge increase in the number of patients who decide to make a psychiatric advance directive (61 vs 3 per cent of controls). Noteworthy is that at 1-month follow-up, those with a facilitated psychiatric advance directive reported a much better 'working alliance' with their clinicians and were more likely to say that they received the services they needed. A later report from this study[11] found that the number of 'coercive interventions' over the succeeding 2 years for those who made an advance directive was considerably fewer compared to patients who chose not to make one. The interventions assessed were (1) being picked up by the police and transported to an emergency facility; (2) being placed in handcuffs; (3) being involuntarily committed to a hospital for psychiatric treatment; (4) being placed in seclusion in a locked hospital room; (5) being placed in physical restraints; and (6) receiving forced medications. It was also found that an advance directive was more effective in reducing such interventions in those patients who had suffered a loss of 'capacity' during the crisis.

Overall then it appears that some forms of 'advance statement' can reduce coercion in mental health care and improve outcomes. Patients may be empowered by the process. From a practical point of view, the information contained in an 'advance statement' may ensure that the most appropriate treatment is given when information from other sources is sparse—for example, in the middle of the night in an accident and emergency department. Independent facilitation, either in a 'joint crisis plan' or a facilitated psychiatric advance directive, may be important for success.

It is likely that the dialogue between the patient and mental health professionals engendered by the planning process is a key ingredient. My personal experience, having negotiated a fair number of joint crisis plans, was that I tended to establish a deeper kind of relationship with the patients involved. I felt I knew them much better and that they trusted me more. Even when circumstances did not permit the terms of the plan to be followed, the relationship could be quite easily salvaged.

Reducing coercive measures on hospital wards

A number of studies, though non-controlled and instead relying on 'before versus after' comparisons, have suggested that the use of seclusion on psychiatric wards can be significantly reduced. The interventions have been varied, multiple, and usually involved changes to the wider system of care—for example, policy changes specifically aimed at reducing seclusion; monitoring and analysing episodes that have resulted in seclusion; strengthening clinical leadership; staff education in methods of defusing tense situations that may lead to violence; changing the ward environment; increasing staff-to-patient ratios; creating special emergency response teams; and treating patients as active participants in interventions to reduce the likelihood of seclusion.[12] There is also evidence that similar measures can achieve a reduction in the use of restraint.[13] A study in which a focused intervention attempted to increase the involvement of inpatients in planning their treatment did not affect the 'perceived coercion' experienced by the patients.

Recently, a large 'cluster' randomized controlled trial involving 31 wards at 15 hospitals, that aimed at changing the ward nursing teams' attitudes and the ways in which they related to the patients reported a significant reduction in coercive interventions.[14]

An important study from Germany that examined the rates of inpatient suicide and absconding from 21 psychiatric hospitals over a 15-year period from 1998 to 2012 found that there were no differences in the rates when 'open' and 'locked' wards were compared.[15] The statistics though were complex, and the extent to which the findings can be generalized to other countries is unclear. Given that the suicide rate in the study was less than one in 1000 admissions, and absconding was about 2 per cent, one wonders how it is justified to place all inpatients on locked wards? (Voluntary patients are allowed out but someone, usually a nurse, must unlock the door for them.) In some countries, England being an example, it has become increasingly common for wards to be locked. A reduction in bed numbers and an increasing proportion of inpatients on a compulsory order play an important role; as does the reputational risk to the hospital of a serious incident in a highly risk-averse society. Comparing countries, custom and convention seem to play a large part in accounting for the significant variation in policies concerning locked wards.

The dearth of strong studies on coercive interventions in both hospitals and the community is very disappointing.

References

1. **Priebe S, Katsakou C, Amos T, et al.** Patients' views and readmissions 1 year after involuntary hospitalisation. *British Journal of Psychiatry* 2009; **194**:49–54.
2. **Katsakou C, Rose D, Amos T, et al.** Psychiatric patients' views on why their involuntary hospitalisation was right or wrong: a qualitative study. *Social Psychiatry and Psychiatric Epidemiology* 2012; **47**:1169–1179.
3. **Lidz CW, Hoge SK, Gardner W, et al.** Perceived coercion in mental hospital admission. Pressures and process. *Archives of General Psychiatry* 1995; **52**:1034–1039.
4. **MacArthur Research Network on Mental Health and the Law.** *The MacArthur Coercion Study: May 2004 Update of the Executive Summary.* 2004. http://www.macarthur.virginia.edu/coercion.html

5. **Henderson C, Flood C, Leese M, Thornicroft G, Sutherby K, Szmukler G.** Effect of joint crisis plans on use of compulsory treatment in psychiatry: single blind randomised controlled trial. *British Medical Journal* 2004; **329**:136.
6. **Thornicroft G, Farrelly S, Szmukler G**, et al. Clinical outcomes of joint crisis plans to reduce compulsory treatment for people with psychosis: a randomised controlled trial. *Lancet* 2013; **381**:1634–1641.
7. **Borschmann R, Barrett B, Hellier JM**, et al. Joint crisis plans for people with borderline personality disorder: feasibility and outcomes in a randomised controlled trial. *British Journal of Psychiatry* 2013; **202**:357–364.
8. **Ruchlewska A, Wierdsma AI, Kamperman AM**, et al. Effect of crisis plans on admissions and emergency visits: a randomized controlled trial. *PLoS ONE* 2014; **9**:e91882.
9. **de Jong MH, Kamperman AM, Oorshot M**, et al. Interventions to reduce compulsory psychiatric admissions: a systematic review and meta-analysis. *JAMA Psychiatry* 2016; **73**:657–664.
10. **Swanson JW, Swartz MS, Elbogen EB**, et al. Facilitated psychiatric advance directives: a randomized trial of an intervention to foster advance treatment planning among persons with severe mental illness. *American Journal of Psychiatry* 2006; **163**:1943–1951.
11. **Swanson JW, Swartz MS, Elbogen EB**, et al. Psychiatric advance directives and reduction of coercive crisis interventions. *Journal of Mental Health* 2008; **17**:255–267.
12. **Gaskin CJ, Elsom SJ, Happell B.** Interventions for reducing the use of seclusion in psychiatric facilities: review of the literature. *British Journal of Psychiatry* 2007; **191**:298–303.
13. **Hellerstein DJ, Staub AB, Lequesne E.** Decreasing the use of restraint and seclusion among psychiatric inpatients. *Journal of Psychiatric Practice* 2007; **13**:308–317.
14. **Bowers L, James K, Quirk A, Simpson A**, et al. Reducing conflict and containment rates on acute psychiatric wards: the Safewards cluster randomised controlled trial. *International Journal of Nursing Studies* 2015; **52**:1412–1422.
15. **Huber C, Scneeberger A, Kowalinski E**, et al. Suicide risk and absconding in psychiatric hospitals with and without open door policies: a 15 year, observational study. *Lancet Psychiatry* 2016; **3**:842–849.

Part IV

How practice would change

Chapter 11

'Mental disorder' and public protection

In the next two chapters, I shall look at some significant changes in medical practice that would follow the adoption of the Fusion Law proposal. In this chapter, I shall examine the intersection between the Fusion Law and the criminal justice system. In many discussions with forensic colleagues about the Fusion Law, the question usually arises of how 'mentally disordered offenders' would fare under this approach. I shall also comment briefly on involuntary treatment of persons with addictions.

Protection, preventive detention, and treatment

Two types of criticism have been levelled at the 'fusion' proposal in respect of its interaction with the criminal justice system. First, that there would be inadequate protections of other people from dangerous persons with mental disorders; second, that some offenders with mental disorders, even if they retain capacity, would be much better off in a hospital than in a prison environment.

However, before addressing these issues, let's look at preventive detention in medicine outside psychiatry. A number of people have pointed to another group of patients who can also be lawfully detained if presenting a risk to others—those with infectious diseases.

Preventive detention for infectious disease and discrimination

Indeed there is legislation permitting the detention of persons with infectious disease to protect others[1] (though it is used rarely in England—five times in 2012–2013; seven in 2013–2014). The wide-ranging powers to do so are currently subject to criticism, but that is not the issue for us here. What concerns us is whether this is discriminatory in the same way as involuntary detention for the protection of others in mental health care (as I have argued in Chapter 5).

In fact, I agree that the case for infectious diseases is not discriminatory in the same way as it is for those with a mental illness. This is because there is no category of persons *within* the group of those who present a risk to others by virtue of their infectiousness who are singled out for detention. All persons who present an equal risk due to their infectiousness are equally liable to be detained. That is, there is no law that authorizes detention only of a category of those who are infectious—for example, those who are drug dependent or who are homeless or who have a mental disorder. This is quite different to the situation in respect of people who present a danger to others by virtue of their apparent potential for violence. Imagine that we knew everyone in the community who has exceeded a particular threshold of risk of violence to others. Of this group of 'risky' people, it is only those with a 'mental disorder'—not, for example, those who are habitually short-tempered, aggressive when drunk, or who regularly assault their partners—who are a priori singled out as subject to preventive detention (under civil commitment legislation), even when no offence has been committed. It is the formalized unequal treatment of people who pose an equal risk for violence that constitutes the discrimination (and contrasts with the equal treatment, in theory at least, of all people who pose an equal risk of being infectious).

Some people claim that a preventive intervention for dangerous people with a mental disorder is not discriminatory because it is appropriate to allow autonomy to be restricted, proportionately, when someone presents a risk to others.[2] However, they fail to use the right comparator. For a person with a mental disorder who has decision-making capability and who presents a significant risk to others, the right comparator is a person who presents the same level of risk but who does not have a mental disorder (and presumably has decision-making capability). Both have the same ability to appreciate what is at stake regarding the potential consequences of their behaviour. If preventive interventions are thus restricted only to those with a mental disorder, this is again clearly discriminatory.

I said in Chapter 5 that non-discrimination in relation to the risk of violence to others could only be ensured through generic dangerousness legislation—or through no preventive detention, including none for people with mental illness. It is the level of risk that would determine that an intervention is required—not the assignment of the person to a particular category (for example, the 'mentally disordered') within the larger group of those who present such a risk.

In fact, some countries have introduced laws permitting a range of preventive sentence options. In England and Wales, for example, there are 'discretionary life sentences' and 'extended sentences' available for those convicted of specified categories of serious offence and who are deemed to pose a risk.[3] There are thus means for protecting the public (in England at least) that are not discriminatory. I do not necessarily support preventive detention of this type, but at least it offers the possibility of non-discriminatory preventive detention if that is what we are to have.

Protection from dangerous people with a 'mental disorder'

I present examples of two fairly common types of case that may arise.

James

James was 42 years old when he suffocated his wife, Maria, with a pillow while she was in an induced sleep caused by a spiked drink he had given her earlier.

Since his late teens he had suffered severe mood swings, both 'highs' and 'lows', and was diagnosed as having a 'bipolar disorder' (previously called a 'manic-depressive illness'). Despite these, he did well at university and graduated with a good degree in engineering. Since then, he had been employed by a car manufacturing company and was regularly commended for his work and promoted to a middle-grade managerial level. There was no history of antisocial behaviour, violence, or drug or alcohol abuse. They had no children, partly because James was worried about transmitting his illness. James' father was a wealthy businessman who died as a result of suicide when James was 16. His mother, who died when James was 34, had a family history of depression affecting two uncles. Maria came from a humble family in the Philippines. James met her there when he was in his mid-thirties and they had now been married for 5 years. Maria was 10 years younger than James and was a shy and submissive woman. She did not work and had no friends of her own.

Since the age of 38, James had experienced two severe episodes of depression, both of which had required hospitalization, each for around 6 weeks. Four weeks before the tragic event James had become progressively severely depressed again. He developed the delusional idea that he was about to suffer a 'catastrophic end' as a punishment for 'grievous sins' he had committed in the past. Knowing he was soon to die in some kind of 'horrific' manner, he became consumed with worry about what would happen to his friendless, isolated, and dependent wife. He decided to kill her so she would not suffer these horrible events, and then to kill himself before the catastrophe was to overtake them.

Immediately after killing Maria, James threw himself in front of a train at his local station, but somehow survived. Although he suffered multiple fractures and required the amputation of a leg, he did not incur a serious head injury.

Cheryl

Cheryl was convicted of arson when she was 27 years old.

Her childhood was characterized by physical and emotional abuse from her drug-dependent mother. She never knew her father. Although she was regarded by her teachers as a bright girl, she did badly at school and left with no qualifications. During her teens she fell in with some bad company and was charged and convicted on a number of occasions for disturbing the peace and theft, but never received a custodial sentence. There had been no arrests since she was 20 years of age. Cheryl started self-harming when she was 15 years old. Numerous scars from transverse cuts disfigured her arms and legs. She had also taken many drug overdoses, one of which could have been lethal if she had not been discovered, unconscious, by a man walking in the park with his dog. She occasionally indulged in binge drinking, when she could become abusive, but was not a regular drinker or a regular abuser of drugs.

Cheryl had no stable relationships. There were some brief affairs with older men who invariably abused her. She had a number of brief jobs as a shop assistant, but they usually ended following an argument about her timekeeping or her short temper and abusive language.

At the time of the arson offence, Cheryl had been under the care of her local mental health services for 5 years. Her diagnosis was 'Borderline Personality Disorder'. The features supporting this diagnosis included overwhelming feelings of distress or rage; intense, highly changeable moods; difficulty managing such feelings without self-harming or binge drinking; stormy relationships with others; impulsive behaviours such as engaging in unsafe sex; chronic feelings of emptiness; a fear of abandonment; losing touch with reality, especially when under stress; and occasionally threatening others. Cheryl had at times shown all of these behaviours. There had been numerous visits to hospital accident and emergency departments following overdoses and self-mutilation. She had been admitted to psychiatric wards on three occasions. Twice there were brief stays of a few days after which she had discharged herself following complaints that staff did not care about her. The third admission was on an involuntary treatment order following the serious suicide attempt mentioned earlier. This admission lasted 3 months. For the first month, Cheryl continued to make attempts at self-harm—usually by cutting with pieces of glass or any other sharp object she could find—and for much of this time required 'one-to-one' nursing care to stop these attempts. Gradually Cheryl became more settled, but throughout her admission was not keen on engaging with staff in any kind of psychological intervention. Often, staff were criticized by her as not really caring.

Before discharge she was referred to a community mental health team. A highly experienced community nurse, Joy, who shared a similar social background to Cheryl's, was allocated to be her primary care worker and started to visit her while she was still in hospital. Cheryl agreed to continue seeing Joy after discharge. The consultant psychiatrist said he would also see her, initially, every 2 weeks. A hostel place was arranged, as Cheryl had no permanent accommodation. A referral, with Cheryl's agreement, to a day centre run by a voluntary organization was also made and she was accepted. At the time of discharge Cheryl was not self-harming, but remained surly and critical of hospital staff for much of the time. No medication was prescribed.

Following discharge, Cheryl infrequently kept her appointments with Joy or the consultant. On most occasions when Joy had arranged an agreed time and day to visit Cheryl at her hostel, Cheryl was not there. The hostel manager, while sympathetic to Cheryl, found her 'a handful'. Cheryl managed to attend one out of four appointments to see the psychiatrist. During this visit she was quite agreeable, but complained that the help she was receiving was poor. Weekly sessions with Joy—many of which Cheryl missed—were, she complained, 'not really enough'. Following a visit to the day centre, Cheryl decided it was not for her—'they just sit around and talk; it's not what I need. I need people who really care about me and really want to help'. Cheryl had sent threatening letters to a charge nurse at the hospital and later one to Joy saying they had shown her 'no respect' and that they had 'better watch out as something very bad could happen' to them.

Six months after her discharge from hospital, late one night, Cheryl threw a lighted petrol-soaked cloth through a broken window of the community mental health clinic building, immediately setting an office alight. A neighbour, hearing the shattering of glass, called the fire brigade. Two rooms and the adjoining corridor were burnt out. Cheryl had been seen in the vicinity by the neighbour and she was arrested in the early hours of the morning.

Cheryl was later found guilty of arson endangering life. Adjacent to the community mental health centre, on each side, were residential buildings.

I shall come back to James and Cheryl after first discussing the implications of the principles of the 'fusion' proposal in forensic cases.

Currently, in many places, including England, a person with a mental disorder who has committed an offence can be detained in hospital and treated involuntarily under a court order for an indefinite period (but, of course, subject to reviews and with the possibility of appeals). Furthermore, if that person is regarded as particularly risky, a 'restriction order' can be imposed that allows the person to be recalled to hospital following discharge if certain conditions imposed on the person are breached. Such 'mentally disordered offenders' almost always spend much more time in detention—sometimes hugely more time—than non-mentally disordered offenders who have committed a similar offence.

How the Fusion Law would deal with such cases

In the 'fusion' proposal, there would be two options for the court when a person with an impairment or disturbance of mental functioning has committed a serious offence, and when that person has impaired decision-making capability and involuntary treatment is in that person's best interests (that is, accords with the best interpretation of their will and preferences). You will recall from the explanation in Chapter 6 that if the person retains decision-making capability, involuntary treatment is ruled out. Such a person can decide to have treatment on a voluntary basis if such a treatment is offered; otherwise they would suffer the same penalty as a person with no mental disorder. The two options are as follows:

1. *Hospital order:* a compulsory hospital treatment order on exactly the same basis as for a person who has not committed an offence. That is, the person would be discharged on the basis of a medical decision as would a non-offender, when well enough; or the person could discharge themselves, if they did not wish to continue treatment on a voluntary basis, when their decision-making capability had been restored.
2. *Hospital-prison sentence:* a sentence, the duration of which is determined by the seriousness of the offence and comparable to that imposed on a non-mentally disordered person who has committed a similar offence; then there would be a number of possibilities:
    a. Involuntary hospital treatment for the person who lacks decision-making capability until he or she regains it, when they might continue as a voluntary patient.
    b. If, when decision-making capability has been recovered, the person were to decide against further treatment, a transfer to prison for the remainder of the sentence would occur.
    c. If at the end of the sentence, the hospitalized person were still to lack decision-making capability and treatment were in their best interests, an ordinary civil involuntary treatment order

would be appropriate if the person were to refuse treatment on a voluntary basis.

d. This type of order could be applied to an offender *with* decision-making capability who had a mental disorder for which a treatment were available, and who accepted that treatment voluntarily. If the offender were to change their mind, or if the treatment were to be completed before the termination of term of the sentence, they would be returned to prison.

Importantly, under the 'fusion' proposal, there would not be a long-term—possibly life-long—'restriction order' allowing the person to be recalled to hospital if certain conditions were breached. As I mentioned earlier, a non-discriminatory equivalent does exist in some jurisdictions, England and Wales being an example. Discharge of those under a *hospital-prison sentence* from hospital or from prison would not mean that a person deemed by the court to be a continuing risk would be discharged with no further ado. In jurisdictions permitting 'extended sentences' or 'discretionary life sentences' for people who have committed a serious violent offence and who are considered to pose a continuing risk, such sentences would apply equally to offenders with or without a mental disorder. They would apply to people sentenced under option 2 listed. An extended sentence means that the person will subsequently be under some form of supervision in the community for an extended period of time following discharge from hospital or release from prison. In the case of a life sentence, such supervision in the community is life-long. The total period of the sentence covering hospital treatment, time in prison, and time in community supervision post discharge will be the same as for a person who has committed the same offence and is deemed dangerous but does not have a mental disorder. This is why it is non-discriminatory.

Such continuing compulsory supervision in the community, however, would not, on its own, be able to compel treatment. A number of conditions can be imposed, one of which could be that the person must be regularly monitored. Prompt action could then be taken if there were signs of a relapse of illness. This could be a mental health assessment to determine whether the criteria for detention and compulsory treatment were met. Or if there was evidence of increasingly risky behaviour, this could prompt a return to the court and an appropriate disposal. In effect, this is a type of 'restriction order'—but one that is non-discriminatory as such supervision is applicable to all offenders similarly sentenced, whether or not they have a mental disorder.

A problem that could arise in relation to extended sentences concerns the weight that might be given in the court's assessment of risk to the presence of a 'mental disorder'. It may be that the court will rate the risk as higher in someone with a mental disorder simply because the person is categorized as having such a disorder. This would constitute a form of 'indirect discrimination' (as discussed in Chapter 8). Given the common stereotype of people with a mental illness as being dangerous, it would not be surprising if this were to occur. Much attention will thus need to be given to the nature of risk assessments under such a regime and attempts made to ensure that they are as objective as possible and that prejudicial stereotypes do not intrude.

So, what then would these considerations mean for James and Cheryl?

James

Under existing law in England and Wales—and as would occur in many other jurisdictions—James was placed on a court-ordered remand in a secure psychiatric hospital until his case was heard. At trial he was found guilty of 'manslaughter with diminished responsibility' and was transferred under the Mental Health Act for an indeterminate period to a secure hospital, together with a 'restriction order'. The restriction order meant that the Ministry of Justice determined when James could be discharged, conditionally and then fully. However, he could appeal to a Mental Health Review Tribunal. In fact, he spent 3 years in a medium secure hospital and was then transferred to an ordinary psychiatric ward where he spent another year, and then was conditionally discharged to the community. He was not fully discharged for another 4 years.

While on remand he was treated with antidepressant and antipsychotic medications and by the time of his court case his psychotic symptoms were improved. He became aware of the enormity of what he had done and was deeply remorseful. After a year he was no longer clinically depressed but continued to be distressed and remorseful. He was determined to not suffer any further relapses and engaged in all forms of therapy that were offered. He was quite well during the final years on his order.

If James were to have been considered as posing a continuing significant risk to others (or himself), he could have been on an involuntary order for very much longer.

Under the 'fusion' proposal, his management would be different. Immediately after the offence he would have been found to lack decision-making capability and would have also been transferred on remand to a psychiatric unit where he could be treated involuntarily if it were necessary in his best interests. Following a conviction of 'manslaughter with diminished responsibility' the court would have two options:

A hospital order: if we assume he still lacked decision-making capability for treatment and treatment was in his best interests according to the best interpretation of his will and preferences, he could be transferred to a psychiatric unit for involuntary treatment under the same terms as would occur under a civil involuntary order. Discharge would be up to his responsible clinician. He could not be treated involuntarily after his decision-making capability had been restored. To remain in hospital he would have to agree to do so voluntarily. There would be no legal powers to demand his attendance for any aftercare arrangements. It is very likely that James would under these conditions have been discharged from hospital after about a year, for some of which time he would have been a voluntary patient. A great deal of his treatment involved helping him to come to terms with and cope with what he had done. There is little doubt he would have engaged with aftercare services. He would have done anything to avoid a recurrence. However, given the gravity of his offence, this option would probably not be judged appropriate.

A hospital-prison sentence: adopting this option, the court would impose a sentence proportionate to the seriousness of the offence. For a homicide this could be for a term up to a life sentence. A manslaughter-diminished responsibility verdict gives the judge a large degree of discretion in sentencing. Given that James's offence was a homicide, even in the absence of any previous history of violence, the sentence could be as long as 10 years, but probably shorter, nearer to 5 years. If we assume again he still lacked decision-making capability, he could be transferred initially to a psychiatric unit for involuntary treatment. Following recovery of decision-making capability, he would have to stay in hospital as a voluntary patient or be transferred to prison. Again, I think he would probably have stayed as a voluntary patient for at least a year, probably longer as he would be faced with transfer to prison while still under his sentence. Transfer to prison would then occur unless he was released under supervision on probation. Treatment could not be imposed under a probation order, but he would need to meet the conditions of probation. James would be required to meet his probation officer regularly and his mental state could be closely monitored. If there were signs of relapse, he could be urgently referred for a mental health assessment. If James showed his willingness to comply with ongoing psychiatric treatment, it might increase his chances of release on probation. (If we think back to the difference between a 'threat' and an 'offer', this would be an offer since the moral baseline would be prison.) Probation would continue until the end of his sentence.

Cheryl

Under existing law in England and Wales, Cheryl was placed in prison on remand. Her behaviour there was unproblematic. At trial she was convicted of arson and a hospital order with restrictions was imposed. She was transferred to a high secure hospital where she spent 8 years.

Under the 'fusion' approach, if she were to lack decision-making capability, remand arrangements would be as for James. If she had decision-making capability, a remand placement in a hospital would depend on whether this would help to determine whether there might be a treatment that would benefit her and, if there was one, whether she would accept it voluntarily. Otherwise she would be remanded to prison. At the trial stage she would very likely be found to have decision-making capability. Given the seriousness of her offence and the long-standing nature of her problems, she would very likely be given an ordinary fixed-term prison sentence appropriate for the offence. Alternatively, if it were deemed that treatment in a psychiatric unit might offer benefit, she could be given a hospital-prison sentence for the same length of time, but with hospital treatment being on a voluntary basis. The rest of the sentence would be spent in prison. Even if Cheryl received an ordinary prison sentence but became ill during her imprisonment, she could be transferred to hospital under a separate hospital order. Cheryl would be eligible for probation in the usual way.

Some of my forensic psychiatrist colleagues have been concerned that the 'fusion' approach to these matters leans too much towards the principles of the criminal justice system without paying sufficient regard to the beneficent principles of the health system. This applies especially to the ability of persons with decision-making capability to refuse psychiatric treatment and to opt for prison instead. They argue that prison is a poor environment for someone with a mental illness. It may not please me that prison might be their choice, but the self-determination of people with decision-making capability should be respected. Some people might prefer prison to a secure or medium-secure hospital. Though I personally hope this would not be the case, they might decide that in some way they would be better off in prison. The stigma of a mental illness might prove to be a factor.

In relation to the unsuitability of prison for people with a mental illness (who retain decision-making capability), we should recall some principles set out in the United Nations (UN) Convention on the Rights of Persons with Disabilities. Of special relevance here is the need for the state to make reasonable accommodations to minimize the extent to which impairments become disabilities. Prisons should thus be expected to make appropriate provisions for persons with mental health disabilities.

'Fitness to plead' and 'not guilty by reason of insanity'

In Chapter 6, I noted problems associated with these 'mental condition defences'—'unfit to plead' and 'not guilty by reason of insanity'. I believe that it is almost inevitable that at some points where they intersect, the different perspectives on human conduct from healthcare (therapeutic values) and criminal justice (legal principles) will not allow a tidy reconciliation. The problem resides just as much with the criminal law as with health law. As we have seen in Chapter 8, from the viewpoint of the UN Committee for the Convention on the Rights of Persons with Disabilities, the legal structure requires complete dismantling and rebuilding—there is no place for 'fitness to plead' or 'not guilty by reason of insanity'. The Committee states that any laws relating to deprivation of liberty must remove 'mental disability' as a determining factor. Thus, if a deprivation of liberty is to occur, the grounds must be de-linked from mental disability and be neutrally defined so as to apply to all persons on an equal basis. As I discussed in Chapter 8, what this would mean in practice is thus far quite unclear.[4] One pointer though could be instituted now: providing support for the defendant through the trial process. This might indeed suffice to make the person fit to stand trial.

For the moment I will go along with the long-established view that there is validity to the 'mental condition' defences. People deemed 'unfit to plead', that is, unfit to be tried in a court because they do not have the abilities required to contribute to their defence, or found not guilty by reason of insanity at the time of the offence, cannot be convicted and thus in the majority of jurisdictions cannot be imprisoned as they are technically 'not guilty'.

Thus the potential problem that arises here concerns the person with a mental impairment who is deemed dangerous, who, on the one hand, now has decision-making capability and who therefore cannot be subject under the 'fusion' approach to an involuntary treatment order, and who, on the other hand, at the same time cannot be sentenced under the criminal justice system because they cannot be convicted—even if found to have committed a serious offence on a 'trial of the facts'.

My colleagues and I, in formulating the Fusion Law, accepted reluctantly, as a stop-gap measure, that detention and treatment even of a person with decision-making capability could occur provided certain conditions were met (see Chapter 6). Let's see how this could be applied to James:

It would perhaps have been possible for James to have been found 'not guilty by reason of insanity'. Under English law, and in many other places, this requires that as a result of a 'defect of reason' due to a 'disease of the mind' the offender 'did not know what he was doing or, if he did know, he did not know that the act was wrong' (known as the M'Naghten rules). If the plea were successful, this could have meant indefinite detention in a secure hospital. Such a plea is rare because of the long-term detention and the stigma.

Under the compromise proposed in the 'fusion' approach, James could have been detained in hospital following such a verdict, even if he had now recovered decision-making capability. This would be permitted if (1) he had committed a serious offence—which he clearly had; (2) a serious mental impairment or disturbance has contributed significantly to that conduct—it clearly had; and (3) an effective treatment can be offered that could be expected to reduce the risk of that disorder's reoccurrence—there was. A time limit would be set for any such hospitalization, commensurate with the seriousness of the offence.

However, a more satisfactory solution needs to be found, one where all equally dangerous people are treated equally—assuming we can accurately forecast who is likely to be dangerous. As I have previously noted, one possibility is that such people could be detained and managed under a generic 'dangerousness' or 'preventive detention' law where *any* person deemed to be dangerous could be detained or subject to special supervision, regardless of the cause of their dangerousness. However, as I have mentioned previously, many of us are troubled by the idea of preventive detention. Another possibility might be a form of compulsory community supervision order that can be reconciled in law with an offence having been committed but with a non-conviction. Indications of a possible relapse would trigger a referral for a mental health assessment, and if the criteria for involuntary treatment were met, a civil compulsory treatment order could be made if the person were to reject voluntary treatment. Such a supervision order would need to be for a definite term, proportional to the sentence that would normally be given for the offence committed.

'Mad' versus 'bad'

Though I would have preferred it, I don't think I can avoid some discussion of the 'mad' versus 'bad' distinction that is often postulated when it comes to particularly brutal offences. How would the Fusion Law deal with this problem?

This is the sort of person who provokes controversy:

Trevor

Trevor, aged 35 years, viciously assaulted, using an iron bar, and robbed a 50-year-old woman after forcing entry into her home when she answered his knock at her front door. She was left unconscious with a fractured skull, causing a haemorrhage around the brain.

Trevor came from a disrupted home and was received into care from the age of 5 years. He truanted from school and left with no qualifications. He was a regular offender from the age of 13 and was sentenced to a youth detention centre when aged 15. From the age of 18 he had spent most of his life in prison. His many offences included dishonesty, robbery, possession of a firearm, malicious wounding, wounding with intent, and burglary. The longest prison sentence was 7 years. On a number of occasions he had been violent in prison as a result of which he forfeited remission. He was, however, out of prison during the year before the current offence.

From the age of 16 years Trevor had regularly misused drugs, especially stimulants, latterly mainly 'crack cocaine'. He was admitted to a drug dependency unit when he was 20, but discharged himself after 2 days. At times he appeared to have had brief paranoid psychotic episodes, most likely related to his drug use.

Trevor had no contact with any family members nor did he have any close friends. He had never held a job for more than a few weeks and all his jobs had been unskilled.

Over the previous 2 years, Trevor had had intermittent contact first, with a community mental health team, and over the previous year with a specialist forensic community team. The diagnosis was of an 'antisocial personality disorder' with 'psychopathic traits' and substance abuse. Usually when seeing staff he presented as an intelligent, pleasant and cooperative man, even quite charming, and apparently grateful for the help being offered. But at the same time, he appeared cold, lacking in empathy for others, and was generally unremorseful for his violence or dishonesty. He rarely accepted responsibility for his behaviour and was quick to blame others for his difficulties. He kept most of his appointments. Reports from other agencies such as probation and social services with which he had contact revealed that he lied to the mental health teams about many aspects of his past history and his life. It was clear from those reports that at times he could be very intimidating and had been violent on occasions during the previous year, possibly in association with drug use.

When interviewed by a psychiatrist after the current offence, he showed little remorse. He admitted that the attack on the woman 'got out of hand'—he said he was sorry, but went on to say that she had earlier that day been 'offensive, treated me like scum' and had 'basically asked for it'. There was no evidence of psychosis at the time.

Trevor's history is fairly typical of what is called 'psychopathy'. So-called psychopaths form a subset of people with an 'antisocial personality'—that is, people who repeatedly behave in an antisocial manner (indeed, essentially a tautology). An influential authority, Robert Hare, has produced a checklist of symptoms characterizing 'psychopathy'.[5] These include callousness and lack of empathy; a lack of remorse and guilt; a glib and superficial charm; grandiose self-worth; lying; conning and manipulativeness; a need for stimulation and proneness to boredom; irresponsibility; a failure to accept responsibility for one's own actions; impulsivity; many short-term relationships; and an inability to plan for the future. These features certainly characterize those with these traits who come to the attention of the criminal justice system. However, there are probably many people with 'psychopathic traits' who are successful in business or in the professions, who are able to plan their careers well, but show the lack of empathy and callousness that typify the group I am talking about. The reader no doubt knows some.

Serious offenders with psychopathic traits are usually sent to prison, but some may be placed by the courts on a hospital order in a secure or medium-secure psychiatric unit for an indefinite period.

When it comes to people like Trevor, the question is often posed: is 'psychopathy' a mental disorder? Surely, many people say, 'psychopaths' cannot be mentally 'normal'. Can such a person be regarded as 'responsible' for their brutal acts? Wouldn't a hospital be a more appropriate place than prison for such a person?

I do not intend to discuss the immensely complex question of criminal responsibility in this book. Our primary interest is in treatment and when it is justified to make it involuntary. This question may arise whether the person is deemed responsible (and usually now in prison) or not responsible (and perhaps in a secure hospital).

It is possible to argue that people with psychopathy suffer from a 'mental disorder'. The abnormality most discussed in such people is a lack of empathy for others (or an inability to put themselves in another person's shoes, to have a sense of what they must be feeling). It is this lack of empathy that leads to their inability to have what we could call a 'moral sense' (or to have 'moral rationality'); callousness and remorselessness would be obvious consequences of such an 'impairment'. We could draw an analogy with intellectual disability. Just as people with an intellectual disability have impaired cognitive abilities, so, some might say, people with 'psychopathy' have impaired 'moral abilities'. In fact, in the nineteenth century, some psychiatrists called the disorder 'moral insanity', a condition entirely unrelated to the intellect, which was usually unaffected. We can easily see why this term was adopted. What makes many authorities uncomfortable about calling 'psychopathy' a mental disorder is the prominence of value judgements in ascribing the 'symptoms'. They are largely antisocial attitudes and behaviours—that is, ones that are socially unacceptable.

'Psychopathy' under the Fusion Law proposal

How would the 'fusion' proposal play out when psychopathy is associated with a serious offence? Would involuntary treatment be possible? How would the determination of decision-making capability and best interests (or best interpretation of will and preferences) be handled?

Let's take Trevor as an illustrative example. Let's assume, for argument's sake, that first, 'psychopathy' is a mental impairment that amounts to a 'disorder', and second, that there is an appropriate treatment that constitutes more than custodial 'care' to prevent further offending. (We will come back to these assumptions later.) Without a disorder and a treatment, an assessment of *treatment* decision-making is an empty notion. Could we see Trevor as having an impairment of decision-making capability?

Decision-making capability: let's start with the conventional assessment criteria. I doubt Trevor would have any difficulty in 'understanding' and 'retaining' any facts offered to him, in an intellectual sense at least, about the nature of his disorder (or problem)—that is, his 'diagnosis' of 'psychopathy' and why this fitted in his case, and about the possible treatment options (for example, some kind of psychotherapy or 'talking treatment'). It is when we come to the ability to 'use or weigh' the information that doubts may start to creep in. What if Trevor cannot understand, in a personal experiential sense, why people behave in a moral way; to him all transactions with others are seen as simply instrumental, serving only his own needs and interests. Could he then truly 'appreciate' the relevance of the information given to him for the predicament he finds himself in? Can he believe something about people's subjectivities that he has never experienced himself? Can he understand in this sense why he should be blamed for acting in ways that he does not, and cannot, feel are wrong, but others do? On the other hand, he would presumably recognize that there are laws that society expects people to observe, whether they agree with them or not. And furthermore that there are unwritten social rules and expectations that nearly everyone else cares deeply about. Most likely, those rules will have been pointed out to him many times since early childhood—perhaps in his mind, too many times. While he may not fully see the sense of those rules and why they should apply to him, nevertheless it is likely that he could give an accurate account of how he should behave if he were to observe those rules. Jonathan Glover's fascinating series of interviews with offender patients detained in the famous Broadmoor high-security psychiatric hospital that aimed to explore their moral thinking supports this view.[6]

I think we would probably conclude, on balance, that Trevor does have decision-making capability using the criteria of the standard test. However, as I described earlier, in the more difficult cases we should look at the person's beliefs and values to determine whether there might have been some kind of disruption in the 'coherence' of Trevor's beliefs and values (or will and preferences) that might undermine his decision-making capability. Finding such a disruption would be, I suspect, very unlikely. Trevor's beliefs and values, though not in accord with our normal social values, have been consistent over time and accord with his life choices—for example, that 'violence is a legitimate means of achieving one's ends, as are deceit and theft'; and 'one's self-interest overrides that of others, even if that causes them distress or pain'. Again, on the basis of an 'interpretation' (as discussed in Chapter 8) it is unlikely that Trevor would be assessed as having significantly impaired decision-making capability.

'Best interests': but let's go a little further. What if Trevor were judged to lack decision-making capability, perhaps on the basis of the depth of his inability to 'appreciate' the nature of a 'moral sense'? There is, in fact, thus far no proven effective treatment that could be offered. An ineffective treatment couldn't be in his 'best interests' (or able to give effect to his 'authentic' will and preferences—which in his case become especially difficult notions). A treatment, almost certainly of a psychological variety, that might have worked with a small number of people in the past, might be offered by an enthusiastic proponent. Given the considerable uncertainty about its effectiveness, this could presumably only be given on a voluntary basis. Trevor would need to go into the treatment knowing there was a high likelihood that it would not work, and that it would require a strong commitment on his part.

But let's go a little further still. What if there were an effective treatment? Let me introduce a little 'thought experiment' at this point. What if my neuroscientist colleagues came up with a new drug that acted on a social attachment hormone system and somewhat miraculously produced a substantial enhancement of empathy in people with psychopathic traits? Let's say it could be given weekly by intramuscular injection. Thus we could be sure that the drug was being absorbed and able to act. If we were to decide that Trevor lacked treatment decision-making capability—say, because of his life-long 'impairment' in being able to really appreciate or believe that we are normally responsive to moral reasons—would we be justified in forcing Trevor to take such a drug against his will? Would it be in his 'best interests'? Or would it be only in the interests of others, who would be spared the serious harms incurred through his antisocial behaviour? Let's apply our tests of 'best interests'. Would the treatment give effect to Trevor's real or 'authentic' values? The answer would seem to be 'no'; in fact it would aim to change them. On all the evidence, his values to date have been consistently and coherently antisocial. Would Trevor have chosen the treatment if he had had decision-making capability at some point in the past? Perhaps this might have been possible in the context of an unusually supportive relationship, an example of 'relational autonomy'. This is a difficult question. We couldn't be certain about his attitude to the new treatment if he had never had the opportunity to reflect upon it or because he could not have imagined being the 'different' person the treatment could make him. Would there be reason to believe, perhaps based on things he had said or done in the past, that his values might have changed if he had had the opportunity to learn then about what the treatment might achieve? Perhaps, knowing that such a transformation of his subjectivity was a possibility, he might have valued a more stable lifestyle and finding a way of spending less time in prison. I imagine this would be extremely difficult to establish.

We could revert again to the analogy with an intellectual disability. What if a drug were discovered that substantially enhanced the cognitive abilities of people with an intellectual disability? In both cases the person—I am only considering adults here—would have substantial difficulty in imagining how their lives would be transformed by an alteration of a fundamental aspect of their being—intellectual on the one hand, moral on the other. Would we give an enhancer with a large effect to such people, not knowing what the impact on their minds and lives might be? Would we be justified in giving it against the person's will? I suspect not. It would be an interesting subject for debate if ever such a treatment was discovered, but perhaps we have wandered into too theoretical a place for now.

We have gone through a fairly complex web of ideas in trying to understand whether we could justify treating Trevor involuntarily, in his *own* interests, even if there were a treatment. The answer seems to be 'no'. A completely different set of considerations would be involved in deciding whether Trevor should be subject to preventive detention to stop further violent offences. I have argued that whether he has a mental disorder or not is irrelevant to whether he should be thus detained. The critical consideration must be the risk of future violence. Detention would be based on sentencing for the crimes committed, as well as possible recourse to the options for extended sentences that can be adopted where the offender is deemed to pose an on-going serious risk to others. If during the course of imprisonment Trevor were to decide voluntarily to take up the offer of a new treatment or if he were to develop a mental disturbance for which there were a psychiatric treatment, transfer to a psychiatric unit or a special prison-based unit should be possible.

Involuntary treatment and addictions

Many countries have legislation that permits the involuntary treatment of persons with addictions. Some, like the United Kingdom, do not allow this. However, most countries that do have such legislation use it rarely. An egregious exception to infrequent use is in South East Asia where an abusive punitive approach that violates human rights is common in some countries.[7] The evidence to date is that compulsory (or forced) treatment for addiction, beyond acute interventions for drug-related delirium or psychosis, is not effective, though the quality of studies has in general been quite poor.[8,9]

Since the 1980s, there has been a growing movement for the establishment of Drug Treatment Courts, especially in the United States. These may be modestly effective in reducing criminal recidivism, and perhaps drug use.[9] However, despite numerous studies the findings are contested, interpretations of results not being helped by substantial variations in the way the courts operate and the inclusion and exclusion criteria determining which groups of addicted persons will appear before them.

How would a 'fusion law' deal with persons with addictions? The key principles are that involuntary treatment can only be justified when the person's ability to make a treatment decision is compromised, and the intervention is in the 'best interests' (that is, in accord with the deep value commitments or 'will') of the person. The addicted person who is in a delirious or psychotic state, usually associated with withdrawal, could be covered by this provision. However, following recovery from that acute disturbance and having re-established decision-making capability, a long-term programme of treatment or rehabilitation would need to be on a voluntary basis. This would be the case even if their decision would appear to others to be unwise and lead to harm to themselves. Of course, there may be immense pressures from family, friends, employers, and so on, but these are outside the scope of this book. The protection of others would only be relevant if it could be construed as falling within the 'best interests' criterion. Otherwise, any interventions would fall under the justice system.

Drug courts raise the issues I considered briefly in the discussion of mental health courts in Chapter 9. I take such courts as proposing an 'offer'. In lieu of a legal sanction for the offence committed (now constituting the 'moral baseline'), a treatment alternative is offered. Rejection of that 'offer' leaves the defendant, in theory at least, no 'worse off' than if the offer had never been made.

However, having accepted the treatment programme, the patient will have to comply with a range of conditions. Failure to comply with them will result in some form of punishment. Benedikt Fischer has raised a number of important questions concerning a fair implementation of drug courts.[10] Do the judges skew the threatened punishment as presented to the person towards the most severe end of the scale whereas the sentence if passed would actually be lighter? Do the judges act in an unbiased manner or do they see their role as being a treatment agent? There is also the problem of the proportionality between the gravity of the offence and the potential level of coercion introduced in the treatment programme and its conditions. Fischer describes cases where the person accepting the treatment programme, by later failing to comply with its conditions, ends up spending more days in prison than would have occurred if they had simply opted for punishment in the first place. The details of the conditions must be understood by the defendant and he or she must have the capability for making the decision—with appropriate support and counsel. I am personally not sure about the place of such courts; the provisos for a fair implementation can be difficult to meet in practice. Many of the ambiguities surrounding the management of persons with addictions reflect a tension between seeing their condition as 'illness' needing treatment versus 'moral failing' deserving punishment or containment. This tension can be played out in the drug court system where it may not be clear whether the essential aim is treatment or punishment or protection of the public.

Under a 'fusion law', there is another possibility for long-term management of an addiction that might allow varying degrees of restraint or coercion. A person with decision-making capability, perhaps following detoxification, may decide to make an 'advance directive' aimed at preventing (or at least containing) a relapse should it occur in the future. Such a directive could detail interventions that could be made by others—including family, friends, members of the treatment team—following the appearance of early signs of relapse. Because this is an unusual application of the advance directive principle, I am not sure of the range of interventions that might be stipulated or how effectively they could be implemented. Examples might include preventing the person from using their credit card (by taking it away or hiding it), making sure they are accompanied when out of the house, searching for hidden drug or alcohol supplies, exerting pressure to attend appointments with the treatment team, and so on. Each measure could be stipulated by the addicted person in their advance directive. Non-restrictive, positive measures that have proven to be helpful in the past could, of course, also be specified. An advance directive acts as a reminder to the affected person and others of the deep value commitments that it is intended should be given effect. It would be unlikely to permit the use of force or a deprivation of liberty.

Advance directives are considered in detail in Chapter 12.

In summary, I hope this chapter has persuaded the reader that a non-discriminatory approach to people with mental illness, as in the 'fusion' proposal, would not increase the risk of harm to others. The most difficult area to manage concerns the mental condition defences—'unfitness to plead' and the 'not guilty by reason of insanity' verdict. As an interim measure, a compromise involving a variation from a strict adherence to a 'decision-making capability–best interpretation of will and preferences' framework might be considered. As I discussed in Chapter 8, the implications of the UN Convention on the Rights of Persons with Disabilities for these defences have still to be worked through.

In Chapter 12, I will consider some other key implications of the 'fusion' approach for medical practice.

References

1. **Martin R.** The exercise of public health powers in cases of infectious disease: human rights implications. *Medical Law Review* 2006; **14**:132–143.
2. **Gledhill K.** The model law fusing incapacity and mental health legislation—a comment on the forensic aspects of the proposal. *Journal of Mental Health Law* 2010; **20**:47–54.
3. **Sentencing Council UK.** *Extended Sentences.* 2015. https://www.sentencingcouncil.org.uk/about-sentencing/types-of-sentence/extended-sentences/
4. **Peay J.** Mental incapacity and criminal liability: redrawing the fault lines? *International Journal of Law and Psychiatry* 2015; **40**:25–35.
5. **Hare RD.** *Manual for the Hare Psychopathy Checklist - Revised* (2nd ed). Toronto, ON: Multi-Health Systems, 2003.
6. **Glover J.** *Alien Landscapes? Interpreting Disordered Minds.* Cambridge, MA: Harvard University Press, 2014.

7. **United Nations.** *Joint Statement: Compulsory Drug Detention and Rehabilitation Centres.* 2012. http://www.unaids.org/en/resources/presscentre/featurestories/2012/march/20120308adetentioncenters
8. **Mitchell O, Wilson DB, Eggers A, MacKenzie DL.** Assessing the effectiveness of drug courts on recidivism: a meta-analytic review of traditional and non-traditional drug courts. *Journal of Criminal Justice* 2012; **40**:60–71.
9. **Hall W, Farrell M, Carter A.** Compulsory treatment of addiction in the patient's best interests: more rigorous evaluations are essential. *Drug and Alcohol Review* 2014; **33**:268–271.
10. **Fischer B.** 'Doing good with a vengeance': a critical assessment of the practices, effects and implications of drug treatment courts in North America. *Criminal Justice* 2003; **3**:227–248.

Chapter 12

Emergencies, general medicine, 'community treatment orders', and 'psychiatric advance statements'

In this chapter, I will look at some other areas of medical practice on which the Fusion Law framework would have a significant impact. In my opinion, in each, the quality of care would improve. In the case of general hospital medicine, while it may appear that there would be substantial resource implications, I do not see the requirements—in the vast majority of cases—as amounting to more than what most people would see as 'good practice'.

'Involuntary outpatient treatment' (or 'community treatment orders') in mental health care, extending compulsion from the hospital to the community, has been very controversial. I suggest that the 'fusion' approach would not in principle rule out this measure, but that it would put it on a sounder, ethically transformed basis.

Once we start to think about a decision-making capability approach to involuntary treatment in mental health care, as well as other medical conditions, particularly those associated with states of impaired consciousness, the huge potential for advance planning by the patient for future episodes of illness where that capability is likely to be lost becomes clear. In the light of the patient's past experience, treatment preferences can be knowledgably incorporated into a treatment plan. The patient thus assumes a significant measure of control over what will happen to him or her at those times. Indeed, a curious paradox may strike us. 'Advance statements' (or 'advance directives') have been used most often in the context of 'end-of-life' decisions where it is clear that decision-making capability will at some time in the future be irreversibly lost. But doesn't its application make as much, if not more, sense for people with relapsing and remitting illnesses—where decision-making capability is lost, then recovered, and then possibly lost again? In such cases, the person (and the clinical team) know from first-hand experience which treatment interventions worked well and which didn't. Planning for the future is thus well informed and treatment plans can be revised if necessary. For persons with early dementia, how they might feel about their experience of life when more severely affected and lacking decision-making capability is largely guesswork.

Emergencies

It is sometimes claimed, particularly when talking about mental health services, that making an assessment that someone suffers from a 'mental disorder' and presents a significant risk to themselves or others fits well with common understandings of mental disturbance that warrant an intervention of some kind. Would decision-making capability criteria be a practicable replacement? In an emergency situation, the Fusion Law model requires the assessor to determine whether there is a reasonable likelihood that the person lacks decision-making capability. This assessment will usually turn on whether a person behaving in an unusual or bizarre manner is able to give a coherent account of their reasons for doing so, whether the person believes some kind of mental disturbance may be a cause (and why), and what kind of intervention (if any) they consider might be appropriate. There is no reason to believe that this assessment is any more difficult than one that aims to establish whether the person has a 'mental disorder' (with its ill-defined boundaries). Indeed, I suggest these questions focus more precisely on what for most of us is of primary (and natural) interest when someone is acting strangely—what account do they give that could help us understand their behaviour?

Intervening when persons are actually engaged in acts of self-harm or of harm to others is usually covered in most countries by a form of general law of justified intervention in an emergency situation where a life is at stake. Such an intervention is not usually based on whether a mental disorder is present or not, but on the need to prevent imminent serious harm. An emergency intervention might involve taking the person to a 'place of safety' for a further evaluation.

General hospitals

In formulating the 'fusion' proposal, John Dawson, Rowena Daw, and I were cognisant of the new demands that would be placed on staff at general hospitals.[1] The use of compulsory treatment orders would represent a major change. We proposed that the range of mechanisms for implementing such orders—second opinions, consultation with a range of others, advocacy, reviews, appeals, and their respective time intervals—should allow a fair degree of flexibility. We argued that a combination of these requirements can be found that will be applicable across the whole range of health services. We also pointed to the accreditation and inspection of health and social care institutions as relevant contextual factors, as well as our level of confidence in these procedures.

In outlining the Fusion Law proposal in Chapter 6, I offered a set of procedures that should be feasible across all health and social care services for people who lack decision-making capability and who object to treatment that is in their best interests (according to the best interpretation of their will and preferences). This comprises a *staged compulsory assessment process*. Immediately necessary treatment could be authorized during an initial period of emergency assessment lasting for up to 24 hours. A structured assessment of the patient's decision-making capability would take place during this time and if an extension of the order were required, a second medical (or appropriate health professional) opinion would be necessary. In addition there would need to be a consultation with those who could contribute to the determination of the best interpretation of the patient's will and preferences. If there was agreement that further involuntary treatment was justified, a care plan would be developed and shared with the patient and those involved in the determination. Treatment could then continue for 28 days. If involuntary treatment were to continue beyond 28 days, authorization by a tribunal would be required. Comprehensive review and accountability mechanisms would apply.

Most patients in general hospital wards, apart from those with dementia or severe brain injuries, are unlikely to have impaired decision-making capability for more than 28 days. I do not consider that the requirements represent much more than what good practice would demand. I think that most of us, if we were to be subject to surgery or to medication with potentially serious effects against our wishes, would welcome safeguards of this type.

'Fluctuating capacity'

'Fluctuating capacity' is sometimes thought to be a reason why capacity-based law would not work well in the case of various medical as well as psychiatric disorders. The fear is that a person might reject treatment during a very brief interval of decision-making capability, but then accept it at another, leaving clinicians confused as to the person's true intentions, will, or preferences. Or the person may refuse treatment during a brief period of capability—perhaps lasting only minutes—but then lapse back into a state of impaired capability. How much weight should be placed on such a refusal?

In practice, this is not a major problem. Psychoses—unless caused by an acute, organic disturbance of brain function such as delirium due to drug toxicity or withdrawal, or a metabolic derangement due to a severe disease—do not fluctuate in this way. Recovery is generally progressive. Fluctuation of conscious level, even over the course of a day, is a well-recognized clinical feature in acute, organic disturbances of brain function and can be taken into account in determining when decision-making capability is stably restored. An issue might arise in relation to the psychoses as to how long a period of restoration of capability would be required before it could be judged 'stable'. One would not usually be thinking here in terms of hours, but of days or even weeks, depending on the pace and trajectory of recovery.

Involuntary outpatient treatment (or community treatment orders)

I introduced the subject of involuntary outpatient treatment in Chapter 5. The focus was on the problematic assessment of risk—or, indeed, the risk of a risk. This is the basis of what one could call 'preventive' involuntary outpatient treatment. The purpose is to ensure, using compulsion, that a person continues to take their treatment—nearly always medication—when they have a high risk of relapse and such a relapse is judged to entail a high risk to self or others. There are two other uses of involuntary outpatient treatment orders. First, to avoid an involuntary admission where involuntary community treatment might be effective; and second, to shorten an inpatient stay if involuntary treatment in the community can ensure treatment adherence following discharge. In these cases, involuntary outpatient treatment is regarded as a 'less restrictive alternative', reducing the need for, or duration of, involuntary inpatient treatment.

The scope of involuntary outpatient treatment powers varies widely by jurisdiction.[2] They nearly always mandate the patient to accept psychiatric treatment (even if there is not a power to restrain and medicate the patient in a non-health care, general community setting). They may direct the patient to accept visits from clinicians and attend appointments, or direct where the patient should reside. They may provide an authority for a clinician to enter the patient's residence at reasonable times for purposes directly related to the enforcement of the treatment regime. There will usually be a power to recall the patient to hospital, and to provide involuntary treatment in a hospital or clinic where such treatment may appropriately and safely be given.

Involuntary outpatient treatment is controversial. Criticisms include potential violations of human rights, such as the right to privacy; the potential to distract attention from the quality of community services and to undermine the development of non-coercive methods for engaging reluctant patients; the potential to divert resources to a small group of patients perceived as 'risky', away from the rest; the possibility that fears of involuntary treatment may deter patients from seeking treatment; and the limited range of treatments that can be enforced, some being perhaps sub-optimal (for example, relying on drugs that can be given by intramuscular injection). There are also concerns (supported by some evidence)[3] that outpatient orders may lead to an increase in the use of compulsion, since unlike inpatient commitment there is no 'ceiling' on the numbers necessarily imposed by a finite number of available beds, previously required for the enactment of a compulsory order. I have earlier remarked on the elasticity of the concept of 'risk', and the potential for its expansion to cover a broad range of 'troubling' behaviours in the community. Just as with inpatient commitment, rates of use vary widely across jurisdictions, fivefold or more.[2]

Of significance is the lack of agreement about the effectiveness of involuntary outpatient treatment in reducing admissions, reducing patient violence, or improving psychological or social outcomes. The same studies, including randomized controlled trials, have been interpreted quite differently by different experts. A comprehensive and detailed review of all studies, randomized and not, in 2007 concluded that the effectiveness of involuntary outpatient treatment was not proven.[4] Since then we have seen a very large randomized trial in England, known as the OCTET study.[5] This involved a total of 336 detained patients, half of whom were randomized at discharge to a community treatment order (as involuntary outpatient treatment is known in the United Kingdom) with the other half receiving care as usual. Over the succeeding 12 months of follow-up, despite the fact that the involuntary outpatient treatment group of patients were on a compulsory order about 20 times as long as the control group, there was no difference on any outcome measure. The authors of the OCTET study, whose lead investigator, Tom Burns, was previously known for his advocacy for community treatment orders, concluded that restrictions on patient liberties associated with community treatment orders cannot be justified unless shown, after rigorous testing, to have benefits. None have so far been convincingly demonstrated.

All studies concerning the effectiveness of involuntary outpatient treatment have been subject to various criticisms. There are many factors that might determine how successful a complex intervention like this might be. Different laws in different countries, together with different service configurations and different cultural attitudes to mental illness and coercion, may all play a part. The introduction of involuntary outpatient treatment has usually been accompanied by an improvement in services—there is no point compelling patients to use services if services are not available. Some have suggested that improved services have been the key factor in improving outcomes, rather than the use of compulsion.

The conventional criteria for involuntary treatment in mental health services—the 'mental disorder' criterion and the 'risk of harm' criterion—prove especially problematic when it comes to compulsion in the community. I have previously drawn attention to the blurred boundary surrounding 'mental disorder' and the uncertain nature of what might be deemed to constitute a 'risk'. Related particularly to the latter is a further problem. When should an involuntary outpatient treatment order be terminated? This question is especially problematic in relation to 'preventive' community treatment orders. There is a susceptibility to a 'catch-22' bind. If the patient is not doing well despite being on the order, it is likely the order will be continued, perhaps with a more rigorous application or a change in the conditions. If the patient is doing well, a general medical principle may kick in—if a treatment is working, don't change it. There is no clear endpoint, and so it is not surprising to find that patients may be on involuntary outpatient treatment for years.

These drawbacks of involuntary outpatient treatment might lead to the conclusion that it should not be used. Under conventional mental health legislation of the type that I criticize in this book, this is a position I would endorse. However, if we think through the treatment options under the Fusion Law proposal, we may find there is a place for community treatment orders, but only in very particular circumstances.[6]

Under the Fusion Law, you will recall, there would be two requirements for involuntary treatment (as well, of course, as a set of protections including appeals and reviews following its initiation). The first is a loss of decision-making capability and the second that in the event of a loss of decision-making capability, treatment should be in the person's 'best interests' (in accord with the best interpretation of their will and preferences). The latter would lean heavily on what the patient would have chosen in relation to treatment under the prevailing circumstances if their decision-making capability had been retained (or giving effect to will and preferences reflected in the person's enduring commitments and values determining their significant life choices). Such a determination, as we have seen, requires the support and involvement of people who know the patient well.

On this account, a community treatment order could be justified if it were used only during a period of impaired decision-making capability and if it were to give effect to the person's will and preferences. The perspective is squarely that of the patient. If there were an 'advance statement', formulated when the patient had recovered from a previous illness episode and now had decision-making capability, this would provide strong evidence of what the person's will and preferences might be. This might constitute a type of 'Ulysses contract': the patient, while having decision-making capability, expresses a 'will' (and associated preferences) for a treatment plan at some time in the future when it is anticipated that decision-making capability will be lost, and, furthermore, he or she agrees that an element of compulsion to ensure adherence to that treatment would be warranted according in an agreed set of foreseeable circumstances.[i] In the absence of a clear preference of this kind, one would attempt to answer the question: would the person have supported the use of this form of compulsion if their decision-making capability had been retained? Would the use of an involuntary outpatient treatment under these circumstances give effect to the person's real or 'authentic' will and preferences, or would it act against them? These issues are illustrated in the following example.

Eileen

Eileen, aged 34 years, had been admitted on two previous occasions to a psychiatric unit on a compulsory treatment order. She had a bipolar illness with severe manic ('high') episodes. During these she believed herself to be specially blessed and destined to marry Christ (she meant this literally), and to have the ability to bring peace to the world. She became 'far too busy' to eat or sleep, gave away her belongings (as she would not need them where she was going), and upset many people on whom she would lay hands when she decided they looked 'sick or troubled'. Some claimed this was an assault and called the police.

---

[i] Based on the Greek myth in which Ulysses made a pact with his crew as they approached the island of the Sirens. Their singing, he knew, was so enchanting that it drove sailors mad, luring them to shipwreck and death in the sea. Ulysses wanted to hear the Sirens' song although he knew that doing so would render him temporarily insane. He therefore put wax in his men's ears so that they could not hear, and had them tie him to the mast. He ordered them not to untie him no matter how much he would beg. Ulysses thus heard the Sirens' songs but survived.

During both previous admissions she had pressed her consultant psychiatrist for an early discharge and was able to give the impression that she was well on the road to recovery. On both occasions she appeared to recognize that following discharge she should continue with her current medication, lithium (a 'mood stabilizer') in the long term, and olanzapine (an antipsychotic drug) in the short term. However, both times she stopped the medication within days of leaving hospital, quickly relapsing. In each case she was readmitted, again on a compulsory order.

Following recovery from the current, now third, episode, Eileen in discussion with her clinical team agreed to a crisis plan. In it she stated that if she were readmitted to hospital in a manic state, she wanted to be an inpatient for the shortest time possible (since she found the experience 'so terribly, incredibly traumatic; trapped and in a strange place, surrounded by strange people. It's really stressful'), and that if the clinical team thought that she was OK to be discharged at an early stage, she should be placed on an involuntary outpatient treatment order. This would ensure she would take her medication and be visited by a home treatment team, and she went on to say she would be happy for virtually any other conditions to be attached.

The type of outcome sought in this case might be quite different to the more 'objective' outcomes that are sought in a clinical trial, such as the OCTET study. Readmissions are generally undesired by most patients, but perhaps some may value other outcomes more highly, such as taking medication on a self-regulated, intermittent basis because of undesired side effects. Another patient, Eileen being an example, might prefer a period under involuntary outpatient treatment to a longer inpatient stay, the order serving as an incentive or control to continue treatment, the patient recognizing from previous experience that this is likely to falter. It is the patient's perspective that counts. The involuntary outpatient treatment order would only be applicable if decision-making capability were impaired, and rescinded when it were stably restored. Unlike the current use of involuntary outpatient treatment, a clear endpoint is defined.

I suggest involuntary outpatient treatment could be justified on this basis. How often such situations would arise is at this time impossible to tell. These are novel criteria, to my knowledge not used so far. The numbers are likely to be small. However, smaller numbers might prove to be an advantage, especially if they involve more personalized care-planning that leads to better outcomes. Smaller numbers might also mean stronger 'teeth' for involuntary outpatient treatment. It might mean, for example, that despite huge bed pressures, an admission can be arranged for a patient who fails to observe the conditions mandated by the order (made with the prior agreement of the patient), even though the level of illness disturbance normally required for inpatient care has not been reached. This was, after all, the preference of the patient.

The justification for compulsion that is being advanced here is strongly at variance with existing mental health law. Unless the law were changed, it would be up to clinicians to follow the principles outlined, I suggest, as a matter of 'good practice'. Given the significant doubts about the effectiveness of involuntary outpatient treatment mentioned earlier, even if the law were to remain unchanged (just for the moment, I hope) clinicians should give good reasons for placing a person on an involuntary outpatient treatment order.

A problem issues from the motivation in some jurisdictions—England being a prime example—for the introduction of involuntary outpatient treatment in the first place: restoring public confidence in 'safe' mental health services, safe especially for the general public. Will a clinician unlucky enough to have a patient who commits a serious violent act be considered culpable if the patient were not on an involuntary outpatient treatment order when there might have been a case under the current legislation for one to have been instituted, probably on the basis of the 'risk' criterion? There is no evidence at all that involuntary outpatient treatment reduces the risk of serious violence, but politicians and the media in a risk-averse society tend to be deaf to such facts.

If the principles outlined were to be adopted without a change in current mental health law, practitioners would need the support of their professional organizations and their codes of ethics.

Advance statements and directives

In Chapter 10, I considered the various types of 'advance statements' that can be used in health care. The essential value of an 'advance statement' is that it allows a patient, when well, to state treatment preferences in anticipation of a time in the future when, as a result of the effects of an impairment in mental functioning, he or she may not be capable of making treatment decisions. The anticipated loss of decision-making capability usually occurs during a crisis due to a relapse of illness (for example, a psychosis) or during a time of especially disturbing events. It gives the person a significant degree of control over their treatment at a time when it would otherwise be absent.

An advance statement can specify treatment preferences and refusals or it can empower a 'proxy decision-maker' to act on the person's behalf when they lack decision-making capability. In the case of the latter, the patient might give a general account of the beliefs and values to which they would like the proxy decision-maker to give special regard. In most jurisdictions, a formal 'advance statement', often called an 'advance directive', can be legally binding, usually for rejections of specific treatments or classes of treatment. Preferences for specific treatments are usually treated as would be a contemporaneous request. Whether that treatment would then be offered would depend on whether the clinician thought it was an appropriate treatment for the particular illness.

Advance directives arose initially as a means of assisting with decisions about care and treatment against the background of the accelerating introduction of new medical technologies. Life could be increasingly prolonged, judged by some unnecessarily so, with burdensome consequences for the patient and the family, as well as the state treasury. In 1990, the US Congress passed the Patient Self-Determination Act which provided support for advance directives, including psychiatric advance directives. This legislation requires publicly funded health care institutions and providers to give information about advance decisions to adult patients upon their admission to the facility. Under the Act, patients are to be encouraged to decide about the treatment they would accept or reject if they were to become unable to make those decisions due to illness. The health care agencies must ask whether the patient has an advance directive, provide information about rights under the law, and recognize the status of advance directives and durable powers of attorney (proxy decision-makers) for health care.

In England and Wales, by the end of the twentieth century, advance refusals were recognized as legally binding. In a case in 2001, the judge summarized the position as follows:

> Accordingly, the first principle of law which I am satisfied is completely clear, is that in the case of an adult patient of full capacity his refusal to consent to treatment or care must in law be observed. It is clear that in an emergency a doctor is entitled in law to treat by invasive means if necessary a patient who by reason of the emergency is unable to consent, on the grounds that the consent can in those circumstances be assumed. It is, however, also clearly the law that the doctors are not entitled so to act if it is known that the patient, provided he was of sound mind and full capacity, has let it be known that he does not consent and that such treatment is against his wishes. To this extent an advance indication of the wishes of a patient of full capacity and sound

> mind are effective. Care will of course have to be taken to ensure that such anticipatory declarations of wishes still represent the wishes of the patient. Care must be taken to investigate how long ago the expression of wishes was made. Care must be taken to investigate with what knowledge the expression of wishes was made. All the circumstances in which the expression of wishes was given will of course have to be investigated.[7]

These principles were placed on a statutory footing in the Mental Capacity Act (2005) in England and Wales. Refusals made with capacity, with adequate knowledge, and clearly applicable in the circumstances must be respected. For life-endangering refusals, these must be in writing and witnessed, and must acknowledge that the person understands that his or her life may be at risk. I think that most judges in such cases would look for a reasonably convincing contemporaneous assessment of the person's mental capacity at the time.

Why have advance statements been ignored in mental illness?

As I said at the start of this chapter, when one thinks about the application of advance statements, mental capability-impairing conditions that are 'relapsing-remitting' (that is, ones that occur in episodes from which the person recovers) would seem to be especially suitable illness candidates. The great advantage they have over the more usual conditions that call for advance directives, such as 'end-of-life' decisions, is that they can be tailored over time, in the light of the patient's individual and often idiosyncratic treatment experiences, to fit more closely to what the patient prefers. In the case of mental illnesses where there may be a number of elements in the treatment plan—for example, therapeutic and supportive relationships of various kinds, medication, home treatment, family meetings, day-care, occupational support, involvement in art therapy—previous experience will point to those interventions that were most effective and those that were not. With most illnesses of this kind, repeat episodes in an individual tend to be remarkably consistent in the form they take. This is enormously helpful in planning for the treatment of a future episode.

End-of-life advance directives obviously miss such opportunities for revision. They may also carry a further problem, one that I mentioned in an earlier chapter when looking at the stability over time of a person's values, will, and preferences. In the case of someone with dementia, for example, their values may differ, or at least appear to differ (as far as one can tell when the person has lost the ability to clearly communicate their preferences), when compared with those of the 'same' person without dementia. The question arises as to why the 'well person' should dictate (by an advance directive) what should happen to the now 'different person' with dementia.[8,9] Should the current preferences of the person with dementia override the advance directive when those preferences clash? As previously discussed, I am afraid there is no rule in such a case. Good arguments can be produced for and against. In the end, the decision-makers in consultation with people who know the person well have to judge the relative weights to be given to the old versus new values and preferences. However, the main point I want to make here is that this is not a major problem in the case of most people with a mental illness. The closest we get to the problem of a 'new identity' as a result of a mental illness is the person with a severe psychosis who does not recover well between relapses. Their personality—and thus beliefs, values, will, or preferences—may change substantially over the years. Such a change can be major. It is common to hear relatives say that the person is 'no longer the same person' as the one they used to know. The mothers of two chronically ill young men I used to see expressed it poignantly: 'my son is my living bereavement'. While the person may not be the same, if the 'new' person's beliefs and values assume a substantial degree of coherence and stability, they might come to be reasonably seen as deserving of our respect.[10] I gave an example in Chapter 8 of such a case in which the court decided this was so.

Why have advance statements not played a significant role in mental health care despite the obvious advantages? One reason, I suppose, is their association with end-of-life decisions. But there are others. I suggest they are the same as those that have accounted for the centuries-long perpetuation of the discriminating mental health law I discussed earlier (Chapter 5). Whether persons with a mental illness are able to make a decision for themselves has not been a criterion for determining whether involuntary treatment is appropriate. The criteria have been, as we have seen, the presence of a 'mental disorder' and the 'risk of harm'. If thinking about decision-making capability is not normally associated with the assessment of people with a mental illness at times of crisis, the idea of an anticipatory patient preference—made when he or she had that capability—does not come readily to mind. The person with a mental illness is automatically assumed to be incompetent, incapable of practical reasoning.

Benefits and drawbacks

Some of the potential benefits of advance statements include providing opportunities for patient empowerment and enhancing 'autonomy';

improving relationships between patients and clinicians, especially if there has been joint discussion about future treatment; preventing future crises, or nipping them in the bud, through careful planning; and clarity about what treatments are to be given in case of relapse. However, some patients express doubts regarding the effectiveness of their statements in practice. Studies on the implementation of advance directives in medicine in general, most often in end-of-life planning, have shown that problems indeed occur. These include staff not knowing that there is an advance directive in existence; staff concerns about whether the advance directive was executed when the person had adequate knowledge of treatment alternatives—including recent developments—and had decision-making capacity at the time; staff concerns about providing an inadequate standard of care if they were to follow the advance directive; staff concerns about the level of decision-making capability necessary to revoke an advance directive; and lack of clarity on the staff's part concerning the relevant law and whether the advance directive is legally binding in all respects, or only in some.

These are essentially practical problems for which there should be practical answers. For example, with electronic records, it is now possible to flag the existence of an advance statement; statements, especially those with serious consequences, can be witnessed, for instance by a doctor or advocate, as being made with decision-making capability; revocation can be clearly stated to require the same level of decision-making capability as execution; education on the law and its interpretation can be provided, and so on.

When, if ever, should an advance directive be overridden?

The question about a clinician's duty of care when an advance directive limits treatment to what, from a purely medical point of view, clearly falls below an adequate standard of care is more difficult to resolve. What should clinicians do if a patient's advance directive rejects all treatment when there are, nevertheless, effective treatments? What if the rejection is life-threatening?

Under current mental health law in the great majority of jurisdictions, an involuntary treatment order will trump an advance directive. There may, however, be a requirement that reasons be given to a supervisory authority, justifying the clinician's decision not to accede to the directive. Under the Fusion Law proposal, there would be no specific mental health law; such trumping would not be an option. An advance directive, made when the person clearly had decision-making capability and with adequate knowledge of the options, would appear to require compliance. With this in mind, how would directives specifying a poor standard of treatment, or a rejection of all effective treatments, be dealt with?

One option is to make advance statements *not* strictly legally binding. An example is the Mental Health (Care and Treatment) (Scotland) Act 2003[11] which recognizes the concept of advance mental health statements, but these are non-binding. The Act provides a comprehensive framework for advance statements which can only be overridden by the clinician after reasons have been provided to the patient, a person named by the patient, a guardian or welfare attorney (if there is one), and the supervisory body, the Mental Welfare Commission. The Act aims to encourage the use and development of advance directives by requiring mental health professionals and tribunals to have regard for their content. However, they cannot bind a doctor or member of the care team to provide or withhold specific treatments. Their value lies in the fact that a competently made advance statement offers a strong indication of a patient's will and preferences regarding their treatment.

What might be the consequences if they were strictly legally binding? Some background factors need discussion here. I think that most people who have studied advance directives will agree that they are best constructed in the light of a detailed discussion of all the options with a clinician. The support of a facilitator may prove especially helpful, both in assisting with the discussion and then with the appropriate paperwork, which can be complex. Such discussion can build a relationship of trust between patient and clinician. There is a further advantage of such consultation. An advance directive to be valid must be 'applicable in the circumstances'. A reasonable doubt about whether the circumstances now in play were anticipated in the advance directive may be reason enough not to follow the directive. A clinician would need to be reasonably certain that the patient made the directive on the basis of adequate information. Furthermore, where an advance directive rejects effective treatments, it would be reasonable to require the directive to be in a written form and witnessed by a person who can reliably attest to the decision-making capability of the patient at the time of its making.

To date, the empirical evidence concerning advance directives made by people with mental health problems is reassuring about their clinical utility. It is rare for a person to reject all treatment. For example, Debra Srebnik and her colleagues reported that 95 per cent of the instructions of psychiatric advance directives made by over 100 patients in Seattle (United States) were rated as 'feasible, useful, and consistent with practice standards'.[12] The area in which there was a potential issue involved those patients who were unwilling to be given medication that was not specifically listed in the directive. Jeff Swanson, who has conducted large studies in the United States, has reported that refusals of all treatment are rare.[13] In our London study of joint crisis plans mentioned in Chapter 10, of 221 patients with a plan, while over 40 per cent included a treatment rejection, alternatives were always accepted.[14] Four per cent refused hospitalization if it should become absolutely necessary from the clinician's point of view. The majority of preferences were general (and notable from the point of view of patient autonomy): for example, to be treated with respect; for the assessor to understand what was 'illness' and what was not; for continuity, consistency, and clarity in the treatment plan; to involve the patient as much as possible in decisions; to be treated at home whenever possible; and to meet the need for support and the opportunity to talk to someone about their experiences.

However, while the research shows that refusals of potentially effective treatment whose omission may have serious consequences are likely to be rare, such cases will certainly arise. The possibility needs to be faced. Would it be justified to override a clearly applicable advance directive made with full capacity and knowledge? In nearly all of the 25 or so jurisdictions in the United States with psychiatric advance directive legislation, as long as the clinician acts in good faith on the basis of their perception of an acceptable standard of care, or makes reasonable efforts to transfer the patient to a clinician who is willing the follow the directive, the clinician is protected from the consequences of overriding the directive. Though there are no clear data available, overriding is apparently not restricted to psychiatric advance directives, but is also not infrequent in the case of non-psychiatric conditions. Such facility in overriding advance directives has come in for criticism; it undermines their basic purpose—to ensure that patients have their treatment preferences respected.

A helpful way of thinking about advance directives is to treat them as far as possible in the same way as a contemporaneous statement of preferences—which is, in effect, the status they claim. If such is the case, there are some reasonable questions a clinician may pose:

1. As in a contemporaneous request, does—or did—the patient have the necessary *information* to make a treatment decision? In the case of an advance directive, did the patient anticipate the present circumstances sufficiently accurately at the time the psychiatric advance directive was formulated?
2. As in the case of a contemporaneous *request*, an advance directive seeking an inappropriate or unavailable treatment would not be met.

A treatment *refusal* has a different standing, however. It carries a strong authority and must be respected unless there is a very strong case against.

3. In the case of an apparently unwise contemporaneous treatment decision, attention would be drawn to the patient's *decision-making capability*. Thus, if an advance directive has been made, one would similarly ask whether the patient clearly had capability at that time. How can the assessor be satisfied, now, that this was the case, then? This suggests that the patient's capability at the time of making an advance directive needed some form of assurance, with a special degree of rigor if the preference could predictably result in serious harm. What we unfortunately miss, to a greater or lesser extent, is the opportunity to enter into a dialogue with the person allowing us to interpret the beliefs and values that underlay their choices.
4. Where there is a high risk of an *imminent suicide attempt*, the approach to an advance directive treatment refusal would be the same as a contemporaneous treatment refusal. How should we respond to a high risk of imminent suicide in a patient who retains decision-making capability? If it were the case that the state's interest to 'protect life' (as for example, under Article 2 of the European Convention on Human Rights) were to prevail, preventing suicide might justify overriding a contemporaneous, competent treatment refusal. The same would apply to an advance directive. Similar considerations would apply where there is a risk of serious *harm to others*, except that there is an alternative regime that might be called on—the criminal justice system. We must bear in mind here the problem of accurately predicting risk as I discussed in Chapter 5. The risk would have to be clear, direct, and imminent and warrant an immediate intervention. (There might follow a problem of a person with a mental illness who lacks decision-making capability who is in custody and will likely remain in custody unless treatment were to be instigated. An important question in such a case would be whether the person, when formulating their advance directive, foresaw the possibility of arrest and long-term detention under the criminal justice system. If not, one might conclude that the directive was not applicable under the circumstances.)
5. I have previously mentioned the difficulties in cases where there has been an irreversible illness that has significantly and enduringly changed the 'identity' of the person when we compare the 'now-ill person' with the person who made the directive and was well enough to do so. There may be occasions when it could be reasonably claimed that present preferences should be given substantial weight.

One must recognize some special pressures that act on clinicians when confronted with a patient who seems to have made an apparently unwise directive. Depending on the society, doctors may harbour greater or lesser degrees of fear of litigation for negligence following a bad outcome for the patient. Immunity from liability in this context, and its boundaries, need to be made clear. Attention has also been drawn to situations where the specific illness that is the subject of a treatment decision is one that has resulted from previous treatment, especially a treatment error or from an unexpected adverse reaction. Not only may the event have been unforeseen when the directive was framed (though common or serious risks of treatment will have been discussed), but doctors may feel a special obligation to act to remedy something they feel they have caused, whether culpably or not.

In a very helpful discussion on overriding psychiatric advance directives, and equally applicable to medical directives, Jeff Swanson and colleagues conclude, with a broadly pragmatic eye.[15] They surmise that successful take-up of psychiatric advance directives may depend significantly on dealing with clinicians' concerns about the consequences for them of their honouring or in some circumstances deciding to set aside psychiatric advance directives requests:

> Having reasonable safeguards for clinicians who decline PAD [psychiatric advance directive] requests or refusals of treatment may be not only prudent, but necessary for clinicians to support broad implementation of PADs and for patients in general — the vast majority of whom will never use PADs to refuse all treatment — to derive any benefit from them.[15]

As this book was largely inspired by my concern with unfair discrimination against people with a mental illness, an important proviso needs to be entered into the discussion. Whatever policies we adopt in relation to overriding advance directives, they should apply equally to everyone, whether they have a mental illness or a physical illness. For example, if the state's duty to protect life were to play a role, it would have to encompass all sources of clear and imminent threats to life where the state or the agents of the state (such as hospitals) are in a position to exercise control over the person and their situation.

How far discretion should be given to doctors (in consultation with important others) to override advance directives when an effective, life-saving treatment is rejected is a matter that each society will need to establish. A case could be made, time permitting, for problematic cases to be heard by a tribunal of the kind that would be established to hear appeals relating to the Fusion Law. Again, it must be insisted that patients' and carers' voices should be clearly heard in formulating policy.

References

1. **Szmukler G, Daw R, Dawson J.** A model law fusing incapacity and mental health legislation & outline of the Model Law. *Journal of Mental Health Law* 2010; Special Issue Ed 20:11–24; 101–128. [See also 'Response to the commentaries' pp. 91–100.]
2. **Dawson J.** *Community Treatment Orders: International Comparisons.* Dunedin, New Zealand: Otago University Press 2005. http://www.otago.ac.nz/law/research/otago036152.pdf
3. **Burgess P, Bindman J, Leese M, Henderson C, Szmukler G.** Do community treatment orders for mental illness reduce readmission to hospital? An epidemiological study. *Social Psychiatry and Psychiatric Epidemiology* 2006; **41**:574–579.
4. **Churchill R, Owen G, Singh S, Hotopf M.** *International Experiences of Using Community Treatment Orders.* Department of Health, 2007. http://www.dh.gov.uk/en/Publicationsandstatistics/Publications/PublicationsPolicyAndGuidance/DH_072730
5. **Burns T, Rugkasa J, Molodynski A,** et al. Community treatment orders for patients with psychosis (OCTET): a randomised controlled trial. *Lancet* 2013; **381**:1627–1633.
6. **Szmukler G.** Is there a place for community treatment orders after the OCTET study? *Acta Psychiatrica Scandinavica* 2014; **131**:330–332.
7. *Re AK (Adult Patient) (Medical Treatment: consent)* 1 FLR 129 (2001).
8. **Dworkin RM.** *Life's Dominion: An Argument about Abortion, Euthanasia, and Individual Freedom.* New York: Vintage, 1993.
9. **Dresser R.** Dworkin on dementia: elegant theory, questionable policy. *Hastings Center Report* 1995; **25**(6):32–38.
10. **Glover J.** *Alien Landscapes? Interpreting Disordered Minds.* Cambridge, MA: Harvard University Press, 2014.
11. *Mental Health (Care and Treatment) (Scotland) Act 2003.* Queen's Printer Scotland: Stationery Office Limited, 2003.
12. **Srebnik DS, Rutherford LT, Peto T,** et al. The content and clinical utility of psychiatric advance directives. *Psychiatric Services* 2005; **56**:592–598.
13. **Swanson JW, Swartz MS, Elbogen EB,** et al. Facilitated psychiatric advance directives: a randomized trial of an intervention to foster advance treatment planning among persons with severe mental illness. *American Journal of Psychiatry* 2006; **163**:1943–1951.
14. **Farrelly S, Brown G, Rose D,** et al. What service users with psychotic disorders want in a mental health crisis or relapse: thematic analysis of joint crisis plans. *Social Psychiatry and Psychiatric Epidemiology* 2014; **49**:1609–1617.
15. **Swanson JW, McCrary SV, Swartz MS, Elbogen EB, Van Dorn RA.** Superseding psychiatric advance directives: ethical and legal considerations. *Journal of the American Academy of Psychiatry and the Law* 2006; **34**:385–394.

Part V

The future

Part V

The future

Chapter 13

Where does this take us?

Change is now essential

I have argued that patients with a 'mental disorder' are being detained and treated against their will on legal grounds that are morally unacceptable. The grounds justifying compulsion contribute to the shadow of coercion that hangs over the practice of psychiatry. Worse still, they have offered a tempting gateway for the abuse of psychiatry by states wishing to silence people deemed to be a threat to the social order. In most countries, including the United Kingdom, the basis of relevant laws date from the late eighteenth century or early nineteenth century. The grounds for instituting involuntary treatment have hardly changed since then.

Two criteria are taken as justifying involuntary treatment in virtually all countries that have mental health law (20 per cent of the world's population live in countries that have none). First, the person has a 'mental disorder' or a 'mental illness', usually broadly defined; and second, there is judged to be a substantial 'risk' of harm to the health or safety of the person, or to other persons.

Despite its universal acceptance, this kind of law discriminates unfairly against people with a mental disorder. It needs to be replaced by an entirely different approach for overriding treatment refusals. I have proposed such an approach, one that offers different grounds for such a serious intrusion into a person's life.

The fact that the same criteria for detention and involuntary treatment have persisted over the centuries might be taken to mean that they work well. But there is a better explanation for the persistence of the old criteria for compulsion: that the persons who are subject to such treatment—those with a severe mental illness—have been so marginalized in society and so lacking in a 'voice' that the unsoundness of the principles justifying their detention have slipped under our human rights radar system.

Treatment without consent is not restricted to psychiatric practice. It is common in general medicine, for example, in preventing patients with confusion—postoperative or resulting from infections or adverse medication reactions—from leaving their hospital ward. However, the justification is completely different. Also striking is the fact that the law in general medicine has not been static—it has evolved with changing attitudes to patients' involvement in deciding about their treatment. The relatively recent notion of 'informed consent' is now widely adopted. Why therefore do we have different rules for involuntary treatment in psychiatry versus the rest of medicine?

The contrast was made especially plain during the 1990s and early 2000s, when the government for England and Wales was examining proposals for new laws establishing the conditions when a 'substitute decision-maker' should be involved in making a decision on behalf of someone who lacked the ability to make decisions for themselves because of a 'disturbance or impairment of mental functioning'. They thus were incapable of giving informed consent. It was decided that this new legislation (resulting in the Mental Capacity Act 2005), one addressing fundamentally the same problem of establishing the grounds for overriding treatment refusals that occurs in psychiatry, excluded patients who fell under mental health law. At the same time a 'root and branch' reform of mental health law was also being debated, but the end result was essentially 'no change'. The old rules were to remain untouched, but were extended beyond the hospital into the community.

In comparing the two sets of rules for involuntary treatment—one for psychiatry, the other for the rest of medicine—the discrimination against people with a mental illness is obvious. For the latter, but not the former, the person's ability (or 'capacity', or 'capability') to make a decision about treatment is key to whether one can begin to justify overriding a refusal. A refusal made with decision-making capability is respected, no matter what the health outcome might be. Furthermore, even when that capability is lacking, an involuntary intervention is only justified if it is in the person's 'best interests'. In assessing 'best interests', the personal values, life goals, and commitments of the patient have increasingly played a major role. These two considerations—'decision-making capacity' and 'best interests'—play virtually no role in initiating detention and, in most places, involuntary treatment in mental health care. Here the 'mental disorder' and 'risk of harm' criteria operate. Thus 'autonomy' (or the recognition of a right to self-determination, or the right to pursue important personal goals and values) for persons with a mental illness is not accorded the same respect as for persons with all other types of illness. Furthermore, the 'protection of others' in the 'risk of harm' criterion makes persons with mental disorders uniquely liable to a form of preventive detention (albeit usually, or eventually, in hospital) on the basis of risk alone. In other words, they can be detained, unlike the rest of us, without first having committed an offence—this, despite the fact that only a few per cent of serious violent offenders have a mental illness.

That we have accepted such discrimination against persons with mental illness for so long speaks to the marginalized standing of people with mental illness in our society. We harbour stigmatizing stereotypes of people with mental illness that remain deeply rooted in our culture. These paint such people as having 'diseased minds' that make them incapable of practical reasoning and whose wishes are thus not to be taken seriously; and, furthermore that 'dangerousness' is intrinsic to mental illness. Mental health law mirrors these assumptions, that people with a mental illness necessarily lack decision-making abilities and are dangerous. However, research clearly fails to support these stereotypes.

A key question then follows: can we come up with a legal framework that is non-discriminatory? I have detailed an approach that meets that imperative. My colleagues and I have called this a 'Fusion Law'. A key point is that it is generic; that is, it applies to all persons who have a problem with decision-making, whatever their diagnosis—'physical' or 'mental' disorder—and in any setting—medical, surgical, psychiatric, or in the community. We see no need for a specific 'mental health' law. The framework is based on 'decision-making capability' and a specific version of 'best interests', but modified in various ways to make it applicable across all medical specialities.

Do we have sufficiently robust assessments of the key elements—'decision-making capability' and the version of 'best interests' proposed—one giving predominance to the person's deeply held beliefs and values? There are challenges that I have described, but there are good reasons to believe that valid assessments can be made. A major concern from sceptics is that when patients disagree with their doctors, they will be judged to lack decision-making capability and their decisions overridden. I have discussed a method for assessment involving 'interpretation', as well as a range of safeguards, to ensure that a person's beliefs and values are given due weight without being ousted by those of the assessor.

I further suggested that the Fusion Law is as close as one can realistically get to meeting the challenges posed by the hugely important recent development in international law, the UN Convention on the Rights of Persons with Disabilities (2006). Two principles in the Convention are especially relevant to involuntary treatment—all persons shall 'enjoy legal capacity on an equal basis with others in all aspects of life'; and, 'the existence of a disability shall in no case justify a deprivation of liberty'. Authorities have interpreted the Convention as effectively ruling out 'substitute decision-making' under any circumstances. I suggest that such a position is not credible and threatens to undermine acceptance of the Convention. The Fusion Law aims to eliminate discrimination, as does the Convention, but leaves a morally defensible place for involuntary treatment as a last resort, when all else, including well-organized support for the patient, has failed. I have argued that an analysis of the meaning of the Convention's touchstone, 'respect for the rights, will and preferences' of persons with disabilities, leads to the conclusion that 'rights', 'will', and 'preferences' may not all point in the same direction, especially when there has been a recent radical change in a person's wishes. Giving effect to a person's authentic 'will' (based on the person's deeply held beliefs and values) may mean overriding the person's present 'preferences' when the latter are clearly in opposition to the former. I propose that the framework underlying the Fusion Law could be termed a 'decision-making capability—will and preferences' approach.

Being a generic law and thus applicable to all patients, the criteria for involuntary treatment need to be workable in all settings. I have described some implications for medical practice. Some people will be concerned that a law based on decision-making capability and best interests (or best interpretation of the person's 'will and preferences') might mean that the public will no longer be adequately protected from persons with mental illness who might be violent. I have shown how those fears can be laid to rest. I have also suggested that adopting the 'fusion' approach will enhance good practice in general medicine by improving communication between patients, clinicians, and other people with an interest in the well-being of the patient. The controversial innovation of involuntary outpatient treatment, so susceptible to what amounts to arbitrary imposition, can be placed on an ethical basis. Advance statements offer real promise of empowering patients, especially in mental health care where they have been ignored until recently, largely, I suggest, as a result of the stereotype of the person with mental illness as never being competent enough for their beliefs and values to be taken seriously.

This book's focus has been on coercion. Thus what have been almost exclusively discussed are persons' so-called negative rights—that is, protections against unwarranted state-sanctioned intrusions into our freedoms. I hope the reader does not form the impression that health law should only be concerned with such rights. Comprehensive law requires equal attention to 'positive' rights—that is, ones that oblige the state to act to ensure that persons have access to a range of economic, social, and cultural 'goods' (for example, health care, housing, education, employment, freedom from abuse and exploitation, and so on). The UN Convention on the Rights of Persons with Disabilities offers an excellent model for the specification of such rights.

Conflicting social policies, but some positive signs

I see two major currents in mental health policy today that conflict. On the one side there is a move to empower patients, to hear their voices, to reduce stigma, to engage them in designing services, and to involve them as partners in the conduct of research—as collaborators not subjects. The 'fusion' proposal, as well as the UN Convention on the Rights of Persons with Disabilities, pulls in this direction.[1] On the other side is the 'risk' agenda. The stereotype of the person with mental illness as dangerous, to self but especially to others, retains its potency. However, its prominence is heightened even further by a general preoccupation with risk now evident in many societies. Eminent sociologists, such as Ulrich Beck[2] and Anthony Giddens[3] talk about the 'risk society'. A feature of 'modernity', they say, is that societies are changing at an unprecedented rate, generating insecurities about 'manufactured' hazards, that is, those resulting from human agency. These include, for example, large, often rapid changes to the environment and to forms of social organization and its institutions. Consequently there is a growing orientation towards safety. A good deal of political decision-making is concerned with managing risks, even risks that do not originate in the political sphere. Risk in psychiatry is perceived as increased by the shift from institutional to community care. A preoccupation with preventing bad things happening leads to provisions for detention, registers, surveillance, monitoring, and supervision for people judged as 'risky'. As I have discussed earlier, professional practice changes in ways that are beyond the control of its practitioners, as mechanisms of accountability are imposed to reassure the public that protective measures are fully engaged. The increasing prominence given to training in 'risk assessment' is an example.

Which current will be the stronger? No one can be sure, of course. However, I am fairly optimistic. We are seeing developments that favour the current that pulls away from discrimination. The UN disability Convention exerts a substantial tow in this direction. Decision-making capability is finding its way into new mental health law. Scotland is one example. Tasmania (2013) and Western Australia (2014) in Australia are others. A Mental Health Care Bill (2013) currently somewhere in the legislative process in India introduces a 'capacity' criterion for involuntary treatment. However, most significant of all is the historic Mental Capacity

Bill passed by the Northern Ireland Assembly in March 2016 which is based squarely on Fusion Law principles—a single, generic law covering all people with treatment decision-making difficulties from any cause and in any setting. Highly inclusive consultations with stakeholders, including service users, was an important feature of the Northern Ireland process.

When it comes to low- and middle-income countries, where abuses of human rights of people with mental health disabilities are common and resources limited, the principles underlying the Fusion Law as reformulated in the light of the UN Convention on the Rights of Persons with Disabilities, I believe, offer far greater potential for meaningful reform than conventional mental health law.[4]

A lecture at King's College London given in 2014 by the Baroness Hale of Richmond, Deputy President of the Supreme Court of the United Kingdom and a distinguished authority on mental health law, was also very encouraging. Lady Hale spoke about the inconsistency of the Mental Health Act with the UN Convention on the Rights of Persons with Disabilities. She also discussed the confusion engendered by having two sets of law in England and Wales, both covering people with an impairment of mental functioning, and a number of situations where it was far from evident which of the two laws should apply. She argued, as she had in an earlier address:

> In fact, it has long struck me that we would have a much more coherent and comprehensible system if we adopted the principles of the Mental Capacity Act for all kinds of mental disorder and disability.[i]

What makes this especially significant is that Lady Hale (Brenda Hoggett QC, as she was then) was at the Law Commission (England and Wales) in the 1990s when it examined the law relating to people who lack capacity, which led to the construction of the Mental Capacity Act. You may recall mention in Chapter 4 that the Law Commission did not see a problem in omitting a consideration of the Mental Health Act from its deliberations since:

> The law relating to mental incapacity and decision-making must address quite different legal issues and social purposes from the law relating to detention and treatment for mental disorder.[5]

---

[i] Lady Hale gave a similar speech with the title 'The Other Side of the Table? in October 2014 to the Mental Health Tribunal Members' Association (https://www.supremecourt.uk/docs/speech-141017.pdf).

I hope it has now become clear that the 'legal issues and social purposes' are not so different after all.

References

1. **Szmukler G, Rose D.** Strengthening self-determination in persons with mental illness. In: Clausen J, Levy N (Eds) *Handbook of Neuroethics*. Dordrecht: Springer, 2015; 879–895.
2. **Beck U.** *Risk Society: Towards a New Modernity*. London: Sage Publications, 1992.
3. **Giddens A.** Risk and responsibility. *Modern Law Review* 1999; **62**:1–10.
4. **Szmukler G, Bach M.** Mental health disabilities and human rights protections. *Global Mental Health* 2015; **2**:e20. http://dx.doi.org/10.1017/gmh.2015.18
5. **Law Commission.** *Mental Incapacity* (Report No. 231). London: HMSO, 1995.

Index

Notes Figures are indicated by an italic *f* following the page number *vs.* indicates a comparison